ProActive
Hospitality & Catering

City & Guilds

Professional
Cookery

S/NVQ Level 2

Series Editor: **Pam Rabone**

'olly Bamunuge • Trevor Eeles • Mark Furr
Shyam Patiar • Dereick Rushton

working together

City&
Guilds

Heinemann
From Harcourt

Heinemann Educational Publishers
Halley Court, Jordan Hill, Oxford OX2 8EJ
Part of Harcourt Education Limited

Heinemann is the registered trademark of Harcourt Education Limited

© Harcourt Education Ltd 2006

First published 2006

10 09 08 07
10 9 8 7 6 5 4 3 2

British Library Cataloguing in Publication Data is available
from the British Library on request.

13-digit ISBN: 978 0 435449 25 4

Edited by Eleanor Barber, Sue Harmes
Designed by Kamae Design
Typeset by Kamae Design
Illustrated by Asa Andersson, Ron Dixon, Steiner Lund, Mark Turner and Kamae Design
Original illustrations © Harcourt Education Limited, 2006
Cover design by Georgia Bushell
Printed and bound in China through phoenix Offset
Cover photo: © City & Guilds
Picture research by Emma Baddeley and Kay Altweg
Original photographs by Jules Selmes and Adam Giles

Acknowledgements
Harcourt Education Ltd would like to thank Phil Dobson, Leighton Anderson, Adam Pickett, Richard Brocklesby, Rod Burton, Colin Cooper,
David Hunter, Ian Monger, Tony Perry and Anthony Wright of the Birmingham College of Food, Tourism and Creative Studies, Iain Baillie,
Gerry Shurman, Rob Zahra and Ben Ross of South Downs College; and Andreas Hein of Farnborough College for their invaluable help.

The authors and publishers would like to thank the following individuals and organisations for permission to reproduce photographs:
Andreas von Einsiedel/Alamy – page 439; Corbis – pages 290, 431, 451; David Marsden/Anthony Blake Photo Library – page 408;
Food Features – pages 238, 254, 265 and 432; foodfolio/Alamy – pages 320 and 379; G. Tomsich/Science Photo Library – page 132;
George Hunter/Superstock – page 420; Getty Images/PhotoDisc – page – 314; Graham Kirk / Anthony Blake Photo Library – page 150;
Hilary Moore/Anthony Blake Photo Library – page 211; Joff Lee/Anthony Blake Photo Library – pages 157 and 218; Jupiter Media/Alamy
– page 344; Lori Alden – pages 251 and 255; Martin Brigdale/Anthony Blake Photo Library – page 189; Maximilian Stock Ltd/Anthony
Blake Photo Library – page 394; Meat and Livestock Commission – pages 164, 165, 168 and 170 – a link has been made available to its
website at www.heinemann.co.uk/hotlinks. Just enter the express code 9257P; Philip Wilkins/Anthony Blake Photo Library – page 319;
Photodisc – page 434; Photodisc/John A Rizzo – page 180; Profimedia.CZ s.r.o./Alamy – page 159; Roddy Paine/FoodAndDrink – pages
150 and 159; Sian Irvine/Anthony Blake Photo Library – pages 193 and 426; Studio Adna/Anthony Blake Photo Library – page 394;
Tim Hill/Anthony Blake Photo Library – pages 191 and 406; Woody Stock/Alamy – page 40

The authors and publishers are grateful to those who have given permission to reproduce material. Every effort has been made to
contact copyright holders of material reproduced in this book. Any omissions will be rectified in subsequent printings if notice is given to
the publishers.
Nash, C. (1998) *Food Safety: First Principles*, Chartered Institute of Environmental Health. Reproduced by permission of CIEH – pages
37 and 41

Crown copyright material is reproduced with the permission of the Controller of HMSO and the Queen's Printer for Scotland.

Steiner Lund would like to thank: Catering Department, East Leigh College, Hampshire; Eugene Hood, The Royal Society for the Protection of
Birds (RSPB); John Robinson, Family Butcher, Stockbridge, Hampshire; David H Batch, Lockerley Hall Farm, Lockerley, Hampshire.

Websites
There are links to relevant websites in this book. In order to ensure that the links are up to date, that the links work, and that the sites
are not inadvertently linked to sites that could be considered offensive, we have made the links available on the Heinemann website at
www.heinemann.co.uk/hotlinks. When you access the site the express code is 9257P.

Tel: 01865 888058   www.heinemann.co.uk

Contents

Introduction

This book has been designed with you in mind. Its purpose is to provide:

○ the knowledge requirements of the key units for NVQ Level 2 in Professional Cookery

○ a reference book for you to use while working towards your qualification and after you have qualified.

The catering and hospitality industry

The catering and hospitality industry is large. There are many roles to choose from and different types of businesses in which to work. The skills and knowledge you will develop while working towards your NVQ will be put to good use in the industry.

Your job title and tasks will be defined by which part of the industry you are working in. The table below shows various job roles which you could undertake with a Level 2 NVQ qualification and the sort of functions or tasks you will undertake.

Sector	Job title	Role	Core functions
Traditional brigade (fine dining)	Commis chef	To prepare, cook and present food (covering all sections of the kitchen)	Prepare, cook and finish basic dishes; ensure quality; manage portion control; participate in stock control; minimise waste
Mainstream	Line/section chef	To process, cook and present food	Process, cook and finish dishes; manage portion control; participate in stock control; minimise waste
School catering	Cook	To prepare, cook and present food	Prepare, cook and finish dishes; manage portion control; minimise waste

Figure i.1 Job title and tasks at entry level

When deciding which part of the industry you would like to work in you need to take into account the different roles and functions as well as the hours of work and terms and conditions.

What is an NVQ?

An NVQ assesses a person's technical competence to perform a job. It can also form part of a Modern Apprenticeship. The assessment is continual but you will only be assessed when you are competent at a task. NVQs are divided into units. In order to pass a unit you need to fulfil various requirements:

○ **What you must do** – details the actions you must undertake to pass the unit.
○ **What you must cover** – details the range of situations, tasks and commodities that you need to demonstrate you can cover.
○ **What you must know** – the statements of knowledge you must show that you understand.
○ **Evidence requirements** – details how much needs to be assessed by observation and how much can be covered by other methods of assessment.

How do I gain an NVQ?

The flowchart below summarises the process of gaining an NVQ. Each stage is discussed in more detail on the next page.

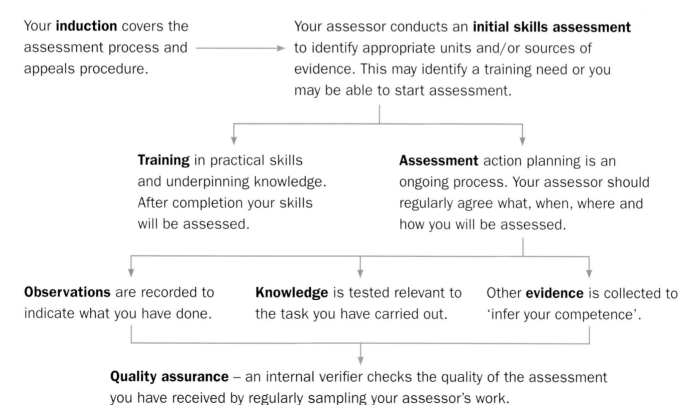

Your **induction** covers the assessment process and appeals procedure. → Your assessor conducts an **initial skills assessment** to identify appropriate units and/or sources of evidence. This may identify a training need or you may be able to start assessment.

Training in practical skills and underpinning knowledge. After completion your skills will be assessed.

Assessment action planning is an ongoing process. Your assessor should regularly agree what, when, where and how you will be assessed.

Observations are recorded to indicate what you have done.

Knowledge is tested relevant to the task you have carried out.

Other **evidence** is collected to 'infer your competence'.

Quality assurance – an internal verifier checks the quality of the assessment you have received by regularly sampling your assessor's work.

Figure i.2 How to gain an NVQ

Induction

You should receive an induction as soon as you start your NVQ. This should include an overview of the assessment process and a detailed explanation of the appeals procedure which you must follow if you meet a problem.

Initial assessment

When you start your qualification you should have an initial assessment. Together with your assessor you will work through the units you have selected to do in order to identify how much knowledge and/or skills you may already have. Your assessor may have a special form to record an action plan so that you are very clear about what needs to happen next.

Training

If your initial assessment identified a training need you will receive training in practical skills and underpinning knowledge before your skills are assessed.

Assessment

Your assessment will be ongoing with your assessor.

Observation

Your assessor will regularly observe you carrying out tasks. The outcomes will be recorded in your portfolio.

Knowledge testing

You will be required to answer questions in writing, orally or online to prove you have the knowledge that underpins your performance.

Other evidence

It may also be possible to collect other evidence including:
○ witness testimonies – from colleagues or managers at your place of work
○ assessment of prior learning or experience – evidence that you may already have some of the skills or experience required by the NVQ, e.g. a food safety certificate
○ work product (naturally occurring evidence) – e.g. menus, recipes, temperature check charts, photographs of dishes you have prepared.

Your assessor will work with you to decide on the best method of collecting evidence for each unit.

Your portfolio

All evidence should be placed into your portfolio and will need to be referenced to the NVQ standards. You may be given a paper logbook showing these standards. There are different styles of logbooks depending upon which awarding body you are registered with. Alternatively you may be using an e-portfolio such as the ProActive e-portfolio which is linked to this course. Your assessor will advise you on whether you will use a logbook or the ProActive e-portfolio.

Who checks my portfolio?

Your assessor will make decisions on your competence and work with you to help you build your portfolio of evidence.

In order to ensure fairness and to monitor the quality of the assessment an internal verifier (quality manager) will check the assessor's work regularly. This may be by observing them assessing you or by sampling evidence already collected and logged in your portfolio.

Shortly after you start your NVQ you will be registered with an awarding body, e.g. City & Guilds. It is responsible for checking the quality of the assessment and internal verification. The awarding body appoints an external verifier to carry out checks before certification.

How this book can help you

Each chapter covers the requirements for one or more NVQ units, so you can use the book to:
○ develop your knowledge for the 'what you must know' sections
○ identify the tools, equipment and ingredients for the practical activities undertaken in the 'what you must cover' and 'what you must do' sections.

Throughout the book there are useful tips and activities that you can use as well as key recipes to help you work towards your NVQ. Photographs identify ingredients and the sequence of complex practical tasks. Clear illustrations identify the equipment and tools that you will need.

Key features

Look out for the following special features as you work through the book.

All important technical words are defined to help you develop your underpinning knowledge.

Interesting and useful culinary facts.

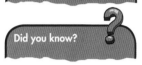

Useful practical ideas and good advice – nearly as good as having a real chef to help you!

Ideas for healthy alternative ingredients and methods.

In the kitchen

These short real-life case studies tell you about the experiences of other people working in the catering industry.

Important points to promote good practice in the kitchen and reminders about safe working practices.

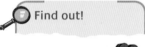

These independent research activities help you explore new areas and extend your knowledge.

When you see this feature you will know that there is a related video clip for you to watch. The ProActive Catering e-learning site can be accessed at http://www.proactive-online.co.uk

Short practical activities for you to try in the classroom. Sometimes they may provide evidence for your portfolio.

At the end of each chapter there is a set of questions to check your knowledge. These are a useful way of revising the underpinning knowledge for a unit ready for assessment.

E-learning

The ProActive Catering e-learning site can be accessed at http://www.proactive-online.co.uk. If your centre has a licence then you will be given a login and password.

There are various types of electronic resources available on the site for independent learning:

○ Video clips clearly demonstrate skills, e.g. how to cut a chicken for sauté.
○ Interactive tutorials teach you about a specific topic, e.g. food safety. At the end of the tutorial there is a short multiple-choice test which checks your understanding.
○ You can print off recipes, menus and worksheets as directed by your assessor.

1 Health and safety

This chapter covers the following NVQ unit:

- Unit 1GEN1 Maintain a safe, hygienic and secure working environment

Working through this chapter could also provide evidence for the following Key Skills:
C1.1, C1.2, WO1.1, WO1.2, PS1.1, PS1.2, PS1.3

In this chapter you will learn how to:

Keep your personal appearance neat, tidy and hygienic	1GEN1.1
Get cuts and scratches treated and report illnesses	1GEN1.1
Practise fire and other emergency procedures	1GEN1.2
Help to keep your customers, colleagues and visitors safe by dealing with hazards	1GEN1.2
Work in a healthy and safe way	1GEN1.2
Maintain hygiene in your work	1GEN1.2
Follow security procedures	1GEN1.2

Health and safety regulations

Working in a safe manner

It is important that all workers are able to carry out their tasks without causing any accident or injury to themselves or others (e.g. work colleagues or members of the public). Many years ago injuries at work were quite common, but since the Health and Safety at Work Act 1974 was brought in, most people take much greater care to work in a safe manner. This means there are fewer accidents in the workplace.

Figure 1.1 All chefs need to know the laws on health and safety

The Health and Safety at Work Act gives everyone certain responsibilities. While at work you must:
○ take reasonable care of your own safety and the safety of others
○ work in the manner laid down by your employer, especially regarding safety
○ tell your supervisor if you see anything that you think may be unsafe and could cause an accident.

Try this!

Try to remember an accident that you saw or one that happened to you.

○ *What happened?*
○ *How many people did it involve?*
○ *What pieces of equipment (if any) were involved?*
○ *Did it involve any of the 'fabric' of the building (e.g. the floor)?*
○ *How was it dealt with?*
○ *Who dealt with it (the manager or Head Chef)?*
○ *What did they do?*
○ *Did the accident result in any changes in the area afterwards, e.g. a change in the position of some equipment or a different floor surface being laid?*

Figure 1.2 What is the cause of this accident?

In the kitchen

A student visiting a fast-food restaurant was electrocuted when she accidentally touched a live wire sticking out of a hand dryer which had been vandalised. The dryer had been damaged at least ten days prior to the accident but had not been repaired.

Figure 1.3 Negligence can result in serious consequences in the workplace

The Health and Safety at Work Act makes sure that employers do not put their staff in dangerous situations where they could hurt themselves or others. Under this Act, employers must:

○ keep all their staff safe while working
○ provide safe equipment, tools and surroundings in which to work
○ train staff how to work, clean and maintain equipment they use
○ produce a policy document telling everyone how to behave safely
○ provide first-aid equipment and help
○ keep an accident book and use it correctly.

Did you know?

During the past ten years over 2,000 workers in the catering industry have had to take more than three days off work to recover from an accident in the workplace. Over 800 of these people suffered a major injury.

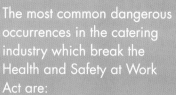

Did you know?

The most common dangerous occurrences in the catering industry which break the Health and Safety at Work Act are:

o missing guards on food slicing machines
o trailing cables
o insecure wiring on plugs
o faulty microwave seals
o broken or worn steps
o poor lighting of work areas.

In the kitchen

A waiter refilling **flambé** lamps turned into a human fireball when the vapour given off from the fuel ignited around him. The flammable liquid had not been stored properly, the waiter had not been trained properly in this procedure and there were no suitable fire extinguishers to use nearby.

Figure 1.4 Training is essential in preventing disaster

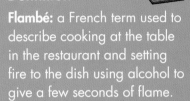

Definition

Flambé: a French term used to describe cooking at the table in the restaurant and setting fire to the dish using alcohol to give a few seconds of flame.

Did you know?

Slips and trips account for more than half of all accidents reported in the catering industry.

Laws relating to working safely

The Health and Safety at Work Act is an 'umbrella' act. This means that it includes other important regulations which relate to health and safety. The table below discusses some of these regulations.

Regulation	Example
Hazard Analysis and Critical Control Point (HACCP) This system identifies the main risks at important stages of work. Any risks found then need to be made as safe as possible. This system is particularly important in the hygiene risk assessment of food production, see page 79, Food safety management systems.	A kitchen prepared meals for a large site. Some customers in the food service area furthest from the kitchen complained that their food was not very hot. This meant there was a danger the food may not be safe to eat. An investigation took place and insulated containers were brought to transport the food. A probe was used to test the temperature of the food before it was packed and when it reached the service area to ensure it was hot enough. Temperature records were kept to satisfy the HACCP Regulations.
Control of Substances Hazardous to Health (COSHH) Regulations 2002 Identifies dangerous chemicals, e.g. cleaning agents. Chemicals must be labelled accurately. They must only be used after suitable training has been given. The correct protective clothing, e.g. gloves and goggles, must also be used.	A kitchen porter was provided with a very effective oven cleaning chemical. He kept it in a spray container under the pot wash sink. The kitchen porter had been trained how to apply the chemical and given a mask and gloves to wear. He kept this protective clothing in his locker. While the kitchen porter was on holiday the trainee chef was told to clean the oven. He tried to use the same chemical, although he had not been shown what to do. This was against the Regulations as he had not been trained how to use the chemical and he had no access to the protective equipment supplied. The chemical should have been kept in a locked cupboard when not in use. 

Reporting of Injuries, Diseases and Dangerous Occurrences Regulations (RIDDOR) 1995
Concerns the reporting of major or fatal injuries to any person in an accident connected with the business where you work. The report must usually be made to the Environmental Health Department of the local council.

A chef slipped over on a greasy kitchen floor while carrying a pan of hot water. She sustained serious burns and had to go to hospital. The accident was recorded in the company's accident book. To comply with RIDDOR the local council was informed. This resulted in a Health and Safety Inspector visiting the premises to carry out an investigation of how the accident happened.

Manual Handling Operations Regulations 1992
Aims to reduce the number of accidents caused by people moving heavy and awkwardly shaped items while at work. Adequate training must be given and equipment provided to help move items safely. See page 29, Safe working practices.

A dinner for 500 guests was going to be held in the exhibition hall of a large conference centre. All the equipment and prepared food needed to be transported from the kitchen to the hall which was several hundred yards away. The last time this type of function was held, the staff had to carry all the items on trays and in large containers. Some items were so heavy that two people had to share the load. After the event had taken place, one of the chefs had to have time off work with a strained back. This time trolleys were provided to move the equipment, and all the staff had received training in lifting heavy items safely to satisfy the Manual Handling Operations Regulations.

Provision and Use of Work Equipment Regulations 1998
Used together with the Prescribed Dangerous Machines Order to make sure people are not injured when they are using machines and other equipment while at work. Before using any type of machinery or equipment the member of staff must be trained in the correct procedures. If the machine is listed under the Prescribed Dangerous Machines Order then no one under the age of 18 may clean, lubricate or adjust it.

A young chef was asked to clean the meat slicing machine after use. He had not yet been trained how to do this but thought it should be easy enough. He dismantled the machine as much as he could but then cut his hand on the sharp blade he had exposed. The chef should not have attempted to clean the machine without first being trained to do so safely. This could have resulted in an offence under the Prescribed Dangerous Machines Order.

Fire Precautions Workplace Regulations 1997 Ensures there are suitable measures in place to protect staff and keep them safe in the event of a fire. There should be appropriate fire extinguishers supplied and a rehearsed evacuation procedure. See page 24, Fire in the workplace.	Some hot fat fell onto the solid stove top in a busy kitchen during service. The fat caught fire and spread over the cooker. The chef at the stove turned off the equipment and looked for a fire blanket to put over the flames. The case on the wall nearby where the fire blanket should have been was empty. By the time the chef had located a foam fire extinguisher the flames had spread up the wall of the kitchen. The fire brigade had to be called to put the fire out. The employer could have been prosecuted under these Regulations because they had failed to maintain the appropriate equipment to extinguish fires. 

Figure 1.5 The different regulations that form part of the Health and Safety at Work Act

Where to find information

It is very important to work in a safe and hygienic way for several reasons:
○ It avoids injuring yourself or others.
○ It is usually quicker and easier.
○ It is more professional.

There should be a Health and Safety representative at your workplace. You should follow any guidelines they give you about safe working practices. If health and safety regulations are not met you or your employer could be fined and your workplace may be closed down until safety improvements have been made. The fine for not following health and safety law is unlimited. You could also be sent to prison for an unlimited length of time! This means that a serious health and safety problem, e.g. a major accident, could be very expensive and also give the person responsible a criminal record.

In due course you will need to know more about health and safety in your workplace. You can:
○ ask your supervisor
○ ask your Health and Safety representative
○ ask your Human Resources Manager
○ look on the staff notice board.

Find out!
○ What year was the Health and Safety at Work Act introduced?
○ If there is a safety problem at work what is the name of the government organisation which will become involved?

Test yourself!

1 What is the best material from which a kitchen uniform should be made?
   a Nylon
   b Plastic
   c Cotton
   d Rubber.

2 What is the correct length at which an apron should be worn?
   a Just above the ankle
   b Just above the knee
   c Just below the hips
   d Just below the knee.

3 What is the purpose of wearing a necktie?
   a It looks smart
   b It absorbs sweat
   c It indicates your job
   d It supports your neck.

4 What should you do if you feel very tired after work?
   a Go to bed early
   b Eat a large meal
   c Go out with your friends
   d Watch more television.

5 What four things should you do if you accidentally cut yourself slightly while at work?

6 What should you do if you burn yourself and a blister forms on the burnt area?

7 What should you do if the skin on your hands becomes itchy and flaky?

8 How often must a first-aid qualification be retaken?

9 Which of these organisations run first-aid courses?
   a Red Arrows
   b Red Cross
   c Red Square
   d Red Aid.

10 Complete this sentence
   All injuries must be reported to _____ _____ and an entry made in the _____ _____.

Hazards in the workplace

Types of hazard

Think of a catering kitchen – what types of **hazard** exist there?
Look at the picture below. How many accidents can you see waiting
to happen?

Figure 1.10 Spot the hazards in this kitchen

From the picture you can see there are several types of hazard.
They can be grouped according to their causes:

○ Hazardous substances
○ Hazardous equipment
○ Hazardous work methods
○ Hazardous work area.

Definition

Hazard: something which
could be dangerous.

Hazardous substances

Any substance that is not in the appropriate place or is not being used correctly may become a hazard. In catering, the types of substances that may become hazardous include:

○ Cooking oil, which may:
  – overheat and catch fire
  – get spilt on a floor and make it very slippery.
○ Cleaning chemicals, which may:
  – be used incorrectly, e.g. not **diluted** sufficiently
  – not be used with the appropriate protective equipment, e.g. goggles and gloves
  – be mixed together and give off dangerous fumes
  – be decanted from a large, labelled container into a smaller, unlabelled container and mistaken for another liquid.

COSHH

The COSHH Regulations form part of the Health and Safety at Work Act. They are rules which control substances which are considered hazardous to health. The COSHH Regulations state that:

○ chemicals that may be dangerous to people must be clearly identified
○ those chemicals must be stored, issued and used safely
○ training must be given in the use of these chemicals
○ suitable protective clothing must be provided when using the chemicals.

When using any type of chemical:

○ always follow the manufacturer's instructions carefully
○ never mix one chemical with another
○ never move any chemical from its original container into an alternative one which is incorrectly labelled or has no label at all
○ never use food containers to store a cleaning chemical
○ always store chemicals in the correct place.

In the kitchen

A pub kept some beer pipe cleaning fluid in an unlabelled, clear glass bottle on the floor. It was placed near the beer pipes ready to use. A new member of staff who was very thirsty opened the bottle and drank from it. The liquid was clear and looked like lemonade but in fact was an extremely strong, **caustic** chemical. The member of staff suffered extensive burning of mouth, throat and stomach and can no longer eat normally.

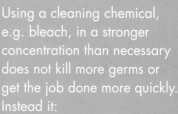

Definition
Dilute: to add extra liquid (usually water) to make the solution weaker.

Did you know?
Using a cleaning chemical, e.g. bleach, in a stronger concentration than necessary does not kill more germs or get the job done more quickly. Instead it:
o wastes the cleaning chemical (which can cost quite a lot of money)
o might damage the surface on which it is being used
o will need more rinsing off after use (which makes the job take longer in the end!).

Definition
Caustic: a substance that will stick to a surface and burn chemically. It is used for heavy-duty cleaning.

Figure 1.11 Never pour a liquid into an unlabelled container

Hazardous equipment

Hazardous equipment can be manual or electrical. Training must be given in the operation of equipment and the equipment must be checked regularly.

Types of manual equipment include:
○ knives
○ mandolins.

Knife care and safety

Poor knife techniques and untidy work methods are often a cause of accidents in the kitchen. Follow the rules below:

○ Store your knives in a specially designed area when not in use, e.g. in a box, case, wallet or on a magnetic rack. Storing loose knives in a drawer can damage the blades and cause injury.
○ When moving knives, transport them in the appropriate box or case. Never leave them loose. This avoids accidents in the workplace. It also stops you getting into trouble with the police when carrying your knives to and from work.
○ When carrying a knife, always point it down and hold it close to your side. Work colleagues can be unintentionally stabbed if this rule is not followed!
○ If passing a knife to a colleague always offer it to them handle first.
○ Never leave a knife on a work surface with the blade upwards.
○ Never leave a knife hanging over the edge of a work surface.
○ Never try to catch a falling knife – let it come to rest on the ground before you pick it up.
○ Never use a knife as a can opener or screwdriver.
○ Do not use a knife which is blunt or has a greasy, loose or damaged handle. A knife in any of these conditions can easily slip and cause a serious cut.
○ It is recommended that you use colour-coded knives to prevent cross-contamination, see Chapter 2.
○ Only use a knife on a chopping board which has a damp cloth underneath to prevent slippage.
○ When wiping a knife clean after use, wipe from the blade base to the tip with the sharp edge facing away from your body.
○ Never leave a knife in a sink. Wash it and remove it immediately.

Figure 1.12 A mandolin

Video presentation
Watch *Choosing the right knife* and *Sharpening a knife* for safety tips.

Figure 1.13 A set of chef's knives. Always take care when handling these

Electrical equipment

Hazardous electrical equipment includes:

- slicing machines
- mixers
- mincers
- blenders.

These are known as **prescribed dangerous machines** and have special regulations relating to their use. See the table on page 5.

Rules for operating machinery

- Always follow the manufacturer's instructions.
- Never operate machinery if the safety guards are not in place. Many machines will not work unless correctly and fully assembled. However, some older models may work without the safety equipment being fitted (be very careful with these).
- If the machine will not work properly seek help from your supervisor.
- Ensure that the correct attachments are being used on the equipment for the task to be carried out.
- Never push food against a cutting blade with your hands – use a proper plunger or the handle supplied. (Many chefs have lost fingers by not following this rule!)
- If using a spoon do not let it touch any moving parts. If it does the spoon and the machine will be damaged.
- Do not use faulty machinery. Label it 'out of order' and unplug it or partly dismantle it so it cannot be used. Report the problem to your supervisor so a repair can be arranged.
- Do not overload electrical sockets. This may cause a fire or cause fuses to blow and could affect everybody working in the building.
- Do not operate electrical equipment with wet hands or near sinks or any other sources of water. An electric shock could result from this action.
- Keep your hands away from sharp blades. Wait for them to stop rotating after switching the machine off before starting any other activity, e.g. cleaning.
- Make sure the power is disconnected before starting to clean electrical machinery.
- Do not use machinery if the plug or flex is damaged in any way.

Remember!
Take great care when operating machinery. No one under the age of 18 may clean, lubricate or adjust a machine if they will be at risk of injury from a moving part.

Remember!
Before using any type of machinery or equipment the member of staff must be trained in the correct procedures. They must be fully instructed about any danger which may arise and be supervised adequately by someone with knowledge and experience of the machine.

Hazardous work methods

Many accidents are caused by poor work methods. Before starting work consider these points:

○ When a range of tasks have to be completed they should be carried out in order.
○ Finish one task before starting the next.
○ Assemble all the equipment necessary before starting the task.
○ Allow sufficient time and space to carry out the task involved.
○ Follow a logical sequence. The flow of work should move one way e.g. left to right.
○ Make sure there are no spillages on the floor. They will make the floor slippery and could cause an accident.

Figure 1.14 An untidy work area showing hazardous work methods

Figure 1.15 How a work area should be organised for safety

Hazardous work area

Some areas of the kitchen may not be the most appropriate to work in, for example:

○ A larder area might be very cold. It is difficult to prepare food with very cold hands.
○ The kitchen may be very crowded if there are several staff on duty. It is easy to collide with other people in a small space. This could be very dangerous if you are carrying a pot of hot liquid.
○ Floors can get greasy and wet if spillages are not cleared up quickly and thoroughly. Staff walking from the kitchen into a walk-in cold room and out again may make the floors slippery.

Did you know?

If a floor is getting slippery during service, you should throw several generous handfuls of salt over the surface. This is a quick, temporary remedy as the salt absorbs the liquid or grease. The floor can then be cleaned properly when there is time.

Reporting hazards

If you see a hazard in your work area which could cause an accident you should do one of two things:

1 Make the hazard safe, as long as you can do so without risking your own safety.
2 Report the hazard to your supervisor as soon as you can, making sure no one enters the area without being aware of the danger.

Two good ways in which you can warn other people about hazards are:

○ block the route past the hazard
○ use a sign.

A sign is usually the best way. Temporary signs may be handwritten if there is no alternative. Many signs involve visual symbols which are best in case people passing the hazard cannot read English. Where signs are in frequent use, e.g. fire exits, they are produced in colours that can be seen by colour-blind people.

Some hazards are temporary so the sign relating to them should also be temporary, e.g. a wet floor sign. Others are there because of the nature of the building, e.g. a low beam may have a permanent sign nearby warning everyone to mind their head.

Did you know?
To warn others in the kitchen that a hot saucepan had just come out of the oven it was traditional to sprinkle flour on the handle or cover the handle with a cloth.

Commonly used hazard warning signs

The colours of the signs indicate the type of hazard involved:

○ A black and yellow sign is used with a triangular symbol where there is a risk of danger, e.g. 'Mind your head'.

○ A red circle with a line through it tells you something you must not do in the area, e.g. 'No smoking'.

○ A solid blue circle with a white picture or writing gives a reminder of something you must do, e.g. 'Shut the door'.

○ A green sign with a white picture or writing is an emergency sign for escape or first aid.

○ A red sign with white symbols or writing indicates fire-fighting information.

When using chemicals that could harm you the following signs may be displayed on the container:

○ Corrosive could burn your skin.

○ Poison may kill you if swallowed.

○ Irritant may cause itching or a rash if in contact with skin.

Find out!

What type of chemicals used in your workplace have these symbols?

What type of protective equipment should you wear when using them?

○ If this is not possible:
  - Telephone 999 (free call – even from a locked phone).
  - Ask for the ambulance service.
  - Give your telephone number so you can be called back.
  - Give the location of the accident.
  - Describe what has happened and give details of the injuries as clearly as you can.
  - Follow any instructions given over the phone. This may be giving some first aid, getting information from the injured person or going to a meeting point to wait for an ambulance.

How to treat a casualty while waiting for help

○ Talk to the person and reassure them. If you do not know them, find out their name and where they live. Be kind and considerate.
○ Tell them that help is on the way.
○ If they feel cold, cover them with a blanket or any available clothing. Try not to cover a major burn.
○ Do not move the person unless they are in danger of further injury.

See how to treat a minor cut or a burn on page 10.

Figure 1.18 Reassure the casualty

Emergency procedures and how to follow them

When there is an emergency it is important that everybody does exactly as they are told and follows the rehearsed procedure. The immediate result of most emergencies is evacuation of the building.

Evacuation procedure

If you have to leave the kitchen as the result of an emergency, remember to do the following:

○ Turn off all the power supplies (gas and electricity). This may mean hitting the red button in a modern kitchen or turning off all the appliances individually.
○ Close all the windows and doors in the area.
○ Never stop to gather personal possessions.
○ Leave the building by the nearest emergency exit (do not use a lift).
○ Assemble in the designated area away from the building.
○ Answer a roll-call of names so that everyone knows you have left the building safely.

External emergency procedure

If there is an emergency, e.g. a bomb alert outside the building, you may have to stop working and take shelter inside. Staff should rehearse for this type of emergency as well as the evacuation procedure. This external emergency procedure should include the following instructions:

- Turn off all power supplies in the kitchen.
- Close all the windows and doors in the area.
- Do not stop to gather personal possessions.
- Gather in a designated safe area. This is usually in central stairwells or corridors away from windows and as close to the middle of the building as possible.
- Stay in this area until told to leave by an emergency official.
- Answer a roll-call of names to make sure no one is missing.

A modern kitchen has a red button that turns off power supplies in an emergency.

Fire in the workplace

Fire is very dangerous and can easily become life-threatening. It is very important that you know what to do in the event of a fire. Respect fire and treat it with the utmost caution.

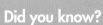

Did you know?

Many fires on catering premises have been started by a spark from the stove being sucked up the extraction canopy. When that canopy is dirty and coated with a layer of grease a fire can easily start. Because the smoke gets sucked up through the extraction system, no one may be aware there is a fire until it has spread to a dangerous level. Some commercial insurance companies will not insure catering premises unless the kitchen canopy is professionally cleaned very regularly.

Causes of fire in the workplace

Fires can quite easily be started in kitchens. There are hot stoves which are left on for long periods of time and hot fat in fryers which can overheat and catch fire. There is a large amount of electrical equipment which can develop a fault and start a fire. Over 28 per cent of fires on catering premises start in the kitchen and are caused by cooking procedures.

Figure 1.19 A fire can start when a spark from the stove is sucked into a dirty extraction canopy

How to minimise the risk of fire

Careful work practices and being observant are the main ways of reducing the risk of fire. These good practices include:

- keeping hot work areas clean of fat and grease
- never overfilling fryers and frying pans
- keeping walls and canopies around stoves clean
- not allowing cloths to dangle over stoves
- not overloading electrical sockets
- never leaving electrical appliances on unattended.

In the kitchen

A **smouldering** oven cloth nearly caused a serious fire in a London hotel. One Sunday afternoon a young chef was very keen to leave work after lunch service. He changed into his outdoor clothes as quickly as he could. Then he threw his chef's whites and cloths into his locker. He did not realise that his oven cloth was smouldering. After a while the fire alarm in the hotel sounded. The sensor board indicated the problem was in the male changing rooms.

On investigation the room was found to be full of smoke with a fire building up inside the young chef's locker. It was put out promptly, which was a good thing as the changing room was located next to the fuel store where tanks of oil were kept.

> **Definition**
> **Smoulder:** to burn slowly with a small red glow and little smoke.

Understand how a fire can start

Fire needs three things to burn. As soon as one is removed, the fire will go out.

Fuel: fire has to be fed and will use any substance that will burn, e.g. gas, electricity, cloth, oil or wood. Once the fuel has been used up the fire will go out.

Oxygen: fire requires oxygen to keep going. If the source of air is removed the fire will go out. This is why a fire blanket can put out a fire.

Heat: fire creates heat. If the heat of the fire is removed the fire will go out. This is how many fire extinguishers work.

A fire can be put out by:

- **starving** it of fuel
- **smothering** it by removing air
- **cooling** it by taking away the heat.

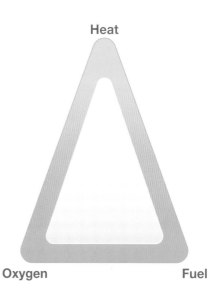

Figure 1.20 The three components that fire needs

The significance of fire alarms

Fire alarms are required in all businesses over a certain size. They save lives and are essential in large buildings. They are required in all businesses that need to have a fire certificate to operate. See Fire safety laws on page 28.

Fire alarms work by fitting smoke and heat sensors in various parts of the building. When any of these sensors are activated an alarm sounds. The sensor that has been activated shows up on the control panel and the area it covers has to be investigated immediately.

Sometimes a sensor may sound the alarm even though there is no apparent reason. This may be due to the system developing a fault. The area covered by the sensor must always be checked, even if nothing is found. A false alarm must never be assumed. If a false alarm continues to occur then an engineer will be called in to check the system.

Testing fire alarms

To ensure the alarm system is working correctly it should be tested regularly. Most businesses check their systems at the same time every week. This involves:

○ all staff being told when the test takes place so they know they do not have to evacuate the building
○ the alarm bells ringing on and off for a few minutes.

If the alarm sounds at any other time, all members of staff should follow the procedure they have been taught. This usually means leaving the building and assembling in a particular area outside. At the assembly point there is a roll-call (a type of register) to make sure that everyone has left the building and is safe.

Some alarms have two stages:

Stage 1: The smoke or fire sensor will set off the first alarm, which sounds briefly. Trained members of staff will then investigate the area. If they can deal with the cause of the alarm, or if it is a false alarm, no further action is taken.

Stage 2: Should there be a fire or other emergency, the second stage of the alarm will be activated. This means the alarm will sound continuously and the building will be evacuated. The fire brigade will also be called.

Figure 1.21 Taking a roll-call

Security procedures

Security procedures on catering premises are important for a variety of reasons:

○ To protect staff, visitors and customers on the premises.
○ To reduce theft and pilferage.
○ To help to keep a workplace safe and secure.

Keeping the workplace secure

Situation	Procedure
Key control	○ Always follow the correct procedure for issuing and returning keys. ○ Never leave keys in locks – replace them in the correct place after use. ○ Never lend keys to someone else – make them sign for them as you have done. ○ Never leave secure areas unlocked and unattended.
Personal possessions	○ Do not take anything valuable to work. If you have to, keep it locked in your locker. ○ Respect workplace rules regarding personal possessions. ○ Do not take personal bags into your work area – you could be suspected of theft. ○ You may be asked by your employer to agree to the right to be searched at random to deter theft.
Visitors and customers	○ Challenge politely anyone who is in your area who you do not recognise. 'Can I help you?' is the best way to start. ○ If the person says they are waiting for a member of staff, check the name and position of the person they are waiting for. Try to contact that person, while keeping an eye on the stranger to make sure they do not wander off. ○ Escort anyone who appears to be lost to the nearest supervisor or manager.
Closedown procedures	○ Make sure you check all doors and windows are closed. ○ Check that all cooking and preparation equipment is turned off and/or put away. ○ Check that all storage areas – fridges, freezers, dry stores and cupboards – are secure.
General observation	○ If you see someone behaving suspiciously, tell your supervisor as soon as you can. ○ Try to remember what any suspicious person looks like as well as what they were doing. ○ If you see an unattended package and you do not know what it is, **do not touch it**. Inform your supervisor as quickly as possible.

Figure 1.26: How to keep the workplace safe and secure

Property
Lost property

Your workplace should have a procedure for dealing with **lost property**. It will involve you giving the item to your supervisor and telling them:

○ where the item was found

○ the date and time the item was found.

If the item you found is not claimed by the owner after a certain period of time, it may be given back to you. Some businesses put unclaimed lost property into a charity box or sell it and put the money into a staff fund.

Security when dealing with customers' property

If you have to handle customers' property you must be very careful. You have a duty to keep the property of others safe and secure. Make sure you record:

○ a description of the item

○ to whom it belongs

○ the date and time it was left with you

○ where it was kept

○ the date and time it was returned to the customer or passed to your supervisor.

This information should help you if there is any query in respect of the property.

Definition

Lost property: an item left behind by someone else.

Find out!

What procedure does your establishment have for dealing with lost property?

Reporting incidents

It is very important that you report anything happening that is out of the ordinary or that you feel is not 'right'. It does not matter if it turns out not to be of concern on this occasion – it could be a very helpful observation for your manager or the police next time.

When you report an incident you must try to remember as much detail as you can. You may be asked to complete an Incident Form with details of:

○ date of the incident

○ time of the incident

○ place of the incident

- who was involved
- what they looked like
- who saw the incident
- a description of what happened
- how long the incident lasted
- whether anybody was hurt
- whether there was any damage to property
- whether the emergency services were called.

You would then be asked to sign and date the form.

Try this!

Study the picture below for three minutes. Close this book and write down all the details that would be needed on an Incident Form.

Figure 1.27 Can you describe what happened here?

Test yourself!

Give one security procedure for each of the following issues:

a Key control

b Personal possessions

c Visitors and customers

d Closedown procedures

e General observation.

Further information

Useful organisations

○ St John Ambulance
○ Health and Safety Executive
○ Royal Society for the Prevention of Accidents
○ Hotel and Catering International Management Association.

You can find out more about these organisations by visiting their websites. Links have been made available at www.heinemann.co.uk/hotlinks – just enter the express code 9254P

within a very short time of consumption. An incidence of food poisoning can affect a large number of people at the same time.

Symptoms of food allergies include:

o vomiting
o difficulty in breathing
o diarrhoea
o collapse
o headache
o rash.

The most dramatic reactions tend to occur in response to peanuts and shellfish.

Some allergic reactions are very severe, come on very quickly and can be fatal. This is why it is extremely important to inform customers of the precise ingredients in any dish they ask about.

Test yourself!

1 Which of the following is not a pathogenic bacterium?
   a Penicillin
   b Salmonella
   c Staphylococcus aureus
   d Bacillus cereus.

2 Which of the following describes the conditions necessary for most bacteria to reproduce?
   a Warmth, oxygen, food, moisture
   b Cool, oxygen, food, moisture
   c Warmth, carbon dioxide, food, dryness
   d Cool, carbon dioxide, food, dryness.

3 Which of the following is not a symptom of food poisoning?
   a Rash
   b Nausea
   c Sneezing
   d Abdominal pain.

4 Which Regulation concerns the safe system of food production?
   a COSHH
   b RIDDOR
   c HASAWA
   d HACCP.

5 Which of the following statements is true?
   a All pathogens cause illness
   b All moulds cause illness
   c All bacteria cause illness
   d All foreign bodies cause illness.

Personal cleanliness and hygiene

Everyone who works in a job that requires them to handle food must:

- be in good health
- have hygienic personal habits
- wear the correct, clean, protective clothing
- be aware of the potential danger of poor hygiene practice.

A high standard of personal hygiene is a requirement under the Food Safety (General Food Hygiene) Regulations 1995.

General health

Some aspects of health have already been mentioned with regard to safe working practices (see page 29). It is important to remember that working in a catering kitchen can involve:

- standing up for long periods of time
- working in a hot, noisy atmosphere
- having to concentrate and multi-task for long periods of time
- starting work early in the morning
- finishing work late at night.

Bearing these points in mind make sure you:

- have sufficient sleep and relaxation during your time off
- eat regular, balanced meals – this is essential as it is too easy to 'pick' which is not good for your digestion in the long term
- drink plenty of water during your shift at work, otherwise your concentration may be affected
- remember that healthy eating applies to staff just as much as to customers, see Chapter 4.

Personal hygiene practice

Hair: Wash your hair regularly and keep it under a hat. Longer hair should be tied back securely or contained in a net. This reduces the danger of flakes of skin or strands of hair falling into food. Beards and moustaches should also be covered. Do not touch your hair while working. When you have your hair cut, make sure you wash it again before you go to work.

Ears: Do not put your fingers into your ears while working in a kitchen. Earwax and bacteria can be transferred to food and work surfaces and equipment this way.

Nose: The pathogenic bacteria staphylococcus aureus, see page 36, is found in many adult noses and mouths. Sneezes and coughs can spread this bacteria over a wide area. This means that work surfaces, food and equipment can be contaminated very easily. A disposable handkerchief should always be used to catch a sneeze or blow your nose. Always wash your hands thoroughly after using a tissue. Nose picking is an extremely unhygienic activity as is wiping your nose on your sleeve, and neither should ever be carried out in a kitchen (or elsewhere!)

Mouth: Tasting food is essential but you must use a clean spoon each time. A spoon used for one taste should not be put back into the food for any reason without being thoroughly washed first. Spitting is extremely unhygienic – never do this. It is not acceptable to eat sweets or chew gum in the kitchen. Do not lick your finger and then use it to open bags, pick up small, light items or separate sheets of paper. All these activities can spread bacteria easily.

Neck: Do not wear strong perfume or aftershaves, deodorant or cosmetics as they can taint food.

Underarms: Daily bathing or showering removes the bacteria that causes body odour. Perspiration smells can be avoided by using a non-perfumed deodorant.

Hands: The most common method of contaminating food is by having dirty hands. Do not use your fingers for tasting. Keep your nails short and clean. Do not use nail varnish. Watches and rings (other than a plain wedding ring) are not allowed as bacteria can live in the food particles caught under them. Gemstones in jewellery may fall out and become foreign bodies in food. It is impractical to wear a watch because of the frequent use of water in the kitchen.

Remember!
Do not touch any part of any glassware, crockery or cutlery that may make contact with someone's mouth. You would not like to drink out of a cup that someone's fingers had touched around the rim, would you?

How to wash your hands properly

1 Wet your hands with a non-hand-operated warm-water spray or fill the wash hand basin with hand-hot water and wet your hands.

2 Use a non-perfumed antibacterial liquid soap or gel to provide a good lather over the top and palms of your hands, between your fingers, around your wrists and lower forearms.

3 Only use a nailbrush to clean under your fingernails if it is disinfected regularly or is disposable.

4 Rinse your hands thoroughly with clean water.

5 Dry your hands well, preferably with disposable paper towels; hot-air dryers take longer and roller towels must be clean to be safe.

Clothing

It is important to remember the following aspects of good clothing practice:

- Clean, comfortable underwear is just as important as a clean uniform.
- Do not enter the kitchen in outdoor clothing; it will be contaminated.
- Do not wear your kitchen uniform outdoors for the same reason.
- Press studs or Velcro fastenings are more hygienic and easier to use than buttons.
- Change your uniform as soon as it gets dirty. This is usually every day for aprons and jackets. Trousers should be changed two or more times a week.

You may need to wear gloves while at work. Types of gloves include:

- thin rubber or latex gloves for fine work with high-risk foods
- non-latex or vinyl gloves if the food handler has an allergic condition.

See Chapter 1 for more information.

Remember!

Always wash your hands:
- when entering the kitchen
- after using the toilet
- between each task
- between handling raw and cooked food
- after touching your face or hair
- after coughing, sneezing or blowing your nose into a handkerchief
- after any cleaning activity
- after eating, drinking or smoking during a break
- after dealing with food waste or rubbish.

Did you know?

There are three items used in hand washing which can contaminate hands rather than clean them! They are:
- a dirty bar of soap used by many different people
- a non-disposable nail brush which is not disinfected very regularly
- a roller towel which is not changed very regularly.

Did you know?

The most hygienic way of putting on your kitchen uniform is to put your hat on first to stop loose hairs falling onto your whites. When taking off your uniform, your hat should be removed last.

Figure 2.12 The correct order to put on your kitchen uniform

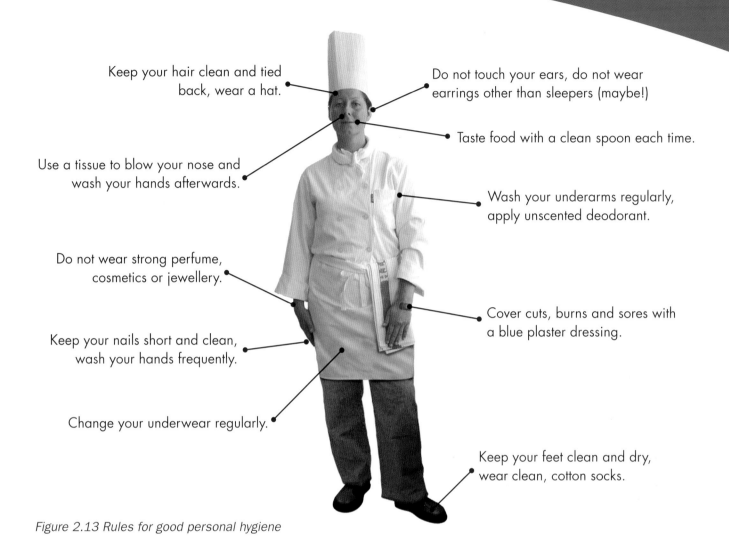

Keep your hair clean and tied back, wear a hat.

Do not touch your ears, do not wear earrings other than sleepers (maybe!)

Taste food with a clean spoon each time.

Use a tissue to blow your nose and wash your hands afterwards.

Wash your underarms regularly, apply unscented deodorant.

Do not wear strong perfume, cosmetics or jewellery.

Cover cuts, burns and sores with a blue plaster dressing.

Keep your nails short and clean, wash your hands frequently.

Change your underwear regularly.

Keep your feet clean and dry, wear clean, cotton socks.

Figure 2.13 Rules for good personal hygiene

Wounds, illness and infection

Working in a kitchen with hot items, knives and dangerous equipment means it is likely that you will suffer a slight injury occasionally. See page 10 for how to treat small cuts and burns and page 22 for more serious accidents.

From a hygiene point of view it is essential that all wounds are covered. This is to:

○ prevent blood and bacteria from the injury contaminating any food
○ prevent bacteria from raw food infecting the wound.

Using a coloured waterproof dressing (blue plaster) keeps the injury clean and protects it. Blue is the best colour for a dressing in food areas as it is easily spotted if it falls off. Very few foods are blue!

Remember!
Always tell your supervisor straightaway if you are wearing a waterproof blue plaster dressing and it goes missing in food!

Spots, blisters and boils are unpleasant skin conditions which can cause problems in food-handling areas because they will be infected with the pathogenic bacteria staphylococcus aureus (see page 36). If you have blemishes on your hands, work in suitable gloves. If they are on your face you must be very careful to avoid touching them with your hands while working. In severe cases your supervisor may give you non-food-handling tasks to carry out until the condition has cleared up.

If you are ill and suffer any symptoms that could be from a food-borne illness you must let your supervisor know as soon as possible. The symptoms concerned include:

o diarrhoea

o vomiting

o nausea

o discharges from ear, eye and nose.

You should not work as a food handler while you display any of these symptoms. It is likely you will have to seek medical help if you suffer severe bouts of these illnesses. You may need clearance from your doctor before you can resume work as a food handler.

Your supervisor also needs to know about any similar symptoms suffered by the people with whom you live. This is because you may be a carrier of an infection without displaying any symptoms of the illness. If you are carrier it means you can transmit the infection to others.

Certain illnesses legally need to be reported to the local health authority. Many of them are identified by the symptoms listed on page 47. Your supervisor or doctor should arrange for this to be done if necessary.

Remember!

Many people pick up 'tummy bugs' while on holiday abroad. If you do so, you need to tell your supervisor before you return to work.

Test yourself!

1 How often should you have a bath or shower during a working week?

2 How many occasions are there when you should wash your hands before resuming work?

3 What is a 'carrier' of a food-borne disease?

4 When changing ready to start work, which item of kitchen uniform should you put on first?

Cleanliness and hygiene in your working area

Cleaning is an essential process of removing dirt. It is vital to the safe operation of food businesses. Cleaning staff are employed in many establishments but it is the responsibility of all employees to make sure:

○ all equipment and work areas remain clean

○ the environment they work in is clean and safe.

Why clean?

Cleaning is essential in an area where food is handled for the following reasons:

○ To reduce the danger of contamination of food from:
  – bacteria, by removing particles of food upon which they can feed
  – pests
  – foreign bodies.

○ To create a good impression for:
  – customers
  – other staff and visitors
  – inspectors.

○ To reduce the risk of:
  – accidents
  – equipment breakdown.

The main principles of cleaning in a kitchen environment

Methods of cleaning

Cleaning has to be carried out in all areas of the kitchen.
These include:

○ **surfaces**: floors and worktops

○ **equipment**: manual or electrical machinery

○ **utensils**: hand-held kitchen tools.

The main stages of thorough cleaning apply to each area:

1 Switch off and unplug electrical machinery.
2 Pre-clean to remove any loose dirt and heavy soiling,
   e.g. soak a saucepan, sweep the floor, wipe down a mixer.
3 Clean by washing the item with hot water and detergent.
   Use a suitable cloth or brush to remove grease and dirt.
4 Rinse with hot water only to remove the detergent and
   any remaining dirt particles.
5 Disinfect with extremely hot water (82°C) or steam
   in a controlled area, e.g. in a dishwasher. Where
   this process is not safe or practical use a
   chemical disinfectant. Apply it to the appropriate
   surface and leave it for the length of time stated
   on the instructions.
6 Final rinse to remove all cleaning chemical residue.
7 Dry – air drying is the most hygienic, otherwise use paper
   towels or clean, dry cloths.

Figure 2.14 Cleaning a slicing machine

Types of cleaning agent

○ **Water** is the most effective cleaning agent. It can be used hot
   or cold and also under pressure. When used in the form of
   steam it can also disinfect. Water leaves no residue and is very
   environmentally friendly. It is also used for rinsing.
○ **Soap** is made from fat and caustic soda. Soap can leave a
   scum on surfaces, so it is not suitable for kitchen cleaning.
   Disinfectants are sometimes added to soap for hand washing.
○ **Detergents** are chemicals manufactured from petroleum. They
   break dirt up into fine particles and coat them so they are easy
   to remove. Detergents can be in the form of powder, liquid, foam
   or gel. They usually need mixing with water before use.
○ **Disinfectants** are chemicals that will kill bacteria if left in contact
   with the surface for a sufficient amount of time. It is better to
   apply them with a spray rather than a cloth. Their efficiency is
   affected if the surface that is being treated is not clean.
○ **Sanitiser** is a chemical which can clean and disinfect. It is often
   used in sprays for hard surface cleaning. It needs to be left in
   contact with the surface to be cleaned for a sufficient amount of
   time to be effective.

You should inform your supervisor if you see:

○ broken floor or wall tiles

○ damaged doors or handles of refrigerators, ovens, cupboards or drawers

○ loose handles on saucepans

○ light bulbs that have failed inside equipment, e.g. microwaves and refrigerators

○ the electric fly catcher becoming ineffective

○ gas equipment that becomes difficult to light or goes off during use

○ blades on machinery that have become blunt or damaged

○ paint flaking from the ceiling and falling on the work surface

○ the chopping boards in use being very scratched and pitted

○ dripping hot or cold water taps which cannot be turned off

○ any blockages, e.g. in preparation sinks or wash hand basins.

There will be many more potential hazards depending upon the size and type of kitchen that you work in.

> **Try this!**   **Worksheet 7**
>
> **Look around your workplace and make a list of all the fittings and equipment that could become a hazard and need attention. The problem could relate to health and safety or food safety. You may be surprised how long the list can be, even in a small kitchen!**

Pest control hazards

Pests are responsible for the majority of closures of food establishments by the Environmental Health Officer. Pests are also responsible for large amounts of food being wasted by infestation or contamination. Staff and customers become very upset if they find any type of pest on the premises. Under the HACCP procedures a catering business is expected to have effective pest control methods in place.

Pests live in or near catering premises because they provide:

○ **food** in store rooms, waste areas, poorly cleaned production areas

○ **moisture** from dripping taps, outside drains, **condensation** droplets

○ **warmth** from heating systems and equipment motors, e.g. refrigerators

○ **shelter** in undisturbed areas, e.g. the back of store cupboards, behind large equipment.

By removing as many of these conditions as possible, pests may be put off living in the area and look elsewhere.

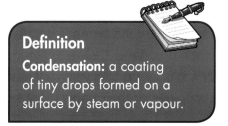

Definition
Condensation: a coating of tiny drops formed on a surface by steam or vapour.

Signs of infestation

How can you tell if there is a pest infestation in your workplace?
Look for:

- dead bodies of insects, rodents and birds
- droppings, smear marks
- eggs, larvae, feathers, nesting material
- paw or claw prints
- unusual smells
- scratching, pecking or gnawing sounds
- gnawed pipes, fittings or boxes
- torn or damaged sacks or packaging.

Pests cause hazards in the following ways:

- Bacterial contamination from pathogenic bacteria found:
  - on the surface of the pest's skin
  - in pest droppings.
- Physical contamination from fur, eggs, droppings, urine, saliva, dead bodies, nest material.
- Chemical contamination from using strong chemicals to kill the pests which then gets into food.
- Cross-contamination which occurs when a pest transfers pathogenic bacteria from one area to another, e.g. a fly landing on raw meat and then moving on to a cooked chicken.

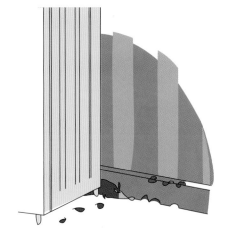

Figure 2.21 Evidence of infestation

Types of pests

Insects

Flies are one of the most common insect pests. They are usually found in places which have not been cleaned thoroughly and where rubbish is allowed to gather. A female housefly can lay up to 600 eggs in her life. An egg takes about two weeks to go through the maggot stage and become a fully grown fly.

Cockroaches are one of the oldest types of insects, said to date from prehistoric times. They do not usually fly and only come out when it is dark. Their eggs take around two months to hatch. They can live for up to a year. Cockroaches can be detected by their droppings or their unpleasant smell.

Weevils are very tiny insects that live in dry goods, e.g. flour, cereals and nuts. They can only be seen with the naked eye if they are moving. It is possible to spot an infestation if there is tunnelling or speckling in the commodity.

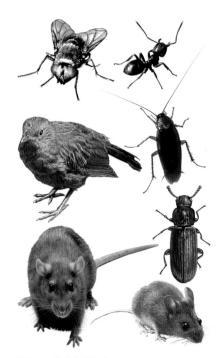

Figure 2.22 Kitchen pests

Ants are attracted by sweet items which have not been stored securely. They usually nest outdoors, and follow set paths to food sources.

Rodents

Rats commonly get into buildings through drains or holes but they also burrow under walls. Rats are a particular hazard as they can transmit Weil's disease, and a worm-type parasite as well as food poisoning bacteria. They also bite. The Norway rat is the most common in the UK. It usually lives outside.

House mice are the main problem in buildings. They can climb very well and cause considerable damage by gnawing to keep their teeth short. Like rats, their teeth grow throughout their lives and unless they wear them down, their teeth will pierce through their heads! Mice dribble urine nearly all the time and leave droppings at frequent intervals. They breed very quickly – a pair of mice can have 2,000 offspring in one year!

Birds

Pigeons, starlings and seagulls can be a problem in outside waste areas where bins are allowed to overflow and are not kept covered. Once in the area, birds may then get into a building through doors and windows and will often try to nest in roof spaces. As well as contaminating food with feathers and droppings, birds can block gutters with nests and spread insect infestation.

Preventing pest infestation

It is almost impossible to prevent pests entering a building. It is possible, however, to discourage them from staying! There are some ways of preventing pests:

- Regular thorough cleaning of areas, e.g. changing rooms and food stores, particularly in corners where pests may be able to hide unnoticed.
- Clearing up any spillages thoroughly and promptly.
- Not allowing waste to build up and keeping bins covered at all times.
- Keeping doors and windows closed or using insect screens across openings.
- Moving cupboards and equipment as far as possible to clean behind and under them regularly (see Safe lifting techniques on page 29).
- Removing any unused equipment and materials from the area.

Did you know?

This is what happens when a fly lands on your food: flies can't eat solid food so to soften it up they vomit on it. Then they stamp the vomit in until it's a liquid, usually including several bacteria for good measure. When it's good and runny they suck it all back in again, probably dropping some excrement at the same time. And then, when they've finished eating, it's your turn.

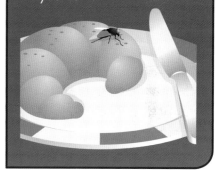

○ Ensuring food storage containers are properly closed when not in use.

○ Checking all deliveries – of all items, not just food – for signs of infestation.

○ Storing and rotating stock correctly.

What does a pest control contractor do?

A pest control contractor will inspect premises looking for evidence of infestation by any type of pest. They will then deal with any pests they discover. Finally, they will complete a report describing what action they have taken. A copy of the report is left on the premises.

A pest control contractor may:

○ lay bait and set baited traps

○ use sticky boards

○ install electric ultraviolet insect killers

○ spray an insecticide chemical over an area.

The contractor will leave instructions regarding the treatments used. It is important not to touch or move any items that have been left to catch pests. Any sprayed areas must be left untouched for the instructed period of time.

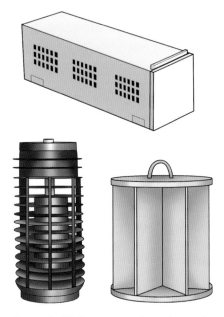

Figure 2.23 Pest control equipment

Test yourself!

1 What is the most important reason for cleaning?
   a To make a good impression on customers
   b To keep the work area pleasant
   c To reduce the danger of contamination
   d To prolong the life of equipment.

3 Which cleaning agent kills bacteria?
   a Detergent
   b Disinfectant
   c Soap
   d Warm water.

2 Which is the correct order for the cleaning process?
   a Pre-clean, clean, rinse, disinfect, rinse, dry
   b Pre-clean, rinse, clean, disinfect, rinse, dry
   c Pre-clean, disinfect, rinse, clean, rinse, dry
   d Pre-clean, rinse, clean, rinse, disinfect, dry.

4 Where might you find an infestation of weevils?
   a Flour
   b Fish
   c Fruit
   d Fennel.

Storing food inside a refrigerator

When separate refrigerators are not available for raw and high-risk foods then these items have to be positioned carefully in one unit. Raw food should **always** be stored below other food so that no blood or juices can drip down and contaminate items on the lower shelf.

Take care with strong-smelling foods (e.g. strong cheese and fish), as they can taint more delicate items (e.g. milk and eggs) and make them taste very strange. All items in a refrigerator should be covered, e.g. in a container with a fitted lid or covered with waxed paper, cling film, greaseproof paper or foil. Do not put food directly in front of the cooling unit if possible as this can affect how efficiently the refrigerator operates.

The following food should be refrigerated:
- raw meat, poultry, fish and seafood
- cooked meat, poultry, fish and seafood
- meat, poultry and fish products, e.g. pies and pâtés
- the contents of any opened cans in suitable containers
- milk, cream, cheese and eggs, and any products containing them (e.g. a flan)
- prepared salads
- fruit juice
- spreads and sauces
- any other item labelled for refrigeration.

Chilled display cabinets

Food in these units is on display for sale but is being kept cold as if it were in a refrigerator. This is achieved by cold air being circulated over the food. The highest temperature permitted for these units is 8°C. The temperature of these units can be affected by:
- draughts which can alter the air flow
- lighting which can increase the temperature
- sunlight which can also increase the temperature.

Under the HACCP procedures this type of refrigeration should be monitored very regularly.

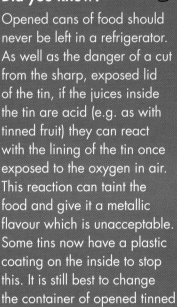

Figure 2.27 A chilled display cabinet

Remember!
Never put hot food into a refrigerator.
Never leave the refrigerator door open longer than necessary.
Both practices will cause the temperature inside the refrigerator to rise.

Did you know?
Opened cans of food should never be left in a refrigerator. As well as the danger of a cut from the sharp, exposed lid of the tin, if the juices inside the tin are acid (e.g. as with tinned fruit) they can react with the lining of the tin once exposed to the oxygen in air. This reaction can taint the food and give it a metallic flavour which is unacceptable. Some tins now have a plastic coating on the inside to stop this. It is still best to change the container of opened tinned items to be stored in the fridge.

Try this!
What problems can you identify with this refrigerator?

Freezers

Food is frozen to make it last longer without spoiling. It also keeps it safely, as pathogenic bacteria cannot multiply in temperatures below −18°C. However as soon as the temperature rises bacteria may start reproducing. Food that has been allowed to thaw should not be refrozen. This is in case the number of bacteria present have been able to reach a dangerous level and cause food poisoning. If a thawed item has been cooked it may be refrozen. This is because the cooking process will have killed any pathogenic bacteria present.

Storing foods inside a freezer

When loading a freezer with frozen food remember to:
- make sure all items are well wrapped
- label items clearly and include the date
- stack items close together to maintain the temperature
- place raw food below high-risk foods
- put stock with the shortest shelf life at the front.

Hot holding of food

Hot cupboards and counter service equipment are designed to store food for a few hours at a safe hot temperature. The heating elements in this equipment are not sufficiently powerful to raise the temperature of the food quickly. This could mean that pathogenic bacteria could survive and reproduce to a dangerous level during the slow heating process.

Did you know?

Unwrapped food in the freezer may suffer from 'freezer burn', i.e. the surface will be damaged as if it has been burnt. When thawed, the quality of the surface of the food will be poor and it may not be usable.

Remember!

If a fridge or freezer breaks down:
- call the service engineer to come and repair it
- do not open the door if at all possible.

Most freezers are fitted with alarms that will sound if there is a malfunction.

Remember!

If food has been cooked, cooled and reheated it should never be cooled and reheated a second time. It should always be thrown away.

The following rules apply when using hot holding equipment:

○ Always preheat the equipment before use.

○ Do not use the equipment to reheat food.

○ Check the equipment regularly if hot water is used; if it needs topping up use hot water (not cold).

○ If heated lights are used, keep the food fully in the lit areas.

Stock rotation

It is very important to use ingredients in the same order that they have been delivered. This is because:

○ food loses quality the longer it is kept

○ food will have to be wasted if it is not used by the 'best before date'

○ food thrown away is money wasted for the business.

Storage systems must ensure that stock is used in the correct rotation. When putting food away it is very important that:

○ older stock of the same item is moved to the front so that it is used first

○ new stock is never mixed up with old stock on shelves or in containers.

Food spoilage

As soon as fruit and vegetables are picked, animals slaughtered and fish caught the process of decomposition starts. Eventually the food will become unfit to eat. This is known as spoilage. Food decomposition is caused by:

○ the action of natural chemicals already inside the food (called enzymes)

○ the action of bacteria, moulds and yeasts that are present on the surface of food.

The speed of decomposition can be reduced by:

○ preservation, e.g. freezing, canning, drying and salting

○ keeping the food at low temperatures, e.g. in the refrigerator.

Decomposition of food can be speeded up by:

○ storage in unsuitable conditions, e.g. warm, damp conditions

○ contamination by pests

○ careless handling causing damage, e.g. the bruising of fruit.

Figure 2.28 A bain-marie, one type of hot holding equipment

Did you know?

In many countries it is now the law to label food with a date after which it is not assured of being safe to eat. It is an offence to change this date without re-treating or processing the food appropriately. Highly perishable foods (those that spoil quickly) must be marked with a 'use by' date. Less perishable items (which are preserved in some way) are marked with a 'best before' date. These dates indicate that the food will be in its best condition before this date. If consumed after this date it may have deteriorated in quality but it will not be a health risk.

Identification of spoiled food

Food that is no longer suitable to eat may:

○ be discoloured at the edges or in patches throughout
○ show mould growing on the surface
○ have a different, often unpleasant smell
○ feel different in texture, e.g. soft, pulpy, dry, cracked and wrinkled
○ taste different, e.g. bitter, sour, with an aftertaste.

Many of the conditions that allow food to spoil also allow pathogenic bacteria to multiply, see page 37. This means that spoiled food is often unsafe to eat and may cause food poisoning.

Ways of preventing spoilage

All the methods of keeping food safe from contamination reduce the speed at which spoilage occurs. These include keeping food:

○ covered
○ cool (refrigerated in most cases)
○ dry
○ free from contamination.

An alternative way of stopping spoilage is to preserve the food. There are several methods of preservation that can delay the process or prevent it altogether. These include:

○ **Heat treatment** by cooking, canning, bottling, sterilising, pasteurising and ultra-heat treatment (UHT). The amount of heat and the length of heat treatment will increase the storage time. UHT products will keep for several months, canned goods will keep for several years.
○ **Low temperatures** used in the chilling or freezing of food.
○ **Dehydration**, i.e. the drying of fish, meat, fruit, vegetables, soups, stocks and beverages. This process excludes water. Dehydrated items stored in airtight containers will last a considerable period of time.
○ **Chemical preservation** by salting, pickling and curing (using sodium nitrate and nitrite salts). This method also alters the flavour of the item. It is often combined with the canning or bottling processes.
○ **Vacuum packing**, also known as 'sous vide', is used mainly for meat, fish and poultry. This process removes oxygen from around the food and greatly extends the shelf life. The items should remain in chilled storage.

Figure 2.29 Fruit that is canned or frozen lasts much longer than fresh fruit

Did you know?
Some tinned foods have been opened after hundreds of years and the contents have still been edible (although not very nice to eat!)

Remember!
If a tin has been badly dented, damaged or is 'blown' the contents will not be safe to eat.

- **Smoking**, used particularly for fish, poultry and meat including ham and sausages. This process imparts a strong flavour to the food. Smoked items last longer than non-smoked items but still have to be kept in the refrigerator.
- **Irradiation**, is a process that kills pathogenic bacteria and spoilage organisms. It works by subjecting the food to a low amount of radiation. It does not kill spores and toxins.

Test yourself!

1 What is the maximum acceptable temperature for a chilled food delivery?
   a 3°C
   b 5°C
   c 7°C
   d 9°C.

2 What is the correct order in which the following delivered goods should be put away?
   a Frozen, chilled, fresh, tinned
   b Chilled, fresh, tinned, frozen
   c Fresh, tinned, frozen, chilled
   d Tinned, frozen, chilled, fresh.

3 Which part of the refrigerator should be cleaned very carefully?
   a Door seals   b Shelves
   c Walls   d Floor.

4 What is the term describing damaged unwrapped frozen food?
   a Contaminate   b Spoil
   c Burn   d Waste.

5 Rewrite these dry store rules correctly.
   a The store should be warm.
   b Flours and cereals may be stored in cardboard boxes.
   c Shelves should be as full as possible.
   d Old stock should be pushed to the back.
   e Store cleaning products in the same area.

6 What does 'FIFO' stand for?
   F_____
   I_____
   F_____
   O_____

7 What is the maximum acceptable temperature for a chilled display cabinet?
   a 5°C
   b 6°C
   c 7°C
   d 8°C.

8 There are three things which can affect temperature of a chilled display cabinet. Write down two of them.

Preparing and cooking food safely

Great care should be taken when preparing and cooking food.

Defrosting food safely

Some food can be cooked straight after being removed from the freezer. If this is the case there will be appropriate instructions on the packet. Otherwise the item must be allowed to thaw before cooking. This is especially important with raw meat and poultry.

The rules for thawing food:

○ Always keep thawing raw meat items well away from other food.

○ Thaw items in a cool room, thawing cabinet or in the bottom of a refrigerator.

○ Always thaw items on a tray where the defrosting juices can collect safely.

○ Once the item is thawed keep it in the refrigerator and cook it within 24 hours.

○ If using a microwave oven to defrost an item be aware of cool spots where it may remain frozen.

○ Never refreeze an item that has been thawed.

Chilling or freezing food not for immediate consumption

If food has been cooked and is not for immediate consumption it should be cooled as quickly as possible. Ideally this should be carried out in a blast chiller (see page 71). Large production kitchens may operate a large cook-chill operation producing hundreds of chilled meals every day. Some cook-chill systems also use the 'sous vide' method for preservation of food in vacuum packs (see page 66). This type of production involves specialist equipment. See Refrigerated storage on page 63.

If food is to be frozen rapidly, specialist equipment is needed to carry out this procedure safely. Blast freezers cool food down to −20°C in 90 minutes.

Did you know?

Be careful with Christmas dinner! Thawing large frozen turkeys has to be carried out very carefully to avoid outbreaks of food poisoning. A 9kg turkey will take several days to thaw. Great care has to be taken to make sure the inside of the bird is defrosted. If not it will not cook to a safe temperature and bacteria will continue to reproduce.

Figure 2.30 Is your Christmas turkey safe?

Did you know?

Some ingredients in dishes do not freeze well. Sauces which are to be frozen should not be made with wheat flour because once defrosted they will separate if not used within a few weeks. Sauce recipes should be adapted to use modified starch instead.

If freezing food you must remember to:

○ reduce the temperature as quickly as possible
○ keep the thickness of the food to be frozen as even and thin as possible
○ wrap the food thoroughly
○ label the food clearly.

See page 64 for more information.

> **Try this!**
> If an item is frozen in a standard freezer it will take much longer to freeze and the ice crystals that form within the item will be much larger. This will cause the texture of the item to be poor. Freeze a strawberry in a domestic freezer and then let it thaw! What happens to the strawberry?

Controlling food safety hazards

Methods of controlling food safety hazards

There are four main areas in the production of food where the risk of contamination by those employed in the kitchen is highest. These are:

○ cooking
○ chilling
○ cleaning
○ cross-contamination prevention.

Cooking

There are many different methods of cookery. No matter which method is used, it is important to cook food thoroughly. The choice of method should suit the food to be cooked, e.g. you cannot grill an egg. The time and temperature at which the food is cooked must ensure that all the harmful bacteria that may be present are destroyed. This must be achieved without spoiling the quality of the item that is to be served to the customer. Overcooked food may be very safe but may also be **inedible**!

Definition
Inedible: unable to be eaten.

Temperature probe

Some food may reach the required temperature on the outside but still be cooler in the middle. This is where a temperature probe is needed to check that the internal temperature has reached the necessary level.

A temperature probe is a type of thermometer on a long stick that is used to take the core temperature from the middle of food. It is particularly useful when:

○ reheating a tray of cottage pie ready to serve on a counter

○ testing to see if the inside of a whole chicken is cooked

○ measuring the temperature of a joint of meat which is being roasted in the oven.

Temperature probes are usually digital and can be battery operated. It is important to keep them very clean. They should always be sterilised before and after each use, otherwise they could transfer dangerous bacteria from one food to another.

Temperature probes are also useful to check whether food has cooled down to the required temperature before being put into the refrigerator or freezer.

Temperature probes need to be checked regularly to make sure they are working correctly. If they are not accurate they should not be used until they have been repaired or replaced.

To make cooking as safe as possible, remember these points:

○ Heat items as quickly as possible to reduce the time spent in the temperature danger zone when bacteria will reproduce quickly.

○ Cut large joints of meat and poultry into smaller portions where possible to ensure even cooking all the way through.

○ Cook stuffings separately (they often do not reach the required temperature quickly enough and have caused many outbreaks of food poisoning in the past).

○ Stir stews and casseroles regularly during cooking to keep the temperature even throughout the pan.

Remember!

All food must be heated to at least 63°C and that temperature held for at least three minutes to make it safe.

Did you know?

To ensure that all heat-resistant spores are destroyed by cooking, a temperature of 75°C must be reached for two minutes. In Scotland it must reach 82°C. Such intense heat may damage the quality of the food. It is also possible to destroy spores by heating food at a lower temperature for a longer period of time.

Remember!

Ideally food should be cooled to below 8°C in under 1½ hours. Only a blast chiller will be able to achieve this. Even this equipment cannot cool a large joint of meat within this time. That is why the law states that food should be cooled 'as quickly as possible'.

The process of monitoring can take several forms, including:

o completing a checklist
o recording specific information on a chart
o filling in particular sections on a schedule
o carrying out spot checks
o questioning staff and contractors
o observing work practices and work areas
o taking samples – of food or **swabs** of work surfaces and equipment
o weighing items
o checking temperatures.

Definition

Swab: a sterile piece of cotton used to take a sample for chemical analysis.

> **Try this!**   **Worksheet 8**
>
> **Which monitoring processes would you use for the following situations?**
>
> o *Keeping the results of refrigerator temperature checks.*
> o *Making sure all areas of the staff changing room have been cleaned thoroughly.*
> o *Checking that a meat delivery is correct.*
> o *Finding out if there is any evidence of mice in the dry stores area.*

Figure 2.35 Completing a checklist

Action to take when monitoring reveals a problem

The purpose of monitoring and checking is to spot a potential problem or risk before it becomes a serious hazard. If checking is carried out regularly then any difference in results should show up very quickly.

The action taken depends on the type of problem. Urgent action is necessary if the problem concerns a possible food safety hazard.

Figure 2.36 What should you do when plated food items do not look like the prepared photograph?

75

The table below shows the type of action that may be necessary to prevent food becoming a hazard.

Problem	Possible action to be taken
Poor standard of work produced by kitchen staff	Retraining and closer supervision by Head Chef.
Refrigerator temperature rises significantly	Check that the refrigerator is not defrosting automatically. If this is not the case: o move items to another refrigerator with the correct temperature o unplug the refrigerator if possible o put an 'out of order' notice on it o tell your supervisor as soon as possible.
A mouse is spotted in the corner of the kitchen	o Tell your supervisor as soon as possible. o The pest control contractor will be called out immediately. o Kitchen staff will need to look out for evidence of mouse infestation. o Make sure that no food crumbs are left around or any food left uncovered in kitchen and stores areas.
Microwave does not heat the food properly	o Check the portion of food is the correct size for the time allowed. o Test the microwave by heating a cup of water. o If it does not perform as it should, unplug the equipment so it cannot be used. o Put an 'out of order' sign on the machine. o Tell your supervisor. o An engineer should attend to rectify the problem.
Chilled produce is delivered in a van that is not refrigerated	o Check the temperature of the delivered items. If over the safe limit of 8°C, refuse the delivery. o Tell your supervisor, as this may have been a problem before and the supplier may be changed.
Out-of-date salad items are found at the back of the refrigerator during a stock take	o Throw the out-of-date items away. o Tell your supervisor, as stock figures will be affected.
A large amount of raw vegetable waste is found in the bin	Head Chef to retrain staff in efficient preparation methods.
A large amount of cooked waste is found in the bin	Head Chef will investigate and take action. Possible reasons: o portions served too large. o quality of food poor.
The plated food items do not look like the prepared photographs	Head Chef will investigate and take action. Possible reasons: o poor quality food used. o staff not trained correctly.

Figure 2.37 Action to take when monitoring reveals a problem

The role of record keeping

Under the HACCP procedures it is important to record readings and actions taken while preparing food. These procedures provide protection for the catering business and its employees in the event of a food safety issue.

The Environmental Health Officer visits all catering businesses regularly to check that food is being prepared according to the Regulations. The Officer will expect to see evidence of how food safety is being maintained. They will expect to see records of a variety of monitoring procedures, including:

○ temperature records of all refrigerators and freezers

○ pest control reports

○ probe temperature records of reheated foods and those held at hot temperatures

○ cleaning checklists and schedules.

If there was an outbreak of food poisoning in a restaurant, the manager should be able to prove that all the food safety procedures have been carried out correctly. This process is known as showing '**due diligence**'. The Environmental Health Officer may decide that the blame for the outbreak is not with the restaurant and investigate other possible causes, e.g. the food suppliers.

> **Definition**
> **Due diligence**: that every possible precaution has been taken by the business to avoid a food safety problem.

The relative importance of different hazards

It is important to be able to identify which situations require urgent action and which problems can be solved a little later on.

All circumstances which put any person in danger should be dealt with immediately. These include any:

○ fire or security alert

○ accident to any person in the area

○ foreign body found in food

○ equipment found in a dangerous condition

○ floor surface found in a dangerous condition

○ food left in an unsafe condition

○ food stored in an unsafe condition.

Try this!

Put the following incidents in the order you would deal with them if they all happened together. Then state the action you would take in respect of each hazard.

○ A carton of cream is past its 'use by' date in the refrigerator.

○ There is a pool of water around the door of an upright freezer and the contents are thawing.

○ A chef cuts their finger and needs a plaster.

○ A fly falls in a pan of soup on the stove.

○ A frying pan overheats and catches fire on the stove.

Figure 2.38 Can you spot all the things that have gone wrong?

Reporting food safety hazards

It is very important to report all possible hazards to your supervisor.

The situation may result in:

○ a serious safety hazard (food or health and safety)

○ a high level of wastage leading to shortages and inaccurate stock records

○ a repair or service call-out to fix or maintain a piece of equipment or to maintain the hygiene of the premises

○ the identification of a need for staff training.

Food safety management systems

In every business that produces, serves or sells food it is vital that there is an organised system to reduce all risk of food safety hazards.

The HACCP procedures require there to be a **documented** system highlighting all areas where special attention should be paid to food safety. The system should cover all food used on the premises and follow the route from the delivery of the raw materials through to the consumption, service or sale of the items.

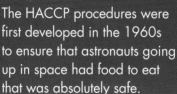

Definition
Documented: making a detailed record of information.

Did you know?
The HACCP procedures were first developed in the 1960s to ensure that astronauts going up in space had food to eat that was absolutely safe.

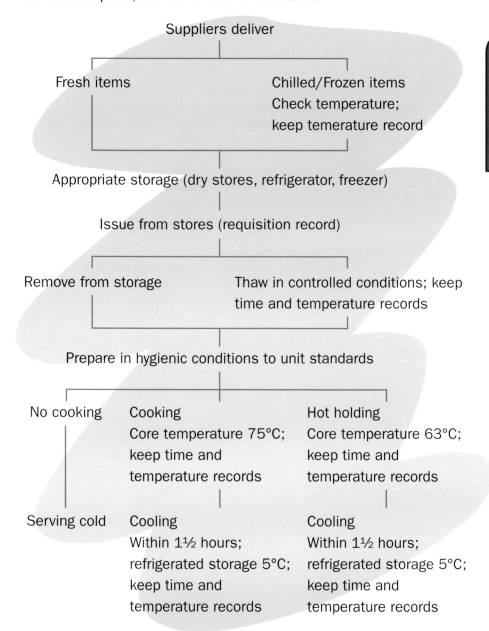

Figure 2.39 Example of isolation of critical control points in a kitchen

Step	Hazard	Action
1 Purchase	High-risk (ready-to-eat) foods contaminated with food-poisoning bacteria or toxins.	Buy from reputable supplier only. Specify maximum temperature at delivery.
2 Receipt of food	High-risk (ready-to-eat) foods contaminated with food-poisoning bacteria or toxins.	Check it looks, smells and feels right. Check the temperature is right.
3 Storage	Growth of food poisoning bacteria, toxins on high-risk (ready-to-eat) foods. Further contamination.	High-risk foods stored at safe temperature. Store them wrapped. Label high-risk food with the correct 'sell by' date. Rotate stock and used by recommended date.
4 Preparation	Contamination of high-risk (ready-to-eat) foods. Growth of food-poisoning bacteria.	Wash your hands before handling food. Limit any exposure to room temperatures during preparation. Prepare with clean equipment and use this for high-risk (ready-to-eat) food only. Separate cooked foods from any raw foods.
5 Cooking	Survival of food-poisoning bacteria.	Cooked rolled joints, chicken, and re-formed meats e.g. burgers, so that the thickest part reaches at least 75°C. Sear the outside of other, solid meat cuts (e.g. joints of beef, steaks) before cooking.
6 Cooling	Growth of food-poisoning bacteria. Production of poisons by bacteria. Contamination with food-poisoning bacteria.	Cool foods as quickly as possible. Don't leave out at room temperatures to cool, unless the cooling period is short, e.g. place any stews or rice, etc, in shallow trays and cool to chill temperatures quickly.
7 Hot-holding	Growth of food-poisoning bacteria. Production of poisons by bacteria.	Keep food hot, above 63°C.
8 Reheating	Survival of food-poisoning bacteria.	Reheat to above 75°C.
9 Chilled storage	Growth of food-poisoning bacteria.	Keep temperatures at right level. Label high-risk ready-to-eat foods with correct date code.
10 Serving	Growth of disease-causing bacteria. Production of poisons by bacteria. Contamination.	COLD SERVICE FOODS – serve high-risk foods as soon as possible after removing from refrigerated storage to avoid them getting warm. HOT FOODS – serve high-risk foods quickly to avoid them cooling down.

Figure 2.40 Critical control points – Department of Health.

The stages a food safety management system should cover are:

o quality, packaging and temperature of the food at delivery

o packaging, temperature, location and method of storage

o method of preparation

o type and length of storage between preparation and cooking

o method of holding hot food after cooking

- o method of cooling and storing after cooking
- o method of reheating cooked food
- o method of serving.

Identify types of food safety hazard

Food safety hazards can come from the most unlikely sources – some of them quite unexpected. When trying to identify possible food safety hazards you need to be very open-minded.

The table below shows the questions you need to ask when trying to identify food safety hazards:

Question	Possible answers
Where could harmful bacteria be found in the workplace?	o Poor cleaning of equipment. o Insect or rodent infestation. o Poor hygiene practices of staff – not washing hands sufficiently, staff being ill and still coming to work.
What can cause cross-contamination?	o By using the same chopping boards for raw and cooked foods. o By storing raw food above cooked food in the refrigerator. o By food handlers not washing their hands thoroughly in between dealing with raw and cooked foods.
What other possible ways are there for food to be contaminated in the workplace?	o Cleaning chemicals getting into food from poor storage or not rinsing properly. o 'Foreign bodies' getting into food from breakages not being cleared away carefully.
Which high-risk foods come into the kitchen in an uncooked state?	o Chicken o Eggs o Meat o Vegetables o Rice. These are high-risk due to the food poisoning bacteria or toxins that may be found in them in their raw state.
Is it possible for harmful bacteria to be able to multiply to a dangerous level?	o Is any food cooked and then left out at room temperature for a long time before being put in the refrigerator? Is there a better procedure that can be used? o Is any high-risk raw food left out for a long time at room temperature? Can this be avoided? o Is there ever a significant delay between cooking food, keeping it hot and it being served? Is there an alternative to this practice?
Is a probe used correctly to ensure thorough cooking and reheating of food?	If no, what happens instead?

Is food ever served before it has been reheated properly?	If yes, why and how can this be avoided next time?
Is frozen food sometimes not defrosted in time?	If yes, what happens?
Does the correct equipment exist in the kitchen for certain processes? Is it used when it should be (e.g. a blast chiller used to chill food quickly)?	If the equipment is not available, what happens?
What happens when demand is unpredictable? How is extra food provided at short notice?	Is there a stock of stand-by items kept in a freezer? How long does it take to get this ready for service?
What happens when food has to travel some distance between preparation and service? Does this happen when the food is hot or cold?	Is specialist equipment provided? If not, how is the food kept free from contamination and at the correct temperature?

Figure 2.41 Identifying food safety hazards

Try this!

Look at the table above. Now think about your workplace. Make a similar list that identifies risk areas that exist with present work practices. This is the first stage of the HACCP procedures for creating a food safety management system.

Test yourself!

1 Which of the following is an example of monitoring food safety?
   a Taking fridge temperatures
   b Writing weekly menus
   c Washing the kitchen floor
   d Calculating food cost.

2 What is the process of collecting information to prove food safety called?
   a Assessing hygiene methods
   b Monitoring bad practice
   c Copying clear records
   d Demonstrating due diligence.

3 What is the principle involved in stock rotation?
   a First in last out
   b Last in last out
   c First in first out
   d Last in first out.

4 Which of the following is not an example of a HACCP record?
   a Staff rota
   b Temperature chart
   c Cleaning schedule
   d Equipment checklist.

○ fill in 'gap' times when items are cooking or resting, with other tasks

○ clear and clean as you go – include time for this on your work plan

○ include a break in your plan at a suitable time.

Try this!

Write a time plan for a busy day at work. Allow yourself a realistic amount of time to complete the tasks. Schedule a break and time in between tasks for cleaning down.

Did your plan work? Did you find that it helped you become more organised? Did you find that you completed more jobs than usual in the time because you took the trouble to plan it out first?

Time	Job/Activity	Equipment needed

Figure 3.9 A time planning sheet

Organising your work area

To be able to work efficiently you must be organised. Part of being organised is planning ahead to make sure you have everything you need for a job before you start. You also need to position the items you are going to use sensibly on your work area. Remember:

○ Leave yourself sufficient space to carry out the task.

○ Avoid cluttering your work space with any equipment you are not going to use.

○ Use any shelves that may be above or below your work area. Do not overload shelves or position anything on them that might fall off easily.

○ Include waste bowls or trays on your list of equipment. They should be big enough to hold trimmings and peelings without overflowing. They should not be so big that they take up too much space on the worktop and cramp the work area.

○ If working with high-risk foods, avoid any risk of contaminating any of the items (see, page 69 Controlling food safety hazards).

○ Make sure you can work in a safe manner so you do not endanger either yourself or others (see Chapter 1, Health and safety).

Figure 3.10 In which area could you work more efficiently?

Try this!

At work on a fairly quiet day, test how organised you are!

While you carry out one of your routine preparation jobs, make a note of how many times you have to leave your workplace to fetch items you have forgotten. Time yourself from when you start to get ready until the task is finished.

The next time you have the same job to do, take a few minutes to write out all the supplies and equipment you will need, then get them ready. Time yourself from the start of assembling the equipment to the end of the job and see if you have saved any time – you should have!

Test yourself!

1 You have been following a recipe to make bread rolls for the first time. The instructions state that the mixture must be 'proved'. You do not understand this term. Should you:

   a ask for help?
   b miss that section of the recipe out?
   c throw the mixture away?
   d leave the kitchen in search of a textbook?

2 When preparing several different dishes for lunch service do you:

   a start with the first one on the list and work your way through to the last?
   b start with the most difficult and leave the easiest until last?
   c pick the one you enjoy making most to do first and leave the others until later?
   d decide in advance which is going to take the longest and start with that dish, working out a time plan to include the others?

3 You find that you have had to go back to the stores several times for ingredients and equipment for your current task. You could save time and energy by:

   a assembling all the ingredients and equipment together at the start
   b leaving that task until the end of the day next time
   c asking someone else to collect the items you had forgotten
   d requesting your work area to be moved nearer to the stores.

Supporting the work of your team

To be able to work together as a team it is important that members:

○ each carry out a fair share of the workload
○ all work to the same standard
○ show consideration to each other
○ communicate effectively with one another.

Unfair work practices

One problem that can occur when people work in teams is unfair working. Everyone in a team is expected to contribute fairly to the workload of the team. In a kitchen there is no choice about how much preparation work has to be completed before service – it all has to be done, otherwise the meal service will be affected.

The reason someone may not be pulling their weight in a team at work could be:

○ they are new at the job and cannot work at the necessary speed yet
○ they are not feeling well
○ they have personal problems which are affecting their performance at work
○ they are tired
○ they are lazy
○ they are not keen or interested in their job.

Figure 3.11 Should these chefs be at work?

New staff members are usually given a period of induction and training when they start a new job. They are not often given a full workload to complete. If they are struggling, the team leader should notice this and assign another team member to help them until they can cope.

Staff who are not feeling well should not come to work. They should contact their employer as soon as possible. This is particularly the case with those employees whose jobs involve handling food. Their illness could be transmitted through the food to other staff or customers (see Wounds, illness and infection on page 47).

Sometimes staff come to work because they do not want to let their other team members down. If this is the case, the team leader should either send them home or transfer them to duties not involving food handling until they feel better.

Many people have to deal with personal problems outside work. Sometimes this can affect their performance at work. If this is the case the poorly performing person should be encouraged to see their team leader or someone either at work or outside with whom they can talk about their problem. If nothing is done to help, the person could end up losing their job – which would be an additional problem for them to deal with.

Working in food production is tiring (see Personal cleanliness and hygiene, page 44). If employees do not look after themselves properly they will not be able to continue to do their job well. This can cause them to be persistently late or careless and slow in their tasks. After a while the rest of their team will not tolerate this.

In the kitchen

Tom started a new job in a busy restaurant kitchen. He worked in the vegetable section with two other chefs. Tom found the work quite hard. He was very tired when he got home at the end of his shift, but he still enjoyed going out with his friends later. Most nights he went out and did not come back until after midnight. After a few days he started being late for work. Tom kept oversleeping. At first the two other chefs helped him catch up with his preparation so that he was ready for service. Tom liked the help. It meant it did not really matter if he was late. A couple of weeks went by and then the two other chefs stopped helping Tom. This meant that Tom could not finish his vegetable preparation in time for service. He got into trouble with the Head Chef and received a formal warning for being persistently late for work.

Why did the two other chefs help Tom at first? Why did they stop helping him?

Being reliable and considerate to your other team members is very important.

There are also people who do not pull their weight at work because they are not really interested in the job they do. This situation may result in staff:
○ being noisy
○ being thoughtless
○ being inconsiderate
○ being annoying
○ being careless
○ taking shortcuts
○ producing work of a poor standard.

This affects other members of the team in a bad way.

Consideration to other team members

Occasionally members of a team do not get on together or with the team leader for a variety of reasons. These may include:

○ a personality clash
○ members of the team having different standards and principles
○ individuals not accepting criticism very well.

It may take some time for frictions in a team to settle down. As long as all the team members are considerate and motivated this should eventually happen. A positive attitude is required from everyone concerned.

Figure 3.12 The wrong way to deal with a problem

Try this!   **Worksheet 11**

Beverley had been working in the kitchen for ten years. She enjoyed her job and knew she was very good at it. She maintained high standards and expected other people to do the same. Beverley did not tolerate fools gladly and she could be very impatient.

Rob started working in the kitchen. It was his first full-time job after completing his college catering course. He did very well at college and won a prize for achievement. He knew he could be very good at his job, and expected to be promoted very soon.

Rob did not agree with some of Beverley's work practices. He told her some of the things she was doing were wrong. This infuriated Beverley. She started to resent Rob and felt that she was being made to look foolish in front of the rest of the staff. One day the Head Chef asked Rob to make a red wine sauce. Rob left the sauce on the stove to cook and went to the stores to fetch some more ingredients. The sauce started to burn. Despite the smell of burning, no one removed the saucepan from the stove. When Rob returned he found the burnt sauce. He was not sure what to do and asked Beverley. Beverley took great delight in telling Rob in a very loud voice that he had ruined the sauce and should have known better than to leave a pan unattended in the kitchen. She reminded him that there was no more red wine left and told him he would just have to make do. Rob swore at Beverley and stormed out of the kitchen.

What approach did Rob have that upset Beverley?

What approach did Beverley have that upset Rob?

If you were the Head Chef, how would you put this situation right?

Figure 3.13 The right way to deal with a problem

Remember!

Never:
o be rude or swear at anyone
o be malicious or spiteful
o take people for granted
o let your standards slip.

Always:
o show respect for others
o be enthusiastic
o be helpful
o listen carefully to others.

Communication skills

Being able to work well as a team is only possible if you communicate well. This does not just mean talking to each other. Communication can take different forms, including:

○ talking face to face
○ speaking on the phone
○ sending an email
○ sending a text message
○ writing a message or letter
○ body language.

Most communication in the kitchen involves speaking and body language. However, sometimes there is a need to write things down – food orders, stock requisitions, messages for other members of staff.

Talking face to face is the most effective method of communication, as both people can see the expressions on each other's faces as well as hear what they are saying. This helps them understand better.

How to communicate effectively

Most people do not listen carefully to what is being said to them. This is where many problems occur. The best way to find out if someone has understood what you have said is to ask them a question about it. Alternatively, you could ask them to repeat back what you have said to them. If you have been telling them how to do something, you could ask them to do it for you.

The catering and hospitality industry is international. You may have to communicate with someone who does not speak the same language as yourself. To ensure they understand what you are trying to say to them you may need to:

○ show them what you mean
○ draw a picture to help you explain
○ get someone who speaks both languages to help you.

Using the phone at work

Speaking on the phone is something that we are all used to at home. At work communication must be precise and accurate. The phone is used at work because you can receive an instant response to a question from someone who is not in the same area.

Figure 3.14 Listen carefully and be precise

When speaking on the phone you must remember:

○ to speak clearly
○ not to speak too quickly
○ to announce yourself and your position when you answer
○ to smile as you speak (it does make a difference!)
○ to write down any important information you are given
○ to repeat back to the caller any important information to ensure it is accurate. This is particularly important with telephone numbers and prices of commodities, for example.

Always keep a record of:

○ the name of the caller
○ the time of the call
○ the date of the call
○ the contact number to return the call.

Sending an email

Sending a business email should be similar to writing a business letter. These are some of the informal rules to observe:

○ Do not abbreviate or use slang expressions or text language.
○ Always read over the message before you send it to make sure it makes sense.
○ Never use all capitals: IT LOOKS AS THOUGH YOU ARE SHOUTING!
○ Always use a greeting, such as 'Dear Mr Phillips'.

In a kitchen environment emails may be sent internally:

○ to different departments about guest requests
○ to departmental managers about staffing arrangements and new procedures.

or externally:

○ to suppliers with orders
○ to potential suppliers asking for prices and delivery information
○ to service companies to arrange engineers to call.

Figure 3.15 Follow the informal rules when sending an email

Writing a message

It is very important when you prepare a message for someone else to read that:

○ you write as clearly as possible – print if necessary
○ you double-check any names and numbers as you write them down
○ you sign the message with your name and the date and time you wrote it
○ you leave the message in a safe place where you are sure it will be seen by the appropriate person as soon as possible.

Figure 3.16 Write messages carefully

Body language

Body language is the way people communicate with each other without using words, instead they use gestures. It is done subconsciously – without you noticing. You must be aware of the effect body language can have. If you are trying to hide your feelings from someone, be very careful – body language never lies!

Body language differs from culture to culture. If you are working with people from other parts of the world you need to be aware of this. Examples of this include:

○ Japanese people greet each other by bowing very low.
○ Indian people may move their heads from side to side when they mean 'yes'.

Which method of communication is best to use?

It is important to know which form of communication is best to use on which occasion. As more ways of transmitting information are invented – such as email and text messages – choosing the best method can be difficult.

Try this!
Worksheet 12

Choose the best method of communication for the following examples:

○ **To get an order to a supplier for delivery the next morning.**
○ **To ask a member of staff to prepare a dish straight away.**
○ **To instruct a member of staff how to garnish a new main course dish.**
○ **To remind a member of staff to start work early the next day.**

Did your answers cover a range of communication methods? If your answers were exactly the same for each example think carefully. Could any problem or confusion result from your choice of communication method? Would this affect the service to the customer? Could others in the kitchen have to work harder to put the problem right?

What do all these situations have in common?

○ The Head Chef tells you the recipe to use for a new starter about to go on the menu.
○ The vegetable supplier tells you the new telephone number to be used to place daily orders.
○ The Head Chef asks you to provide a list of the ingredients you need to prepare for the service next week.
○ The meat supplier gives you the website address where the up-to-date prices can be found.

Feedback will often result in a change or reward, for example:

- A negative customer comment about a dish may mean it is removed from the menu.
- A positive appraisal may mean an employee is considered for promotion.

Developing and using a learning plan

A learning plan is a useful way of organising your development. As you progress in your job you may improve your skills and abilities on a formal basis – such as a college course. You may also learn different skills in your everyday work.

A learning plan can help you in two ways:

- It can help you to plan out a career path.
- It can help you organise any formal learning you are undertaking.

Planning out a career path

If you are ambitious and want to own your own catering business or manage a large kitchen, you will need a high level of technical knowledge as well as good business and management skills. To obtain these skills you may need to study several courses. A learning plan will help you map these out so that you take the right courses in the most suitable order – either full-time or part-time. You need to match these courses with appropriate jobs at the right level to help you develop your skills.

It is useful to have the help of a Careers Advisor when using a learning plan in this way.

Formal learning

If you are already studying a course a formal learning plan can be very useful. It will:

- help you order the reading and coursework that you need to complete
- allow you to set realistic targets to achieve these stages in your studying
- help to train you in time management
- help you to keep your learning on track so that you can achieve your ambition.

What you need to set up a formal learning plan

You will need a diary and a notebook. In the notebook you will need to record:

- your long-term aims – what you want to achieve finally
- your short-term aims – the achievements you need to fulfil your long-term aims
- the formal short-term aims that you may have set for you by your workplace or college, e.g. passing your Intermediate Food Hygiene examination, or completing a project on different types of poultry.

In the diary, set yourself some realistic target dates such as:

- the date you have to take your Food Hygiene examination
- the date by which you should start revising for the examination
- the date you should hand in your project
- a series of dates by which you should have various sections of your project researched, prepared and produced.

By planning your learning in this way, you are giving yourself the best chance of fulfilling all your ambitions. You are also demonstrating to your employer and others that you can be organised, conscientious, focused and reliable. By completing the learning experiences, you acquire knowledge and skill which can be used to help you later in life.

Test yourself!

1 Name three ways in which you could improve your work performance and further your career.

2 What could happen if you had a bad appraisal interview with your manager?

3 What do you need to set up a formal learning plan?

4

Healthy eating

This chapter covers the following NVQ unit:

- Unit 2FPC13 Prepare, cook and finish healthier dishes

Working through this chapter could also provide evidence for the following Key Skills: C1.1, C1.2, N1.1, N1.2, WO2.1, WO2.1, PS2.1, PS2.2

In this chapter you will learn how to:

Check the ingredients for a dish
Prepare ingredients to minimise fat, salt and sugar and maximise fibre content
Cook the dish to maximise its nutritional value
Present the dish in a way that is attractive to the customer
Serve the dish to give the customer a choice of sauces, dressings, toppings and condiments

A balanced diet

Everyone is constantly told by the press, doctors and the government that healthy eating is very important. People generally live much longer now that they did fifty or one hundred years ago. On average people also grow taller and weigh more. The amount and variety of food available today is the greatest ever. Many food items are much cheaper than they used to be.

Food provides material that our bodies can convert into heat and energy and can use to grow and repair internal systems.

Food is made up of various amounts of carbohydrate, protein, fat, vitamins, mineral salts and fibre. A balanced diet must contain all of these nutrients in the correct proportions. Lack of any one will affect the body in different ways:

○ Lack of carbohydrate → lower energy levels.
○ Lack of protein → poor growth and healing.
○ Lack of fat → poor health and low energy.
○ Lack of vitamins → poor health.
○ Lack of mineral salts → poor teeth and bones and general health.
○ Lack of fibre → poor digestion.

Figure 4.1 Eating healthily can lead to a longer life

If we eat more food than our bodies require, the excess amounts will:

○ build up fat which is stored on our bodies
○ increase the weight which we have to carry around
○ create an imbalance of chemicals in our bodies (e.g. too much salt or sugar).

This leads to problems such as:

○ obesity (from the build-up of fat)
○ joint problems (from the increase in weight)
○ diabetes, high blood pressure, thyroid problems (from the increase in sugar and from particular types of fat which are much more common now in the food we eat).

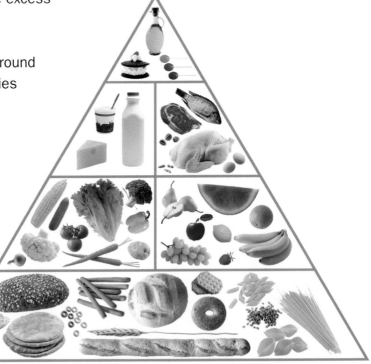

Figure 4.2 A food pyramid

When they are at home, people have the choice of eating healthily. Some people are not in this position and have to eat meals that have been prepared for them. Examples of people in this situation include residents of:

o hospitals
o prisons
o care homes
o boarding schools
o residential homes
o armed forces barracks.

If you work in a food production operation which caters for one of these sectors you have a particular responsibility to ensure that they have a balanced diet.

Nowadays people eat out more than ever before. This places a duty on caterers to ensure that safe, nutritious, healthy choices appear on restaurant menus. Chefs must be aware of the need to offer a choice of dishes with:

o fewer calories
o less fat
o less sugar
o less salt.

Government guidelines for healthy eating

The government, together with experts from the food industry, regularly carries out investigations into the health of the population. From these investigations it produces a series of reports with recommendations.

A 2005 government report states:

'Good nutrition is vital to good health. Poor nutrition is a recognised cause of ill-health and premature death in England – an estimated one-third of cancers can be attributed to poor diet and nutrition. While there is a high awareness of healthy eating, most people consume less than the recommended amounts of fruit and vegetables but more than the recommended amounts of fat, salt and sugar.'

Did you know?
In the UK 65 per cent of men and 56 per cent of women – 24 million adults – are either overweight or obese. This is a form of 'malnutrition' – meaning 'bad nutrition' – although this term is more often used to describe people who do not have sufficient food to eat.

The government issued the following guidelines for everyone to follow:
○ Increase the amount of fruit and vegetables eaten to at least five portions per day.
○ Increase the amount of fibre consumed.
○ Reduce the amount of salt consumed.
○ Reduce the amount of saturated fat eaten.
○ Reduce the amount of sugar consumed.

The Food Standards Agency has developed a programme called 'The Balance of Good Health' to show people what proportions and types of foods make up a healthy, balanced diet.

This programme divides foods into five different groups. For each group it gives a recommended daily serving. This will vary slightly according to the age, sex and occupation of the person. The groups are as follows:
○ Bread, other cereals and potatoes – one to two servings per day.
○ Fruit and vegetables – five servings per day.
○ Milk and dairy foods – two to three servings per day.
○ Meat, fish and alternatives – one to two servings per day.
○ Foods containing fat and food containing sugar – one small serving per day.

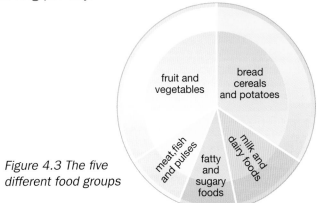

Figure 4.3 The five different food groups

Remember!
The way you cook food can affect how healthy it is to eat. Chicken breast is a healthy food – but not if it is breadcrumbed and then deep fried!

Remember!
Your customers should:
○ enjoy their food
○ eat a variety of different foods
○ eat the right amount to be a healthy weight
○ eat plenty of foods rich in starch and fibre
○ eat plenty of fruit and vegetables
○ not eat too many foods that contain sugar or salt
○ not eat too many foods that contain a lot of fat.

Types and combinations of ingredients that make a healthy dish

Including the following items in a dish will increase its health value:
○ Generous amounts of fruit and vegetables which are an excellent source of vitamins, minerals and fibre.
○ Moderate amounts of meat, fish and dairy foods.
○ Small amounts of fats and oils.
○ Wholegrain items such as oats, wheat and other cereals.

Basic nutrition

Nutrition is the study of the various ways in which food can nourish the body. The human body is very complicated. Nutritional scientists are still discovering ways in which the body uses food. New recommendations about diet are issued when new research has been successfully carried out. These may recommend that we eat more of certain types of food, or identify food items which have been found not to be good for health.

The table below shows which types of food are the best sources of the nutrients that are needed for a balanced diet.

Nutrient	Type of food	Why it is needed
Carbohydrates	Potatoes, bread, pasta, rice – as starch Sweet food and drinks – as sugars	To provide energy
Proteins	Meat, fish, nuts, lentils	For growing and repairing tissues
Fats	Meat, fried food, cakes and pastries	For energy and certain vitamins
Vitamins and minerals	Fruit, vegetables and many other types of food	For general health
Fibre	Fruit, vegetables, unrefined cereals	To aid digestion
Water	Pure water is best but 4 pints per day of water-based liquid (such as low-sugar squash) is recommended	To aid digestion and most other body processes

Figure 4.4 Types of food that provide different nutrients and why they are needed

Try this! Worksheet 13

Protein is essential for growth and the repair of the body. List five types of food that are high in proteins and five that are low in proteins. You can repeat this exercise for the other basic nutrients too.

Did you know?

A prolonged lack of certain substances may lead to particular illnesses, e.g.:
o a lack of vitamin C leads to a skin condition called scurvy
o a lack of iron leads to a blood condition called anaemia.

The digestive system

The body is able to make use of the food we eat by a process called digestion. Most food contains more than one nutrient. Food needs to be broken down by the body into individual nutrients ready for use.

The digestive system breaks down the food we eat into a substance from which it can remove the nutrients. It does this in a series of stages:

1 Your teeth physically reduce the size of the food. If you do not chew your food well you can put strain on your oesophagus (the tube from your mouth to your stomach).

2 The food is then mixed with saliva, which breaks down starch into simple sugars. This is why if you leave bread or potatoes in your mouth for a while before swallowing they start to taste sweet.

3 In the stomach the food is mixed with gastric juices. These juices are made up of hydrochloric acid and substances called enzymes. These break down the complex structure of protein and curdle any milk present.

4 In the small intestine:
   ○ any remaining starch is converted to glucose
   ○ proteins are converted into a range of amino acids
   ○ fats are broken down into a watery solution ready to move into the intestines.

5 Most nutrients are absorbed into the bloodstream through the lining of the small intestine. The nutrients can then be carried round the body to where they are needed.

6 Bacteria are naturally found in the large intestine and they help the body to process food.

7 Any indigestible matter – such as fibre – continues through the colon and passes out through the rectum and anus. A meal may take 24 hours or more to completely pass through the digestive system.

We need to look at the nutrients in food in more detail to be able to appreciate their importance when creating healthy dishes.

Figure 4.5 The digestive system

Did you know?

If you unravelled your intestines they would be the length of a double-decker bus!

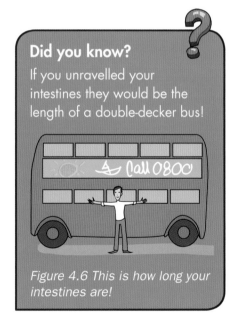

Figure 4.6 This is how long your intestines are!

Did you know?

Some of the acids present in your stomach are as strong as industrial strength cleaner!

Proteins

All proteins are made up from amino acids. There are 22 of them and all are needed by the body to grow and repair itself. When proteins are broken down by the digestive process, the body can manufacture most of these amino acids for itself – but there are a few that it cannot create. These are known as 'essential' amino acids. To ensure the body has all the amino acids it needs it is important to use protein food from both animal and vegetable origins.

These include:

Animal	Vegetable
Meat Game Poultry Fish	Peas Beans Nuts
Eggs Milk Cheese	Wheat products

Figure 4.7 Types of protein

Fats

As well as providing energy, fats also carry certain important vitamins. Both plants and animals contain fats, but they are of different sorts. They include:

Animal fats	Vegetable fats
Butter	Margarine
Cheese	Nuts
Lard	Soya beans
Fish oil	Olive oil

Figure 4.8 Types of fat

Differences between fats are caused by the variety in fatty acids from which they are made. Animal fats are 'saturated' and fish and vegetable fats are 'unsaturated'. Some animal fats also contain vitamins A and D. A manufacturing process called 'hydrogenation' can turn liquid oils into solid fat known as 'trans-fat'. This type of fat can be found in increasing amounts in ready-prepared meals. To be digested successfully all fats have to be broken down into fatty acids and a chemical called 'glycerol'. Animal fats and trans-fats are said to cause a higher amount of cholesterol to be found in the bloodstream.

Carbohydrates

The vast majority of food items in which carbohydrates are found are vegetable. They provide energy for the body. There are two main types of carbohydrates:

○ Sugars are very simple for the body to absorb.
  They include:
  – glucose
  – sucrose
  – maltose
  – fructose
  – lactose.

○ Starch is difficult to digest unless it has been cooked.
  Sources include:
  – all cereals (such as wheat flour)
  – potatoes
  – pulse vegetables such as lentils.

Vitamins

Vitamins are chemical substances which are very important for health. Without the correct balance of vitamins in your body you may not grow properly and will feel generally unwell. If you take in too large an amount of some vitamins you can poison yourself – but it is extremely unusual for this to happen.

The table below gives more information about the main groups of vitamins.

Vitamin	Type of food	Why it is needed
Vitamin A	Dairy products Fish oils Dark green vegetables	Helps growth and resists infection Helps eyesight
Vitamin B group	Yeast (in bread) Meat Cereals	Helps growth and energy levels Helps the nervous system
Vitamin C	Fresh fruit Green vegetables Potatoes	Helps growth and healing of injuries Prevents gum and mouth infections
Vitamin D	Sunlight Dairy produce Oily fish	Prevents brittle bones and teeth

Figure 4.9 What types of food provide vitamins and why they are needed

Minerals

You may be familiar with minerals such as iron, salt and copper and what they can be used for, e.g. manufacturing. But did you know that the human body needs very tiny amounts of 19 minerals to keep it healthy? However, too much of any mineral can be extremely bad for you. For example, most people in Britain eat far too much salt.

The table below gives more information about the most important minerals.

Mineral	Type of food	Why it is needed
Calcium	Dairy products Fish Bread	Helps bones and teeth grow Helps blood clot
Iron	Meat Green vegetables Fish	Helps keeps the blood healthy
Sodium (salt)	Meat Eggs Fish	Helps keep all the fluids in the body balanced

Figure 4.10 What foods provide minerals and why they are needed

Did you know?
Thinking uses up less than one calorie per hour!

Calories

All food has a value in numbers of calories. Calories measure the amount of energy food can produce in the body. If the body does not use this energy it tends to be saved as fat. It is useful to know the number of calories in the food you are eating if you are training for a particular sport when you need to use a lot of energy. It is also helpful when you are trying to keep a balanced diet and control your weight.

Figure 4.11 The more active you are, the more calories you will use

Different activities use up different numbers of calories. For example:
- Sitting watching television – 15 calories per hour.
- Walking moderately fast – 215 calories per hour.
- Climbing up stairs – 1000 calories per hour.

Try this!   **Worksheet 14**

When you are next out shopping for food, look at the label of the item you are buying. It will usually tell you how many calories the food will provide. See which food has the highest in value and which has the lowest. The highest value food is likely to be the most fattening!

What makes a balanced diet?

Now that you know the main nutrients that are needed by the body you may be able to understand the problems that people can experience from not eating a balanced diet.

If people eat too much **fat** they are in danger of:

- obesity
- high blood pressure
- heart attacks.

If people eat too much **sugar** they may suffer from:

- tooth decay
- diabetes
- obesity.

If too much **salt** is consumed, people may experience:

- kidney problems
- high blood pressure.

The government's research has discovered that many people have medical problems brought on by eating too much fat, sugar and salt. This is why it is trying to promote a healthier diet and lifestyle for everyone. A healthier diet would include more starchy food, fruit, vegetables and pulses. Why are these important?

Eating **starchy** foods helps:

- the digestive system work better
- provide many of the minerals and vitamins needed for health.

Eating more **fruit and vegetables** helps:

- general health improve
- the digestive system work better
- provide many of the minerals and vitamins needed for health.

Eating more **pulses helps:**

- the digestive system work better
- provide a useful alternative to meat and fish
- reduce the amount of fat consumed.

Did you know?
Most people eat too much salt – probably around one and a half times more than is good for them. Adults should eat no more than one teaspoonful of salt per day.

Remember!
Starchy foods include cereals, bread, pasta and potatoes.

Remember!
Pulses include butter beans, kidney beans, lentils, soya beans and chick peas.

How to interpret food labels

Labels on packaged food now have a great deal of nutrition information. This is to try to help everyone eat a balanced diet. There is also a lot of information about ingredients which is very important for anyone who is allergic to a particular substance (see Allergies, page 42).

The law now states that food labels must contain:

○ the name of the food – including any method of processing, e.g. dried peanuts, smoked mackerel
○ the weight or volume
○ a list of ingredients – in order of weight from largest to smallest
○ a use-by date for perishable food or best-before date for preserved food
○ storage conditions
○ preparation instructions – to ensure the food tastes its best and that it will be thoroughly heated to the safe temperature of 75°C
○ the name and address of manufacturer, packer or seller – in case further information is required
○ a production lot number – in case there is a problem and the product has to be recalled.

Additional information may also be provided, e.g.:

○ nutrition information
○ cooking instructions
○ serving suggestions.

These are the symbols for the shelf life of frozen foods:

Symbol	Food must be kept at or below	Maximum storage times	Pre-frozen or frozen from fresh
*	–6°C	One week	Pre-frozen food only
**	–12°C	One month	Pre-frozen food only
***	–18°C	Three months	Pre-frozen food only
****	–18°C or colder	Six months	Pre-frozen food; or fresh food frozen from room temperature

Figure 4.12 Shelf life of frozen foods

Allergen information

As well as appearing in the ingredients list, sometimes food types which are known to cause allergy may be listed again in a separate box or highlighted in some other way. Some labels include 'may contain' warnings to indicate the food may contain minute traces of food known to cause an allergic reaction (see Allergies, page 42).

> **Remember!**
> In Britain, most foods sold loose do not have to display all the information required by the food labelling laws for packaged foods.

> **Did you know?**
> A new European Union law will require certain food ingredients to which many people are allergic to be very clearly labelled. The foods include milk, eggs, peanuts, fish, soya, wheat, sesame and sulphur dioxide.

Figure 4.13 Food labels must contain warnings about allergens

Creating and presenting healthier dishes

For chefs producing food in residential situations, such as care homes and schools, offering their customers healthy meals is very important. It is also necessary in hospitals, to help patients recover their health quickly.

Figure 4.14 Healthy meals are especially important for hospital patients

Fresh ingredients are better for health

Many commodities now travel a very long distance from where they were produced to where they will be used. The longer the journey, the more the quality of the produce will drop. Salad leaves picked by a farmer and sold in the local market will be much fresher than those grown in Spain, packed up and transported by a lorry, followed by a plane journey and then another lorry trip!

Figure 4.15 Many ingredients travel a long way to get to our tables

Preserved ingredients such as frozen and canned items are useful, but are not usually as healthy as fresh or chilled items which contain more nutrients. The preservation process can destroy some of the nutrients in the food.

Did you know?

A large hospital in the south-west of England produces meals for 720 patients daily and operates a 250-seater restaurant providing lunches for hospital visitors and staff. The chef uses a low-salt convenience stock in the kitchen. Menu items offered to patients include choices suitable for high-energy, diabetic, low-potassium, low-salt and healthy-eating diets.

Did you know?

At the Yew Lodge Hotel in the Midlands, the chefs use seasonal, healthy food and include ingredients such as beans and lentils in dishes. They use sweet potato and carrot mash instead of creamed potato. They allow the customer to choose if they want a sauce with their food.

Preparing ingredients in a healthy way

If fresh ingredients are prepared a long time before they are used, they lose some of their important vitamins and minerals. The quality also suffers as they may become dried-up and stale. Onions prepared too far in advance will lose their flavour and beetroot will 'bleed'. There is also likely to be more waste from food that cannot be used.

Ways of reducing saturated fat in dishes

- Use olive oil or sunflower oil instead of butter.
- Select lean cuts of meat and trim the fat off other cuts.
- Cut chips as thickly as possible as they absorb less fat.
- Avoid glazing vegetables.
- If frying, make sure the oil is hot enough. Otherwise the food will absorb more fat. Food which has been fried needs to be drained on absorbent paper to remove the surplus fat.
- Use fish such as salmon, trout, mackerel and fresh tuna in place of cod, haddock, plaice and tinned tuna.
- Use semi-skimmed or skimmed milk in place of the full-fat type.
- Use a strong cheese so that you can use less of it.
- Use yoghurt, **quark**, crème fraîche or fromage frais in place of cream.

Definition

Quark: A German cheese with the texture and flavour of soured cream.

Ways of reducing sugar in dishes

- Eat plain fresh fruit as a dessert.
- Always use tinned fruit in natural unsweetened fruit juice rather than in syrup.
- Use fresh or unsweetened fruit juices whenever possible.
- In place of fizzy drinks, try fresh or unsweetened fruit juice with sparkling water.
- Cut back on the amount of sugar used to make desserts (except meringues and ice cream – which cannot be made with less sugar).
- Use sugar-free cereals and low-sugar jams where appropriate.
- If appropriate use a sugar substitute or honey.

Ways of reducing salt in dishes

○ Add less salt – do not automatically add salt when beginning to cook, only use it to adjust the seasoning at the end.
○ Check the labels of any processed foods you use for flavouring dishes. It is surprising how many already contain salt, e.g. mustard, soy sauce.
○ Do not combine foods high in salt together in one dish such as bacon, beefburgers, sausages, cheese and ham.
○ Combine salty foods with fruit or vegetables which contain potassium. This will help to reduce the effect of the salt.
○ Avoid using preserved ingredients that contain high levels of salt such as dried fish, smoked salmon and capers.

Ideas for flavouring dishes using less salt

○ Make your own stock. Ready-made stocks or bouillon are often high in salt.
○ Use lemon juice, lime juice and balsamic vinegar instead of salt.
○ Use lots of fresh herbs and spices.
○ Onions, shallots, leeks and garlic all help to flavour food without using salt.
○ Freshly ground black pepper can be a popular alternative to salt.

Ways of increasing fibre and starch in dishes

○ Use high-fibre, wholemeal or granary bread.
○ Use wholemeal flour instead of white flour.
○ Use wholemeal pasta and brown rice.
○ Include pulses in dishes where appropriate.
○ Offer jacket potatoes.

Healthier types of sauces, dressings, toppings and condiments

As fashions change, so do ingredients and methods of cookery and presentation. With so much talk about healthy eating, many establishments are changing how they prepare their sauces. Traditional sauces use flour, butter and cream, but the following styles of sauces are more healthy and are becoming popular:

○ Herb, olive and walnut oils and dressings.
○ Sauces made from reductions of stocks and flavourings.
○ Yoghurt-based dressings.
○ Fruit-based sauces and dressings.

Did you know?
The concentration of salt in soy sauce is twice that of seawater!

Did you know?
Substituting wholemeal flour for white flour is most successful when making savoury dishes. However, pastry can be very heavy if made with all wholemeal flour. A mix of half wholemeal, half white flour produces a better result.

Did you know?
Brown rice will take longer to cook than white rice.

Blanching

Blanching is the process in which raw food is immersed in boiling water for a short time, then removed and refreshed in iced water or under cold running water. Blanching is carried out for a variety of reasons:

○ To make it easier to remove the skins of vegetables, fruit and nuts.
○ To make ingredients firmer.
○ To purify ingredients by killing the enzymes that cause the quality of food to deteriorate. Food that has been blanched, e.g. garden peas, can then be stored fresh or frozen for later use.
○ To remove the salt or bitterness from ingredients.
○ To reduce the volume of ingredients.

You can blanch chips in hot oil before frying them.

Video presentation
Watch the techniques used in *Blanch a tomato to remove the skin* and *Blanch meat bones.*

Poaching

Poaching, a wet cooking method, means to simmer slowly and gently in liquid. The amount of liquid used depends on the dish to be cooked. A whole chicken will require more liquid than a breast, but generally the minimum amount of liquid is used.

The liquid used to poach food is usually boiled first. When the food is added the liquid is not brought back to the boil, but is kept just below boiling point. The cooking liquid may affect the food being poached, e.g. it may add flavour to a food (stock) or its boiling point may be lower (milk). Liquids commonly used in poaching are water, wine, stock and milk. Fish, vegetables, eggs and some offal are examples of food suitable for poaching.

The equipment used to poach poultry is usually a heavy-based pan with a lid. The heat source can be an open flame, a solid or electric hob or oven. If food is poached in the oven (e.g. fish), this is known as 'oven poaching'. It is a speedy and gentle method of poaching. Overcooking food during oven poaching could lead to the food drying out.

When poaching, the food may be only half-covered by liquid. It is a good idea to cover the food, e.g. with a lid or buttered paper. This will keep the moisture in and prevent the food drying out.

Once cooked, poached food must be well drained. Excess liquid could alter the consistency of a sauce added to poached food and spoil it.

Video presentation
Poach a salmon fillet teaches you how to do this like an expert.

Stewing and braising

Stewing and braising are wet methods of cooking in a pot on top of the stove or in the oven. This is a slow cooking method, which allows food to be cooked gently until it is soft and ready for service. In stewed or braised dishes the food and liquid is served together as a dish.

Use a large, heavy-based saucepan or dish, with a minimum amount of liquid covering the food. Bring the liquid to the boil and simmer it slowly. Take care not to burn the base of the pan, as this will spoil the flavour of the dish. Always ensure there is enough liquid in the pan to prevent burning.

> **Remember!**
> Food that is stewed or braised will be hot and dangerous. Use protective clothing and equipment to prevent accidents from spilling hot liquid and burning yourself.

Frying

Frying means cooking in hot fat, e.g. oil or butter. There are four types of frying:

1 shallow frying
2 sauté
3 stir-frying
4 deep-frying.

Shallow, sauté and stir-frying

Shallow, sauté and stir-frying are all versions of a similar frying process. Food is cooked with a small amount of butter or oil. Cooking this way colours the food and makes it more appealing. Stir-frying is usually associated with Asian food dishes. It is a quick cooking method using a wok and hot oil. The food is cut into small, evenly-sized pieces and tossed in hot oil in the wok for a short period of time.

The equipment required for shallow or stir-frying is:

o a sturdy pan with steep sides
o a cloth to protect you from high temperatures
o utensils, e.g. tongs, palette knives, spoons, to move and agitate the food
o a range or hob to provide the heat source. To achieve even cooking you will need to regulate the heat under the pan; gas hobs make it particularly easy to do this.

> **Remember!**
> Hot oil can inflict serious injury. For safety reasons:
> o make sure the food you are frying is free from water and excess liquid, which may cause the oil to spit and possibly burn you when cooking
> o place the food into a hot frying pan away from your body to avoid splashing yourself with hot oil.

> **Video presentation**
> Watch the video *Stir-fry beef* to find out more about this cooking method. Watch *Deep-fry goujons* to learn how to do this safely.

Deep-frying

Deep-frying food means immersing it in hot oil in a saucepan or deep fat fryer. The temperature of the oil should be approximately 180°C. Deep-frying will colour the food and give it a crunchy texture on the outside. Inside the food remains moist. This method of cooking is popular for breadcrumbed or battered fish, chicken pieces, chips and onion rings.

The equipment needed for deep-frying is:
o a sturdy pan with a heavy base
o a basket or slotted steel spoon to lift the food out of the oil
o utensils, e.g. tongs to grasp the food
o colanders or absorbent paper to put the food into to allow the excess oil to drain off before serving
o a regulated heat source
o a thermostatically controlled deep fat fryer may also be used.

Looking after the oil is the most important part of deep-frying. Make sure you:
o filter oil daily
o wipe the inside of the fryer thoroughly before replacing the oil
o clean the fryer once a week
o switch off the fryer when not in use
o turn the fryer down during quiet periods: the recommended standby temperature is 93°C
o use the correct utensils for handling food and filtering oil: using iron or copper will cause a chemical reaction and harm the oil.

> **Remember!**
> Although chips can be deep-fried straight from the freezer, it is important to shake off all the ice first or the oil will froth dangerously.

> **Remember!**
> Always season food after frying, never before.

> **Chef's tip**
> Do not use olive oil for deep-frying as it can burn easily at the temperatures required to deep-fry and this will taint the food.

Grilling

Grilling is a dry method of cooking by intense heat from above, below or both. The heat source can be electric, gas or charcoal. Food is placed near the source of heat on bars or on a solid metal plate. If the heat source is above the food, the equipment being used is known as a salamander.

Grilling is an extremely popular, simple method of cooking which is appropriate for tender cuts of meat, offal, poultry, fish and vegetables.

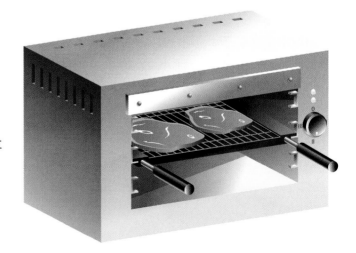

Figure 5.2 Food being grilled on a salamander

Before food is grilled, it is usually seasoned with salt and pepper and sometimes herbs, spices or marinades. Food can be brushed with butter or olive oil to baste it and can be coated in flour to aid the colouring process and give a crispy texture when grilled. Food will colour when grilled, but it is important not to pierce the surface of the food, as moisture or juices will be lost, leaving the food dry. If you overcook food when grilling, it will be dry and tough.

Griddling

Griddling is an American term. It is another form of grilling. The food is placed on a solid iron plate which is heated from underneath. The heat source can be gas, electric or charcoal. Some griddles have bars running across them. This enables the foods to be **charred** or **seared**, providing a distinctive flavour, colour and pattern. Safe procedures must always be followed, as this equipment can cause serious injury.

Too much oil on the griddle can lead to excessive smoke and can hamper the cooking process.

Roasting and baking

These cooking processes make food easy to eat and digest and more appealing to the consumer.

Both use an oven and dry convected heat to cook the food. Ovens can be powered by electricity or gas. Modern combination ovens combine dry and moist heat to ensure the best cooking results. The temperature of the oven will determine the cooking time. The hotter the oven, the quicker the food will colour and cook. A fierce temperature can spoil the food being cooked, so you must regulate it. Food to be baked, e.g. rolls, should be even in size. This ensures they all cook in the same amount of time.

The equipment required to roast or bake dishes includes:

○ Sturdy roasting trays of an appropriate size

Remember!

Grilling is a quick method of cooking food and the heat must be regulated to prevent the dish burning.

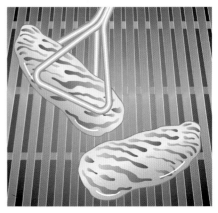

Figure 5.3 Cooking on a griddle

Definition

Charring or **searing**: using the hot bars on a griddle to darken or pattern the item as it is cooking.

Remember!

The temperatures reached when roasting are extreme (120–300°C). Always use oven cloths and personal protective equipment.

RADBROOK LRC

○ Cloths to handle hot equipment

○ Suitable utensils, e.g. a perforated spoon or slice, to agitate the food

○ An oven to roast or bake

The difference between baking and roasting is that for roasting, oil is added to aid the cooking process. For example, roasted Mediterranean vegetables have seasoning and oil added to them. The oven heats the oil, which in turn cooks and colours the vegetables. Roasting also requires you to baste. This means taking the oil and juices from the food and pouring them over it at timed intervals to keep it moist.

Baking is a method of cooking in an oven using dry heat. The dry heat within the confined space of the oven creates the best conditions for cooking the dish. When baking, the heat generated within the baked product (e.g. pies, pastries) creates moisture that counteracts the dry convected air. This self-generated moisture keeps the cooked product in optimum condition for serving. No oil or other additional ingredients need to be added, e.g. baked potatoes need only be washed and pricked before placing in the oven.

Combination cooking

Combination cooking means that more than one method of cooking is used in making a dish. For example, a cauliflower cheese gratin uses two cooking methods. Cauliflower is cooked by boiling and then placed in a dish, covered with a cheese sauce and then finished and coloured in the oven or under a grill.

Some cooking equipment is designed to enable combination cooking methods. For example, combination ovens give the benefits of both steaming and convection during cooking. This cooking process ensures the dish remains moist.

Microwaving

Microwaving is a method of cooking and heating food by using high-frequency power. The energy is used to disturb molecules or particles of food, agitate them and cause friction, which has the effect of heating the food.

Microwave ovens are fast, energy-saving, versatile and easy to operate. Food that is cooked in a microwave oven needs no fat or water. However, microwaves do not brown the surface of the food or make it crispy.

Remember!
Metal objects should never be used inside a microwave oven.

Using a bain-marie

Food can be cooked and kept hot by the bain-marie method. This is done made by placing a pan or bowl of food in a larger pan of boiling water.

This method can be carried out in the oven, on top of the stove or using the kitchen equipment with the same name, a bain-marie. A bain-marie has open wells of water and needs to be heated by steam, gas or electricity to boil the water.

Figure 5.4 A bain-marie

> **Try this!**   **Worksheet 15**
> **Close your book. How many cooking methods can you name?**

Test yourself!

1   Are these cooking methods wet or dry? Put a W next to the wet cookery methods and a D next to the dry cookery methods.
    a   Simmering   _____
    b   Braising   _____
    c   Baking   _____
    d   Stewing   _____
    e   Grilling.   _____

2   What is the recommended standby temperature for a deep-fat fryer?
    a   90°C
    b   92°C
    c   93°C
    d   95°C.

3   There are four types of frying. What are they?

4   What is the difference between roasting and baking?

Chives

Chives are usually used as a herb or garnish and are not served as a dish. Chives are available all year round.

Try this!

Leek and potato soup can be served either hot or cold. Make the soup, taste it hot and then cold to see which temperature you prefer.

Most items are now available all year round from suppliers. However, if a supplier gets a product from abroad it will generally cost more.

Garlic

Garlic is a versatile vegetable. It is not usually served on its own but is crushed or sliced and added to dishes such as soups, sauces, meat dishes or marinades to enhance flavour. Garlic is usually grown in France and can vary in size from a standard bulb to jumbo or elephant garlic.

Chef's tip

Garlic has a very overpowering flavour, which can linger on your hands, breath and clothes. Always ensure you use the correct amount according to the recipe. If you use too much, the dish will be overpowered by the garlic flavour.

Flower heads

Broccoli, asparagus and cauliflower are common examples of flower head vegetables. As the name suggests, the flower head is the part of these plants which is eaten. Flower heads deteriorate quite quickly so it is important to ensure they are fresh.

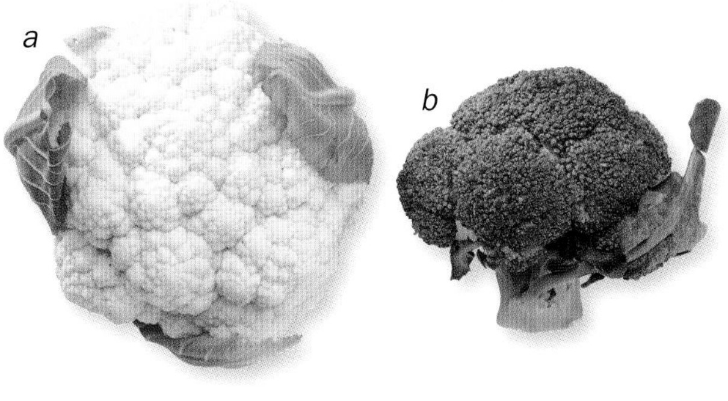

a

b

Figure 6.4 Flower heads: a cauliflower, b broccoli

Cauliflower

A cauliflower has tightly packed florets or flowers making a compact, round, white head. The flower head is usually surrounded by thick green leaves, which are discarded during preparation. Cauliflowers are available all year round, but the price will vary.

Did you know?
Cauliflower leaves can be used to make soup.

Broccoli

Broccoli is a deep greenish-purple colour. Poor quality is indicated by discoloration – the head starts to seed and goes yellow. The stem from which the florets are cut is edible so by leaving the stem intact with the floret you have a greater yield from the vegetable.

Did you know?
The consumption of broccoli is associated with reducing the risk of developing some cancers.

Fungi

Not all fungi are edible. In fact some fungi could kill you or your customer if eaten so it is really important to obtain your fungi from a reputable supplier. Most people do not possess the skills to pick their own mushrooms or fungi in a wood; the consequences of picking the wrong fungi, e.g. a death cap, mean it is not worth taking the risk.

Reputable suppliers will have many different types of edible fungi and mushroom available, e.g. grey and yellow oyster, hon-shimeji, field and paris brown. They will vary in price due to their availability and the season.

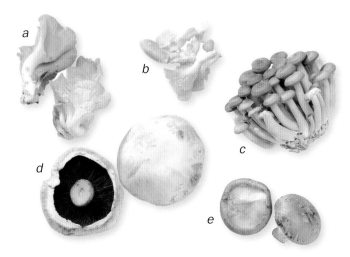

Figure 6.5 There are many types of mushrooms available to caterers, including: a grey oyster, b yellow oyster, c hon-shimeji, d field, e paris brown

Mushrooms

The most commonly used mushrooms are button mushrooms and open flat mushrooms. These are generally white but can be dark brown. Freshness is essential and should be checked before use. Mushrooms must be washed thoroughly as they are found in or around decaying trees and plants or are artificially cultivated in soil heavily treated with manure or animal waste. Mushrooms are usually cooked by frying.

Quorn

This is a high-protein vegetable used by vegetarians as a meat substitute. Quorn is processed from a tiny plant of the mushroom family. It resembles grey mincemeat. It is not suitable for vegans as it contains egg white.

Figure 6.6 A death cap mushroom

> ### Try this!
> Substitute quorn for minced beef and make a cottage pie in the same way. You will be surprised how similar the taste is.

>
> ### Remember!
> Not all fungi are mushrooms. A truffle is also a fungus. It can be black or white, is extremely expensive and is used to add flavour to certain dishes.

Tubers

Tubers are swellings or nodes on the roots of plants. The rest of the plant is discarded for cooking. They grow under the soil. The main vegetable in this group is the potato. Potatoes are round or oval, yellowy-white on the inside with an outer skin, which is peeled or scrubbed before cooking. Sweet potatoes have orange flesh and a sweeter flavour than normal potatoes.

There are at least 40 different types of potato ranging from small Charlotte potatoes to red Desiree potatoes. Maris Pipers make the best chipped potatoes. Potatoes differ in size from bite-sized baby new potatoes to large King Edwards, which can be bigger than your hand.

Potatoes are split into 'new' and 'old'. New potatoes are available between May and August and old potatoes are available between September and April.

Figure 6.7 Potatoes: a baby new potatoes, b maris piper, c desiree

Did you know?
A potato is made up of layers, which can be seen if the potato is cut.

Leaves

Leaf vegetables are the prepared leaves of the plant. They include cabbage, sprouts, spinach and lettuce.

Cabbage

Several varieties of cabbage are commonly used in cooking:

Traditional or **white cabbages** are greenish-white balls of flat leaves tightly packed together. The thick-stemmed leaves are trimmed to aid the cooking process.

Savoy cabbages have a distinct flavour and ruffled appearance. The leaves are green or yellow. They are not as tightly packed as white cabbages.

Figure 6.8 Leaf vegetables: a savoy cabbage, b red cabbage, c spinach, d iceberg lettuce, e green cabbage, f white cabbage

Red cabbages are similar in shape and texture to white cabbages, but the leaves are a deep purplish-red. Red cabbages generally take a little longer than normal cabbages to cook because of their density and the thickness of their leaves.

Sprouts

Sprouts, which we all traditionally turn our noses up at during Christmas, are a type of miniature cabbage with a very distinctive flavour. The small, tightly-packed balls of leaves are attached to the long sturdy stem of the plant. Extremely nutritious, Brussels sprouts are a valuable source of folic acid which is important for pregnant women.

Spinach

When cooked, spinach reduces to a dark-green, soft texture. Because it reduces in volume so much on cooking, a great amount is needed if a large yield is required.

Lettuce

Lettuce is traditionally used in salads. Lettuce must be washed thoroughly, as soil can easily get into the heart. Lettuce leaves should be firm, clean and fresh.

Stems

This group of vegetables includes celery, asparagus and seaweed.

Celery

Celery is the most commonly used stem vegetable. It has a distinctive taste and is often used in salads, although it can be braised or made into soup. The long green stem has a fibrous string-like outer skin, which should be removed to enhance its quality.

> **Chef's tip**
> Fruit, e.g. apple, is a good accompaniment for red cabbage.

> **Chef's tip**
> Nutmeg is a great addition to spinach.

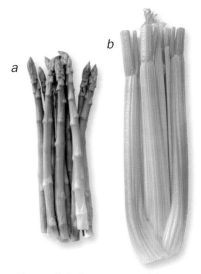

Figure 6.9 Stem vegetables: a asparagus, b celery

Asparagus

The base of asparagus is quite woody, so cut it away. The remaining stem has a small flowering head, which has usually not flowered before cooking.

Seaweed

With the increased interest in Asian cooking, especially Japanese cooking, seaweed is used in many kitchens. Many types of seaweed are used in cooking and it is used in a variety of dishes including salads, ice cream, puddings, bread, soups and stocks. These are some different types of seaweed:

- **Kombu**: also known as kelp, this can be used in rice or bean dishes, or used to make soups or stock.
- **Wakame**: this can be added to soup.
- **Nori**: can be eaten on its own, in soups or sprinkled over food.
- **Arame** and **hijiki**: traditional Japanese seaweeds.
- **Agar agar**: occasionally used in desserts. Processed agar agar can be used as a gelatine substitute for vegetarians.
- **Dulse** and **sea palm**.
- **Samphire**: is a common and popular seaweed which is used to flavour soups and salads.

Seaweeds are very rich in minerals. For example, they contain between seven and 14 times as much calcium as milk, depending on the type of seaweed. Seaweed is eaten cooked, dried or fresh depending on the dish, and can be obtained from Asian restaurant suppliers.

Did you know?
Asparagus is classed as a flower head if just the tips are cooked. However, asparagus is usually cooked whole with its stem.

Chef's tip
Finely shredded deep-fried seaweed is a great accompaniment to an Asian dinner.

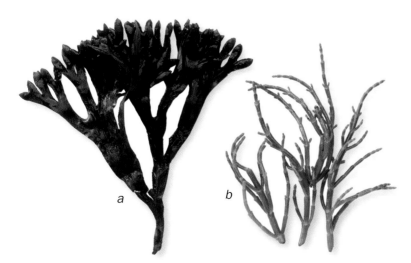

Fig 6.10 Seaweed: a nori, b samphire

Vegetable fruits

These vegetables are the ripened fruit of the plants they grow on. They include aubergines, capsicums (peppers), cucumber, avocados, tomatoes, courgettes, marrow and sweetcorn.

Aubergines

Aubergines have a firm to spongy texture. They are bell-shaped and black or purple in colour. They are generally used with other vegetables, e.g. tomatoes, courgettes, garlic and onions for ratatouille. Aubergines can be grilled with olive oil for an hors d'oeuvre (starter) or used as the vegetable layer in moussaka. Aubergines are a Mediterranean vegetable and are a popular element in that style of cookery.

Figure 6.11 Vegetable fruits: a aubergine, b capsicums, c cucumber, d avocado, e beef tomato, f tomato, g cherry tomatoes

Capsicums

Capsicums are commonly known as sweet peppers. They can be red, orange, green or yellow. The colour depends on the age of the capsicum, i.e. a green capsicum will eventually turn red. These versatile vegetables are used in salads and many Mediterranean dishes. They can also be blanched and stuffed with other food, e.g. rice, to create vegetarian dishes (see page 291).

Cucumbers

Cucumbers are long green baton-shaped vegetables, which are not usually cooked but are used for cold food and salads.

Avocados

Avocados originally came from South America but are now grown in many different countries. They are oval in shape and are a green or brown colour. The skins are tough and inedible. Once peeled, avocados may discolour rapidly. Avocados contain a large seed or stone in the centre. When ripe the flesh feels soft to touch. It can easily be puréed. They have a high fat content for a vegetable.

> **Try this!**
> Take a piece of raw red capsicum and taste it. Now brush it with oil and grill it till the skin is black. Remove the skin and taste the capsicum. The difference is astonishing – the sweet flavour of the capsicum really comes through.

Tomatoes

Tomatoes are very versatile and are used in many dishes and salads. They are instantly recognisable from their round red appearance, although they do come in other shapes as well, e.g. the long plum tomato from Italy. Their colour varies and a good indicator of flavour is a deep red colour. Tomatoes supplied on the vine are considered to be better quality and the flavour should be sweeter. Cherry tomatoes are baby tomatoes and have a sweeter taste than normal tomatoes. Beef tomatoes are the largest variety. They are very fleshy and juicy with a sweet flavour. They are ideal in Greek salad and can be cooked by grilling or shallow frying as an accompaniment to a meal.

Courgettes

Courgettes are similar in appearance to marrows, but they are smaller. They taste quite bland so they are usually sautéed or stir-fried with other vegetables, e.g. onion and garlic, to add flavour. Overcooking courgettes makes them soggy and unattractive.

Marrows

Marrows are much larger versions of courgettes with similar preparation and cooking methods. Marrows are not popular as their high water content makes their flavour quite bland. Overcooked marrows are extremely unappealing and mushy.

Fresh peas and beans

Peas and beans are the seeds (e.g. garden peas) and the seed pods (e.g. mangetout, French beans, runner beans and broad beans) of plants. Vegetables such as garden peas are usually blanched and then frozen.

Some seed pods grow to yield large seeds, e.g. broad beans, from which the pod is discarded and only the seed is used for cooking. Other types, e.g. runner beans and French beans, are picked with the pod and seed still intact and are prepared together. These vegetables contain high levels of vitamin C.

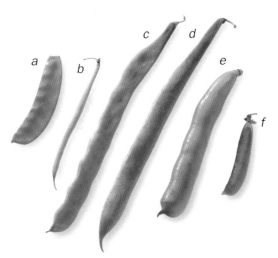

Figure 6.12 a mangetout, b French bean, c flat bean, d runner bean, e broad bean, f garden peas

Mangetout is a pea pod inside which the peas have not yet grown. They are very delicate and do not take long to cook. Quick cooking methods such as stir-frying are suitable for mangetout as they can become wilted and mushy very quickly.

Pulses

Pulses are the edible seeds of plants, harvested for drying.

Pulses, e.g. chickpeas, lentils, split yellow peas, split green peas and beans, can be obtained dried or cooked and canned. The pulses you are likely to use at NVQ Level 2 will be dried, and most of these will need soaking before use. Pulses are a high source of fibre, protein, iron and B vitamins.

Peas

- Split green peas disintegrate easily and are very starchy. They are often used as an ingredient in soups and broths.
- Chickpeas hold their shape well and are used, as with other pulses, in vegetarian dishes. In some parts of the world they are ground into flour to make breads, batters, etc. They have a slightly nutty flavour.
- Marrowfat peas, like split green peas, disintegrate easily and are very starchy. They are often used as an ingredient in soups and broths.

Beans

Many types of beans are available to caterers, e.g. red kidney beans, white haricot beans, mung beans, butter beans, borlotti beans, broad beans and soya beans.

- Red kidney beans contain an enzyme which if not destroyed will cause food poisoning. Rapid boiling for ten minutes destroys the enzyme. This cooking time enables the heat to penetrate the bean and kill the enzyme.
- Haricot beans are used in baked beans.
- Butter beans are also known as lima beans. They are large, flat and yellowy-brown. They have a buttery taste when cooked.
- Borlotti beans are similar to kidney beans and are a good substitute for kidney or haricot beans in dishes. They are very moist and tender and have a nice texture in dishes.

Try this!   **Worksheet 16**
Close your book and list as many vegetables as you can for each category.

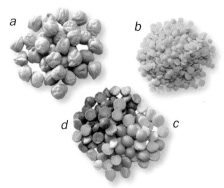

Figure 6.13 Dried pulses: *a* chickpeas, *b* lentils, *c* split yellow peas, *d* split green peas

Healthy eating
Pulses contain no saturated fats and are a healthy alternative to meat.

Remember!
Red kidney beans must always be boiled for at least ten minutes before use.

○ Soya beans are high in fat and protein. Soya bean products are increasingly popular. They are processed into flour, milk, meat substitutes (e.g. tofu or tempeh), margarine and even soy sauce.

Lentils

Lentils are the seeds of a small branching plant. They resemble small peas. They can be used whole or split and do not necessarily need to be soaked before cooking. Lentils are rich in protein. They are named and identified according to their colour: red, yellow, green and brown. Red and yellow lentils disintegrate when cooked, while green and brown remain whole.

> **Find out!**   **Worksheet 17**
>
> Find more information about pulses. For each type of pulse write a description, a note of its uses, nutritional information and any other key facts you discover.

How to judge quality of vegetables and pulses

It is essential that you can recognise good quality vegetables and select those suitable for use. Common sense should always be used when selecting vegetables of appropriate quality. Always consider size, shape, colour, smell, damage and texture. The table below lists vegetables and the quality points to look for.

Vegetable or pulse	Quality points
Potato	No excessive soil, no eyes or roots growing from the tuber, no weeping, bruising or damage to the skin. Good even size for type required.
Carrot	Good tapered straight shape, vibrant orange colour, no woody appearance, no insect or spade damage or wrinkling of skin.
Turnip	Firm with no damage to the exterior. Outer skin is not wrinkled, no insect or spade damage. Pliable to touch.
Swede	Firm with no insect or spade damage to the exterior. Outer skin is not wrinkled and pliable to touch.
Parsnip	Firm with no insect or spade damage to the exterior. Outer skin is not wrinkled. Pliable to touch.
Radish	Even size, good red colour. No insect or spade damage to outer surface. Healthy fresh-looking green leaves.
Onion	Firm and dry exterior, no moisture at top. No sign of stem growth.
Garlic	Firm and dry exterior, no moisture at top. No sign of stem growth.
Chives	Good green colour, no discoloration, no signs of wilting.

Spring onion	Bulb and stem clean in appearance, no damage to stem, leaves or bulb. No slime, no moist leaves.
Leek	No excessive soil, no damage or slimy feel to exterior layers or leaves.
Cabbage	No discoloration or evident damage, clean and fresh appearance. No wilting.
Courgette	No bruising or damage to the exterior surface. Firm flesh.
Marrow	No bruising or damage to the exterior surface. Firm flesh.
Sprouts	Compact leaves, no yellow discoloration, clean fresh appearance.
Lettuce	No wilting leaves, no excessive soil, no contamination from insects such as snails and slugs. Colour should be bright and vibrant.
Spinach	Crisp leaves, fresh appearance, no slimy leaves, deep green colour.
Cauliflower	Tightly packed heads, no discoloration or damage to the head. Leaves surrounding the flower head intact and not wilting. Not too many leaves.
Broccoli	Fresh green colour, no discoloration (yellow). Stems firm and crisp, not spongy or flexible.
Asparagus	Firm flower heads, good size, base not too woody, no discoloration or damage.
Celery	Firm stems with no damage or discoloration to the vegetable. Stems tightly packed together. Breaks crisply when separated.
Mushrooms	No slime or bad odour, appears clean and dry, no discoloration to the cap.
Tomato	No damage to skin, firm to touch, good colour.
Avocado	Good green or brown colour, skin firm but with some give to show ripeness. No damage to exterior.
Aubergine	Firm, no damage or soft spots.
Cucumber	Long firm and straight. Skin clean and a good green colour. No sign of wilting or wrinkling. No soft spots.
Capsicum	No wrinkling, good vibrant colour, no soft spots or damage.
Broad bean	Pods undamaged and not too large. Evenly sized.
Mangetout	Crisp, flat, evenly sized pods, good green colour, no discoloration.
Peas	Plump and crisp, no discoloration.
Runner beans	Even size, not too big, good green colour, no discoloration, snaps crisply when broken.
French beans	Even size, not too big, good green colour, no discoloration, snaps crisply when broken.
Dried pulses	Free from contaminants such as insects; feels clean, dry and smooth.

Figure 6.14 Quality points to look for in vegetables and pulses

Food value and healthy eating

Pulses and vegetables are an essential part of a healthy, well-balanced diet. The wrong cooking method or cooking time will affect the nutritional value of the food so it is important to understand and apply the correct preparation and cooking methods.

Most vegetables contain large amounts of vitamins B and C. These vitamins dissolve in water; therefore over-boiling vegetables to a mush means they will not be as nutritious.

The table below identifies the nutritional value of vegetables.

Type	Fats (grams per 100g)	Protein (grams per 100g)	Carbohydrates (grams per 100g)	Vitamin content
Potato	0.2	3.9	31	B, C
Carrot	0.3	0.6	7.9	A, B, C, K
Turnip	0.3	0.9	4.7	B, C
Swede	0.3	5.0	1.9	B, C
Parsnip	1.1	1.8	12.5	B, C, K
Beetroot	0.3	0	9.0	A, B, C
Radish	0.1	0.8	2.9	C
Onion	0.2	1.2	7.9	B, C
Garlic	1.0	7.0	15.0	C
Spring onion	1.0	2.0	3.0	B, C
Leek	0.5	1.6	2.9	B, C
Cabbage	0.5	2.1	3.9	B, C
Courgette	0.4	1.8	1.8	C, K
Sprouts	1.0	2.8	2.0	A, C, K
Lettuce	0.3	0.7	1.9	C
Spinach	0.8	2.8	1.6	A, B, C, K
Cauliflower	0.9	3.6	3.0	B, C, K
Broccoli	0.9	4.4	1.8	A, B, C, K
Asparagus	0.6	2.7	1.1	C

Celery	0.3	0.3	0.9	C
Mushroom	0.5	1.8	0.4	B, C, K
Tomato	0.4	0.7	2.8	A, B, C
Avocado (145g)	28	2.0	2.0	B, C, E
Aubergine	0.4	0.9	2.2	B
Cucumber	0.1	0.7	1.5	C
Capsicum	0.4	1.0	6.4	A, B, C
Broad beans	0.8	5.1	5.6	B, C
Peas	0.7	4.8	7.8	B, C
Runner beans	0.4	1.6	2.0	A, C
Haricot beans	1.6	21.4	49.7	B
Lentils	1.5	24.0	48.8	B
Soya beans	7.3	14	5.1	B
Chickpeas	5.4	21.3	49.6	C

Figure 6.15 Nutritional value of vegetables

Preparation tools and techniques

Washing

Vegetables grow in, on or above the ground. They can become contaminated by the soil, which contains many types of harmful bacteria, e.g. clostridium perfringens and bacillus cereus, so it is important to wash them carefully. Also, insects and other animals, e.g. slugs, can be trapped within the leaves. Another reason for washing vegetables is to remove any residue from chemicals and pesticides, which may have been sprayed onto the vegetables to deter birds and insects.

It is important to inspect the product first to make sure it is the right quality. Then strip away any unnecessary leaves or remains from when the vegetable was joined to the plant, e.g. removing the tomatoes from the vine.

Figure 6.16 A brush can be used to clean potatoes

Next wash the vegetables in cold running water. The type of vegetable will determine how robustly you clean it. You may use a brush to scrub the mud from potatoes but you would be more careful washing a tomato. Once the items have been washed thoroughly, they should be drained of any excess water.

Peeling

Peeling is the removal of the outer layer of a food item (which is generally inedible or unappealing) to reveal the edible flesh beneath, e.g. peeling a swede will reveal the yellow flesh. Peeling also improves the presentation of the vegetable.

Not all vegetables need to be peeled. Vegetables such as tomatoes, cucumbers, mushrooms, beans, mangetout, capsicums, cabbage and spinach grow above the ground, and their outer skins are edible. They do not need to be peeled unless it is a dish requirement.

Vegetables which grow in or on the soil often develop tough outer skins. These need to be washed and then peeled. As a general rule, root vegetables and tubers require peeling. Some fruit vegetables, e.g. avocados, also need peeling due to the toughness of their skin.

The tools used to peel vegetables vary from a hand vegetable peeler, a 3-inch vegetable knife to a 7-inch vegetable knife. Carrots require a hand peeler, whereas a turnip will need to be peeled using a 7–10-inch vegetable knife. Always use a brown board when peeling vegetables.

Large industrial equipment may be used to peel vegetables such as potatoes. Potatoes are usually required in large quantities, so rather than peeling hundreds of potatoes by hand, a potato rumbler can be used. This is a large mechanically operated drum which has a rough interior and spins at a fast rate. Water is flushed through the rumbler constantly. The rapid spinning of the drum removes the skins of the potatoes. The water washes them and also washes away the peelings. This process saves a lot of time. Potatoes can also be purchased pre-prepared.

Video presentation
Watch *Washing and peeling vegetables.*

Remember!
In all cases, if you are unsure of how to peel an item, seek assistance from your supervisor.

Figure 6.17 Tools used to peel vegetables

Figure 6.18 Potato rumblers are a quicker way of peeling large quantities of potatoes.

For vegetables such as broad beans or peas, peeling means to shell the whole vegetable from its pod. Break open the pod, and remove the peas or beans and wash them.

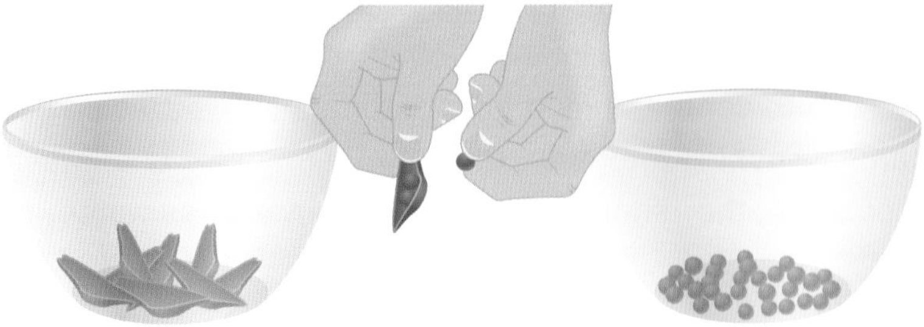

Figure 6.19 Shelling fresh peas

Rewashing

Constantly handling vegetables when peeling may mean they become re-contaminated with soil or other impurities. Re-washing the vegetable after peeling or other preparation methods will remove any unwanted impurities and leave it ready for the next stage. This process is good practice when food handling.

Cutting

Cutting vegetables into the required size or shape is a necessary part of preparing vegetables. Many vegetables need to be cut into bite-sized pieces, which may also speed the cooking process.

There are many different cuts which can be applied to vegetables (but not usually pulses). To cut you need a knife and a chopping board. The knife should be appropriate to the task. The board should be brown, stable and flat. As the knife handler, it is important that you act in a safe manner, always considering your safety and that of others.

Remember!
Cutting root vegetables into smaller pieces will allow them to cook more quickly.

Traditional French cuts

There are six traditional French cuts for cutting vegetables:
○ **Jardinière:** vegetables are cut into baton shapes 15mm × 4mm.
○ **Macedoine:** vegetables are cut into dice 5mm × 5mm × 5mm.
○ **Julienne:** vegetables are cut into thin strips like matchsticks, 3–4cm in length by 2–4mm thick.
○ **Mirepoix:** vegetables are chopped roughly into pieces of no specific shape or size, although they are normally quite large pieces.
○ **Paysanne:** vegetables are thinly sliced into strips, circles and triangles cut to 1cm in diameter.
○ **Brunoise:** vegetables are cut into small dice, 2mm × 2mm × 2mm.

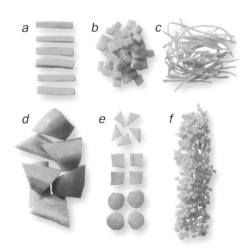

Figure 6.20 Traditional French cuts: a jardinière, b macedoine, c julienne, d mirepoix e paysanne, f brunoise,

Mastering these cuts takes time because they are very precise and a lot of skill is involved. Good knife skills are essential for a chef, and practising these cuts is good preparation for developing other knife skills.

Clumsy knife skills and poorly cut vegetables will detract from the presentation of a dish. They could even affect the cooking, as larger pieces will cook more slowly than smaller ones.

> **Try this!**   **Worksheet 19**
>
> Draw a simple sketch of the vegetable cuts to scale then find out five uses for each.

Slicing

Slicing is a general term for cutting food with a knife. Vegetables such as onions are usually sliced. If the bulb is whole, slicing across the diameter of the onion will create onion rings. Halving the bulb will produce slices of onion, which are suitable as general garnish, e.g. with steaks.

Slice to the specific size or shape stated in the recipe. Slicing can be done by hand or by a mechanical food processor, depending on the size of the catering outlet.

Trimming

Trimming is the removal of food parts not required for a particular dish. For vegetables this includes peeling, removing the thick stems in the centre of cabbage leaves and removing the outer leaves of a cauliflower.

Grating

Root vegetables and other vegetables of a firm texture may be grated to yield fine strands of vegetable. Carrots are grated for salads and coleslaw.

A grater is a metal utensil which has a sharp rough surface and is perforated. As a vegetable is passed over this surface, strands of it are shaved through the perforations. Graters come in all shapes and sizes, from hand graters to industrial machinery which will grate large quantities in a short space of time. Food processors normally have grating utensils.

> **Video presentation**
>
> *Choosing the right knife* and *Sharpening a knife* will give you important background information. *Classic cuts* shows you how these essential cuts are made.
> Watch *Preparing and chopping an onion* to see a skilled chef doing this.
> Watch *Preparing leeks* for a demonstration of trimming.

> **Remember!**
>
> At all times ensure your own and others' safety. Never use any equipment you have not been trained on how to use.

Figure 6.21 An industrial food processor

Soaking

Pulses are generally dried. They need soaking or reconstituting before cooking. This means soaking them in water to put the water content back into the vegetable to make it soft.

The type of pulse will determine how long it should be soaked for. Usually pulses should be soaked in twice the volume of water to pulses and between 4 and 8 hours.

It is advisable to soak pulses in the fridge as warm temperatures during the soaking process can have an adverse effect on them.

Once pulses have been soaked they should be re-washed, as there will be some sugars in them which are hard to digest.

Cooking methods, tools and equipment

Blanching

Blanching is used to kill the enzymes in vegetables that cause their quality to deteriorate. Blanching can also be used to remove skins from vegetables and nuts.

Video presentation
Blanch a tomato to remove the skin shows you how to do this.

To blanch vegetables immerse them in boiling water for between ten seconds and two minutes depending on the type. Remove them from the boiling water and refresh them (make them cool again) by immersing them in iced water or running cold water over them.

Once drained, vegetables which have been blanched may be stored fresh or frozen for later use or the next stage of preparation.

Over-blanching a vegetable will cook it for too long and the quality will be affected. If a tomato is blanched for too long the flesh after peeling will be very mushy and unsuitable for use.

Have to hand:
- a cloth to stop you burning yourself
- a pan with boiling water
- a spider or perforated spoon
- a perforated basket if the quantity is large enough
- an industrial boiler if the quantity is large enough
- a container with iced water or cold running water.

How to blanch tomatoes to remove their skins

1 Use a paring knife to remove the eye of the tomatoes. Make a cross-incision on the underside of the tomatoes.

2 Use a slotted spoon to plunge the tomatoes into boiling water for ten seconds.

3 Remove the tomatoes and immediately refresh them in a bowl of iced water.

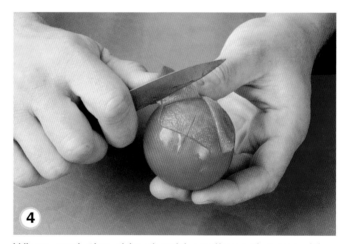

4 When cool, the skin should easily peel away with the help of a paring knife.

Capsicums can also be blanched to remove their skins. Oil rather than water is used because the skins are very tough and difficult to remove. There are three ways to remove the skins:

1 Brush the capsicum with oil and grill it until the skin is black, then peel it off.
2 Deep-fry the capsicum until the skin comes off.
3 Roast the capsicum, then deep-fry it and put it in a plastic bag. The skin will come off.

The equipment needed for blanching capsicums is either a grill or a deep fryer, a spider or perforated spoons, cloths and suitable trays to lay out the vegetables. For more information see page 121.

Ratatouille

tomatoes	200g
onion, diced	100g
garlic, chopped	hint
green capsicums	100g
red capsicums	100g
olive oil	50ml
herbes de Provence	good pinch
courgettes	200g
aubergines	200g
salt and pepper	to taste
chopped parsley	good pinch
Cooking time	1 hour
Serves	10–12

Method

1 Blanch the tomatoes (see method above). The skin should split for easy removal. Peel off the skin and chop including the seeds.
2 Chop the onion and garlic.
3 Clean the capsicums, cut into small strips.
4 In a large cooking pot with thick bottom, put in olive oil, onions and chopped garlic. Add the capsicum. Cover to keep in the moisture. Cook for 20 minutes, stirring frequently, and add olive oil as necessary to prevent burning.
5 Add the peeled tomatoes and herbes de Provence. Stir well and cook for another 15 minutes.
6 Cut the aubergines and courgettes into chunky bite-size pieces.
7 Add the aubergine and courgettes to the pot. Cook for another 25 minutes.
8 Season to taste and garnish with parsley.

Boiling

Not all vegetables are suitable for boiling, e.g. courgettes have a high water content and will disintegrate if boiled. Vegetables which are suitable for boiling include:

- potatoes
- carrots
- runner beans
- broad beans
- dried pulses, e.g. lentils, beans and peas
- fresh peas

- broccoli
- cauliflower
- beetroot
- Brussels sprouts
- cabbage
- parsnips
- turnip
- swede.

Boiling lowers the nutritional value of the vegetable. Vitamins B and C are commonly found in vegetables. These vitamins dissolve in water and are absorbed into the hot liquid during boiling.

Over-boiling can leave a vegetable limp and lifeless, so correct cooking times are important to ensure a good-quality product. Different types of vegetables have different cooking requirements. For more information see page 119.

Boiling root vegetables and tubers

The flesh of root vegetables and tubers, e.g. potatoes, is firm and dense. The boiling process breaks down the structure of the vegetable, making it pleasant and easy to eat. These types of vegetables should be put into cold water and brought to the boil. They will need boiling for 15–20 minutes. Test them by inserting a sharp implement, e.g. a skewer, into the flesh. It should enter easily. Some root vegetables, e.g. carrots, should not be too soft. They should still be quite firm with a slight crunch.

Remember!

Root vegetables must be cooked in cold water brought to the boil. Green vegetables must be cooked in water that is already boiling.

Glazed baton carrots

carrots	600g
butter or margarine	50g
sugar	15g
salt	to taste
chopped parsley	good pinch
Serves	6–8

Method

1 Wash and peel the carrots and cut them into **batons**.
2 Place them in a pan and add the butter, sugar and salt.
3 Add enough water to half cover the carrots.
4 Cover them with a lid until the liquid boils.
5 Remover the lid. **Skim**.
6 Serve in a hot dish, season to taste and sprinkle with chopped parsley.

Definitions

Baton: a cut of a vegetable, evenly sized 2.5cm long × 0.5cm × 0.5cm.
Skim: to remove any surface impurities from a liquid using a spoon or similar implement.

Boiling stem vegetables

Asparagus is expensive and care must be taken to cook it correctly. The tips cook quicker than the stem so use a special asparagus kettle which boils the stem and steams the tips. If an asparagus kettle is not available, bundle the stems, tie them with string and cook them standing up in a wide pan.

Figure 6.22 An asparagus kettle

Asparagus and prosciutto

fresh asparagus	1kg
salt	5ml
prosciutto, cut into thin slices	250g
parmesan cheese, grated	60ml
butter	200g
Oven temperature	180°C
Cooking time	8–10 minutes
Serves	10

Method

1 Preheat the oven to 180°C.
2 Clean the asparagus, cutting off the tough ends. Add salt to the boiling water. Place the asparagus in the water, cover and cook for five minutes.
3 Lift out with tongs and drain the asparagus on paper towels.
4 Divide the asparagus into bundles, wrap each bundle with two strips of prosciutto, securing with a toothpick or similar implement.
5 Place the asparagus and ham bundles in a greased ovenproof dish and sprinkle with the parmesan cheese.
6 Heat in the oven for three minutes.
7 Melt the butter in a saucepan. Put the bundles on a warm serving plate and pour melted butter over them.

Boiling leaves

Leaf vegetables are less dense and require a much shorter boiling time. They should be added to water that is already boiling and cooked for only a few minutes. This also helps to reduce the amount of vitamins and minerals lost during the cooking process.

Potatoes dauphinoise

mixture of milk and whipping cream	250 ml
salt	¾ tsp
pepper	½ tsp
garlic, minced	1 clove
potatoes	1kg
gruyère cheese, grated	200g
Oven temperature	190°C
Cooking time	45 minutes
Serves	8

Method

1. In a heavy saucepan, combine the milk and cream, salt, pepper and garlic.
2. Bring the liquid to the boil over a medium heat.
3. Immediately remove from the heat. Set aside and keep warm.
4. Peel the potatoes and then using a sharp knife or mandolin, cut into very thin slices.
5. Pour 75ml of the milk mixture into a greased 10-inch (25cm) dish. Layer with half of the potato slices, overlapping slightly. Repeat this layering.
6. Pour remaining milk mixture over the top of the potatoes.
7. Cover the potatoes with gruyère cheese.
8. Bake in the oven for about 20 minutes or until milk mixture starts to bubble up the sides. Using a spatula, press down the potatoes to submerge.
9. Bake for about 25 minutes longer or until potatoes are tender and the top is golden brown.
10. Let the dish stand for 15 minutes before serving.

Remember!
Always use a dry cloth when handling trays from the oven to reduce the risk of burning yourself.

Roast potatoes are a popular dish for Sunday roast lunch. To make roast potatoes, peeled potatoes are covered in oil and put into a hot oven. The oil fries the potatoes while in the oven, producing brown and crispy potatoes ready for the table.

Roast potatoes

potatoes	5kg
oil	75ml
salt	to taste
parsley	for garnish
Oven temperature	190–200°C
Cooking time	60–90 minutes
Serves	10–15

Method

1 Pre-heat the oven.
2 Wash, peel and re-wash the potatoes.
3 Cut the potatoes into even sizes.
4 Fry and colour the potatoes in shallow hot oil.
5 Season the potatoes with salt. Place them on a tray and put them in an oven.
6 Baste the potatoes at regular intervals.
7 When they are soft inside and crisp on the outside, place them in a dish. Sprinkle them with parsley and serve.

Braising

A vegetable dish such as braised celery is started on the top of a stove. The vegetable can be fried to give colour (brown braising) or left as it is (white braising), before being added to a liquid, e.g. white stock or jus-lié (see Chapter 11). The ingredients are brought to the boil, covered with a lid and then placed in an oven.

Vegetables suitable for braising are:

○ celery
○ onions
○ artichokes
○ pulses such as chickpeas
○ stuffed cabbage
○ leeks.

For more information see page 122.

Combination cooking

A cauliflower cheese gratin dish is a good example of combination cooking as it uses two methods of cooking. The cauliflower is boiled, then put in a dish and covered with cheese sauce. It is finished and coloured in the oven or under a grill. For more information see page 125.

Cauliflower cheese

cauliflower	1 whole
butter	25g
plain flour	25g
mustard powder	½ tsp
warm milk	300ml
cheddar cheese	150g
salt and pepper	to taste
Oven temperature	180–200°C
Cooking time	20–30 minutes
Serves	4–6 depending on size

Method

1 Cut the cauliflower into florets. Cook the cauliflower by boiling or steaming and place it in a dish suitable for the oven.
2 Melt the butter in a pan.
3 Add the mustard powder and flour.
4 Cook into a white roux.
5 Add the warm milk and make sure there are no lumps.
6 Add the grated cheese and stir until smooth. Season to taste.
7 Pour the sauce over the cauliflower and bake it in the oven until a good glaze appears.
8 Sprinkle with chopped parsley and serve.

Holding and serving

Holding vegetables and pulses at the right temperature is very important. The Food Safety Act 1990 states that hot food must be served and held at a temperature of at least 63°C. Cold salads must be served at or below 5°C. These temperatures make sure that potentially harmful bacteria will not multiply and harm the consumer.

If vegetables must be kept warm (e.g. if they are bulk cooked), they can be stored in a thermostatically controlled hot cupboard for no longer than 90 minutes. Ideally, however, food should be served freshly cooked so it is at the optimum temperature of 63°C and above. If the dish is covered in tin foil it will hold heat for a short period.

Test yourself!

1 What are the six traditional French cuts of vegetables?

2 What general quality points should you check for in vegetables and pulses? Write a description.

3 What particular quality points should you check for in the following vegetables and pulses?
  a Potatoes
  b Radish
  c Courgette
  d Mangetout
  e Dried pulses.

4 What should you do if you have any problems during the preparation of vegetables or pulses?

5 What are bulbs?

6 What are root vegetables? Write a description.

7 Which vitamins are water-soluble?

8 What should you do if you have any problems during the cooking of vegetables or pulses?

9 What is blanching?

10 What equipment do you need to blanch tomatoes?

11 At what temperature should vegetables be deep-fried?

12 Why must kidney beans be boiled rapidly for ten minutes before use?

7 Meat and offal

This chapter covers the following NVQ units:

- Unit 2FP3 Prepare meat for basic dishes
- Unit 2FC3 Cook and finish basic meat dishes
- Unit 2FP6 Prepare offal for basic dishes
- Unit 2FC6 Cook and finish basic offal dishes

Working through this chapter could also provide evidence for the following Key Skills:
C1.1, C2.2, N1.1, N1.2, WO2.1, WO2.2, PS2.1, PS2.2, PS2.3

In this chapter you will learn how to:

Check the meat and offal meet dish requirements	2FC3.1 and 2FC6.1
Combine meat and offal with other ingredients ready for cooking	2FC3.1 and 2FC6.1
Cook meat and offal	2FC3.1 and 2FC6.1
Check flavour, colour and consistency and quantity of dishes	2FC3.1 and 2FC6.1
Garnish and present the dish	2FC3.1 and 2FC6.1
Make sure the dish is held at the correct temperature	2FC3.1 and 2FC6.1
Safely store cooked meat and offal not for immediate use	2FC3.1 and 2FC6.1

You will learn to cook basic meat and offal dishes, including:

- classic roast beef
- steak and kidney pudding
- liver and onions.

Types of meat

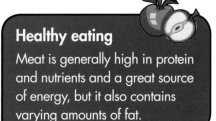

Healthy eating

Meat is generally high in protein and nutrients and a great source of energy, but it also contains varying amounts of fat.

Figure 7.1 Domestically farmed animals

Meat is the flesh of domestic farmed animals. It is taken from the carcass in various cuts and joints. The following types of meat are relevant to your NVQ Level 2 award:

○ beef
○ veal
○ lamb and mutton
○ pork
○ ham
○ bacon.

Beef

Beef is a red meat from cattle. Cattle are usually slaughtered between the ages of 18 months and two years. Different breeds of cattle (Aberdeen Angus, Welsh Blacks, Hereford, Sussex and shorthorn) may be used and the quality of the beef can vary according to the age and type of cattle.

Once the animal is slaughtered, the carcass is hung for between 7 and 21 days. A carcass which has been hung for longer will produce a more tender meat as the natural enzymes within the carcass will start to break down the meat tissue. This hanging process is strictly controlled in both temperature and process and regular checks are carried out so there is no risk to consumers. The outcome is tender meat for cooking.

Figure 7.2 Aberdeen Angus cattle produce high-quality beef

Cuts and joints of beef

The quality of meat varies depending on which part of the **carcass** the meat is taken from. You must know where on an animal a cut of meat is from, as this will have a bearing on how the meat is cooked, as well as its preparation method.

After **slaughter** the head is removed and the carcass is split in half lengthways giving two sides. Figure 7.3 is of a side of beef, showing where the different cuts and joints are to be found.

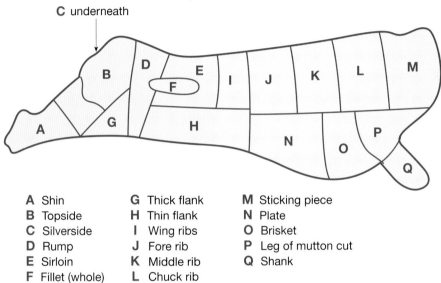

A Shin	**G** Thick flank	**M** Sticking piece
B Topside	**H** Thin flank	**N** Plate
C Silverside	**I** Wing ribs	**O** Brisket
D Rump	**J** Fore rib	**P** Leg of mutton cut
E Sirloin	**K** Middle rib	**Q** Shank
F Fillet (whole)	**L** Chuck rib	

Figure 7.3 The different cuts and joints that can be found on a side of beef

The table below gives more information on the cuts and joints from Figure 7.3 that you will use most often. It provides information on cooking methods and suitable portion sizes. Each cut or joint has a distinctive shape. Remember these shapes to help you recognise the different cuts.

Position	Name of cut/ joint	Appearance	Suggested cooking methods	Weight per portion
A	Shin		Boiling, stewing	180g
B	Topside		Roasting, braising, stewing	180–200g
C	Silverside		Roasting, braising, stewing, boiling	180–200g

> **Definition**
> **Carcass**: the dead body of the animal.
> **Slaughter**: the killing of an animal for food.

> **Healthy eating**
> Lean cuts of beef (less than 5 to 9 per cent fat), are almost as healthy as a chicken breast. In some cuts such as fillet, beef has only 1g more saturated fat than a skinless chicken breast.

> **Healthy eating**
> Beef is extremely high in nutrients, especially vitamins B12 and B6, riboflavin and iron.

D	Rump		Roasting, braising, grilling, frying	180–360g
E	Sirloin		Roasting, grilling, frying	180–300g
F	Whole fillet, chateaubriand, tournedos, filet mignon		Roasting, grilling, frying	120–360g
G	Thick flank		Braising, stewing	180g
H	Thin flank		Boiling, stewing	180g
J	Fore rib		Roasting	120–210g
O	Brisket		Braising, boiling, stewing	120–210g
Q	Shank		Stewing	120–160g

Figure 7.4 Identifying and preparing the different cuts and joints of beef

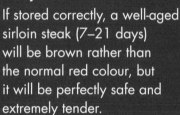

Did you know?

If stored correctly, a well-aged sirloin steak (7–21 days) will be brown rather than the normal red colour, but it will be perfectly safe and extremely tender.

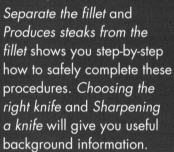

Video presentation

Separate the fillet and *Produces steaks from the fillet* shows you step-by-step how to safely complete these procedures. *Choosing the right knife* and *Sharpening a knife* will give you useful background information.

Checking beef quality

When checking beef before preparation you must make sure it is of the right quality. A poor-quality piece of meat will inevitably end up as a poor-quality dish. If you are unsure about the quality, always check with your supervisor.

The following points should be considered when checking the quality of beef:

○ It should have a fresh aroma and not smell stale or unpleasant.
○ There should be a sufficient amount of fat in proportion to the meat present.
○ The fat should be smooth and creamy in colour.

- The meat should be clean and bright in appearance. It should not look slimy.
- Flecks of fat run through some cuts of meat, this is called 'marbling'.
- It should be an appropriate temperature (1–5°C if fresh and –18–25°C if frozen) and stored correctly.
- It should be firm and a deep red colour with a sheen.
- It should be the correct cut or joint for the dish you are preparing.

Problems with beef are usually associated with the condition and quality of the meat. Cattle are now subject to rigorous checks by vets prior to slaughter.

Veal

Veal is the flesh of a calf (usually **culled** at three months of age). The meat is classed as white meat and is usually pale pink as the calf's diet is cow's milk. The texture of the meat is fine and lean because of the age of the animal.

Cuts and joints of veal

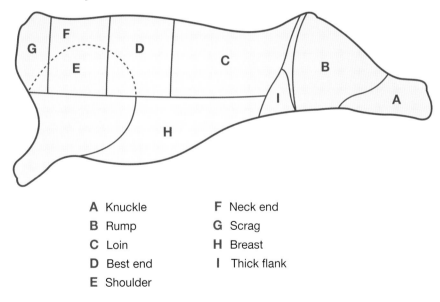

A Knuckle	**F** Neck end	
B Rump	**G** Scrag	
C Loin	**H** Breast	
D Best end	**I** Thick flank	
E Shoulder		

Figure 7.5 The different cuts and joints on a side of veal

The table on page 166 lists the cuts and joints from Figure 7.5 that you will use most often. It provides information on cooking methods and average weights of each cut.

> **Remember!**
> Meat may well have a lot of fat or glands on it as well as bones still within the cut or joint, and as the chef you will need to know how to prepare it. Some cuts of meat are expensive, so mistakes can be costly.

> **Definition**
> **Cull**: to kill an animal.

Position	Name of cut/joint	Suggested cooking methods	Average weight
A	Knuckle	Boiling, stewing	1–2kg
B	Rump	Roasting, frying, braising	4–6kg
C	Loin	Roasting, frying, braising, grilling, griddling	4–6kg
D	Best end	Roasting, frying, braising, grilling, griddling	5–7kg
E	Shoulder	Roasting, braising, stewing	3–5kg
F	Neck end	Boiling, stewing	3–4kg
H	Breast	Stewing	2–3kg
I	Thick flank	Roasting, frying, braising	6–8kg

Figure 7.6 Preparing the different cuts and joints of veal

Checking veal quality

Issues regarding selection, quality and potential problems concerning the use of veal are similar to those of beef as the origins are the same (see pages 164–165).

Lamb and mutton

Lamb is meat from domestically farmed sheep which are less than 12 months old. Meat from sheep over the age of 12 months is classed as mutton.

The breed of sheep used for lamb and mutton is varied and can depend on the region. The meat from sheep usually has a delicate, sweet flavour and the flesh can vary in colour from pink to a deep red. The fat is usually quite hard and white in colour.

Lamb can be slaughtered at three different ages. This will have a bearing on the colour and flavour of the meat. The ages are:
o 30–40 days, weighing 8–10kg
o 70–150 days, weighing 20–25kg
o 180–270 days, weighing 30–40 kg.

Mutton can be from rams (male sheep) or ewes (female sheep). Rams produce better quality mutton than the ewes, whose meat is of an inferior, fattier quality. The best quality mutton is taken from a **castrated** ram over 12 months old.

Did you know?
The loin and best end of veal are joints, which are used in the same manner as lamb (see page 168).

Did you know?
Lamb or mutton generally has a higher fat content than beef. Its calorific value can be as much as 250 calories per 100g of meat.

Healthy eating
Lamb and mutton are a rich source of protein and vitamin B12.

Definition
Castrated: testes removed before sexual maturity.

Bacon

Bacon usually comes from a large pig bred specially to produce bacon called a 'baconer'. The meat is cured (salted in brine) or smoked. There are two types of bacon: green, which is usually unsmoked bacon, and smoked. Bacon is usually cooked by frying and grilling but if kept in larger joints, as opposed to rashers, it can be boiled.

Cuts of bacon

There are usually four cuts from a baconer pig: back bacon, streaky bacon, middlecut bacon and gammon steaks. Back bacon is cut from the loin of the pig, while streaky is cut from the belly. Middlecut bacon is from the loin and the belly.

Checking bacon quality

Consider the following points:
- Streaky bacon has a higher fat content than back bacon because it is taken from the belly.
- Bacon should be firm to touch and dark pink.
- It should not be slimy to touch.
- It should not have an unpleasant smell.
- The fat should normally be creamy, but smoking can give the fat a brown tint.

Types of offal

Offal is the edible organs and parts taken from domestic farm animal carcasses. It is usually cooked in the same way as meat. The following types of offal are relevant to your NVQ:
- oxtail
- kidney
- heart
- tongue
- liver
- sweetbread.

You will need to know what parts of the animal offal comes from, as this will have a bearing on how the offal is prepared and cooked.

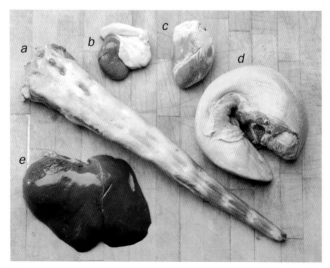

Figure 7.13 a oxtail, b kidney, c heart, d tongue, e liver

Find out!

Worksheet 20

Find out about other types of offal, e.g. ox tongue and lamb hearts. How big are they? How much do they weigh? How are they cooked? Find a recipe for each type.

Liver

Liver is taken from many different types of animal and can be cooked in a variety of ways, but it is usually fried, grilled or braised. The size of the liver varies depending on the size of the animal which it comes from. Calf's liver is the most popular type, followed by lamb's liver. Ox liver is also used, but it is lower in quality and has a much stronger flavour. Pig's liver is also used, but generally in braised dishes and pâtés.

Checking liver quality

The following quality points should be checked before using a piece of liver:

○ It can deteriorate quite quickly if not stored correctly, so it is important that it is stored at the correct temperature (see Pork quality on page 169 for temperatures).

○ It should be deep red, have a clean appearance and smell pleasant.

○ Signs of discoloration, bad smells and a slimy appearance are indicators of poor quality.

Kidney

Kidneys are organs which vary in size depending on the animal from which they are taken. Calf's kidneys are the best quality. Lamb and pig kidneys are also good. Ox kidneys are used, but these take longer to cook and need to be blanched before cooking. See page 121. The usual cooking methods for kidneys are frying, grilling and braising.

Checking kidney quality

Consider the following points when selecting a kidney:

○ It should be clean, reddish brown and have a pleasant aroma.

○ The kidney should not feel slimy.

○ The kidney should be below 5°C prior to preparation.

○ If encased in fat the fat should be a creamy colour.

Remember!

Offal may have a lot of fat or glands on it as well as bones left inside it, and as the chef you will need to know how to prepare it.

Healthy eating

Liver has a high level of vitamins and minerals especially vitamins A, B and C, and iron.

Did you know?

Liver is at its best if cooked and served pink.

Healthy eating

Kidney is high in vitamins A and K and has a strong flavour.

Sweetbreads

Sweetbreads are the throat and pancreas glands of calves and lambs. Lamb sweetbreads are usually an average weight of 100g. Calf sweetbreads can weigh as much as 500g.

Checking quality of sweetbreads

These are the points to consider when checking the quality of sweetbreads:

○ They are usually creamy white.

○ They should be soft to touch, dry and clean.

○ A good aroma is a sign of quality.

>
> **Find out!**   **Worksheet 21**
> Find out and record why vitamins B6, B12, C and the minerals iron, riboflavin, zinc and protein are important for health and which types of meat and offal contain them.

Healthy eating
Sweetbreads are a very good source of protein.

Preparing meat and offal dishes

Preparation methods

The table below lists the most popular cuts for each type of meat or offal.

Meat or offal	Cut or joint
Beef	Dice, steaks, strips
Veal	**Escalopes**, cutlets
Lamb	Leg, cutlets, chump chops, shoulder
Mutton	Dice
Pork	Chops, cutlets, dice, leg, loin
Bacon	Rashers, gammon
Ham	Slices
Kidney	Sliced, diced
Liver	Sliced
Sweetbreads	Sliced, pressed

Figure 7.14 Popular cuts of meat and offal

Definition
Escalopes: large slices of veal cut from the leg and flattened before cooking.

Cutting

It is essential that the correct knife and equipment is used and that you observe safe working procedures.

Ask yourself:

- Have I been trained to cut this food item?
- Do I know what to do next? (If not, ask!)
- Have I got the right knife?
- Is my knife sharp enough?
- Am I using the correct board?
- Am I dressed correctly?
- Have I selected the right equipment?
- Is my workstation tidy and suitable to prepare the food?

If your answer is 'Yes' to all of the above questions, it is safe to proceed.

In most cases a red chopping board is used for raw meat and the knife could be a red 7-inch boning knife, 10-inch chef's knife or 12-inch steak knife. Generally, you will need a knife with a sturdy blade so that it does not move when you are cutting the meat, as this could cause an accident. For slicing and dicing you will need a knife with a large heel.

Dicing

Meat which is off the bone can be diced. The meat or offal is cut into square cubes or evenly sized pieces to allow it to cook evenly.

Remember!
Make sure you use the correct knife and chopping board for the procedure, that your work space is clean and tidy and your hands are washed prior to cooking.

Remember!
Always cut away from yourself for safety reasons.

How to dice beef

① Use a 10-inch chef's knife. Cut across the beef (here a thick flank) to leave thick slices. You can trim off the end of each slice to neaten it.

② Cut each slice into strips. Trim the end of each strip to make a neat square end.

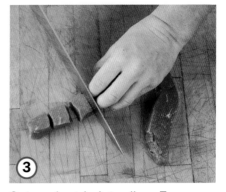

③ Cut each strip into dice. Ensure they are evenly sized. Store on a tray and refrigerate until required.

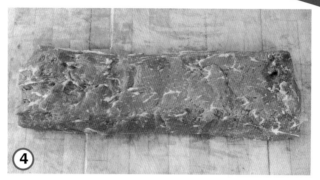

(3)

Turn the meat over. Lift the end of the fat with your fingers. Slice the fat away with a sawing motion.

(4)

The trimmed sirloin.

You must observe the following safe working procedures:

o Ensure your workplace is clean and tidy.
o Use a red chopping board for raw meat.
o Use a 10-inch chef's knife.
o Always cut away from yourself to avoid accidents if the knife slips.
o Have a container ready to put the trimmings into and a dish to put the finished product into.

How to trim liver

Liver varies in size. It is surrounded by a fine, transparent membrane which should be removed, because if it is left on during the cooking process it will shrink. The liver may also have some small glands (green or brown jelly-like spheres) and tubes or gristle. These should also be removed before cooking. After trimming liver should be cut into even thin slices – cut at a slant or angle. This is to ensure consistent cooking.

> **Remember!**
> Some trimmings may be suitable for stock, so do not just throw your trimmings in the bin.

> **Video presentation**
> *Prepare a whole lamb's liver* shows you how to trim and slice a liver. Also watch *Prepare a chicken liver.*

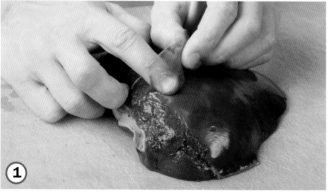

(1)

Use your fingers to remove the membrane without damaging the liver.

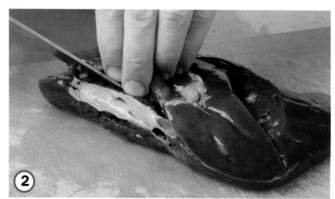

(2)

Remove excess fat, glands or valves. You will be left with a deep red liver with a soft gelatinous texture.

177

How to trim kidneys

Kidneys are usually cut through the centre to expose the white core, which must be removed. If large enough, they can be sliced thinly before cooking. Like liver, kidneys are surrounded by a membrane, which if left on during the cooking process will shrink, so this should be removed. They may also have some small glands (green or brown jelly-like spheres) and tubes or gristle, all of which should also be removed before cooking.

> **Video presentation**
> Watch *Prepare kidneys* to see the skills you need.

Pressing

Sweetbreads are usually blanched before cooking by bringing them to the boil. They are then washed, dried and pressed before being cooked. Calves' sweetbreads are sometimes passed through flour, egg and breadcrumbs then shallow-fried.

> **Video presentation**
> Watch *Prepare sweetbreads* to find out more.

Mincing

Mincing means passing meat or other ingredients through a piece of equipment which cuts and grinds the product into a fine texture. Mincing meat enables cheaper cuts of meat to be used and cooked using quick cookery methods, such as grilling or frying.

Minced meat can vary in quality depending on fat content of the meat and the cut of meat minced. Minced fillet steak for steak tartare is high-quality and low in fat compared to other cuts.

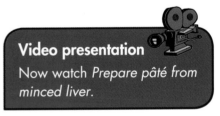

Figure 7.16 Minced beef

Mincing or grinding is used to make sausages. The meat is finely minced and then blended with other ingredients to make sausagemeat. Sausage skins are then filled with sausagemeat.

Another word for minced meat is forcemeat, as the meat is forced through a mincing machine, changing its appearance and texture.

> **Video presentation**
> Now watch *Prepare pâté from minced liver.*

Skinning

Pork and bacon have a very tough skin, which is usually scored (for crackling) or removed or to expose the fat layer beneath, which is in turn removed to an acceptable level. To remove the skin from a pork loin you need a sturdy firm-bladed knife. The process is the same as removing the fat from a sirloin of beef, but the pork fat is tougher.

> **Try this!**
> Rather than throwing away the skin from the pork loin, replace it over the skinned loin when roasting as it keeps the pork moist and the skin crisps into a tasty accompaniment.

How to remove the skin from a pork loin

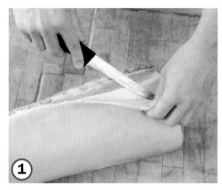

① Keep the knife blade away from you and make a cut to separate the skin from the fat.

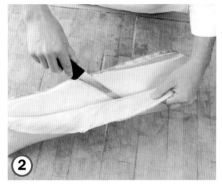

② Remove the skin by cutting across the horizontal loin. Use gentle sweeping motions.

③ At the edge make sure you cut away only skin and not meat. The bone edges give you a clear cutting guide. Do not remove too much fat as this aids the cooking process and keeps the meat moist.

Coating

Coating can be as simple as covering a piece of liver in seasoned flour during preparation. It can also refer to covering meat e.g. a veal escalope in flour, egg and breadcrumbs to meet the requirements of a dish.

Coating with seasoned flour

This is commonly done when preparing pieces of offal for cooking, e.g. liver and kidneys. Each piece of meat or offal is dipped in a dish of seasoned flour, then the excess is shaken off. The flour helps to give colour to the meat or offal when it is fried.

Coating with flour, egg and breadcrumbs

Nearly all types of meat and offal can be coated in flour or breadcrumbs. The dish requirements will dictate whether or not this is necessary. Before you begin have ready three separate bowls: one bowl of well-seasoned flour, one bowl of beaten egg and one bowl of fine breadcrumbs. You should always follow the process below to make sure that the meat or offal is evenly coated.

Video presentation
Coat goujons of plaice demonstrates these skills but uses fish rather than meat.

How to coat a pork escalope with seasoned flour, beaten egg and breadcrumbs

1

Coat the pork with seasoned flour.

2

Gently pat the pork to remove the excess.

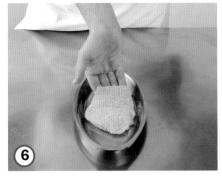

3

Put the pork in the beaten egg. Make sure it is completely covered.

4

Allow the excess to run off. Clean your hands.

5

Put the pork in the breadcrumbs. Ensure it is well coated. Gently pat off the excess.

6

Put the breadcrumbed portion on a suitable tray until it is required for cooking.

Once the meat or offal has been coated, it must be cooked fairly soon or the coating will become soggy. Do not stack portions of breadcrumbed products on top of each other as they may stick together and affect the appearance of the coating. Use greaseproof paper to layer many portions of coated meat or offal.

Coating meat in flour, egg and breadcrumbs helps it to remain moist during cooking, as it is sealed within a crispy coating, e.g. pork schnitzels.

Stuffing

Stuffing meat adds to its flavour, appearance and texture. Stuffing is added to the meat during the preparation stage. Ingredients such as meat, vegetables, rice and even fruit can be used for stuffing.

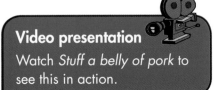

Video presentation
Watch *Stuff a belly of pork* to see this in action.

How to stuff a pork belly draft

Before you begin make light cuts in two-thirds of the skin to improve the flavour of the finished product. Trim the belly to form a square.

(1)

Trim to remove any excess fat.

(2)

Make the stuffing into a sausage shape. Put it in along the centre of the meat and spread it out.

(3)

Start to roll the meat around the stuffing.

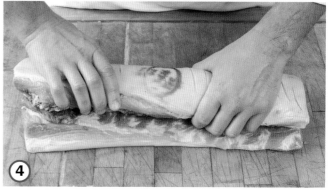

(4)

Continue to roll. The skin with the light cuts in it should be uppermost. Tuck the uncut skin inside the cut skin.

The equipment and tools used to stuff meat are:

○ Suitable knife

○ Chopping board

○ Piping bag to fill cavities in the meat (optional)

○ Spoons to prevent unnecessary handling of stuffing

○ String to tie the joint

○ Gloves

Before stuffing meat, it is important to check the quality of the product. If necessary, wash and dry the meat before stuffing. The stuffing or filling should always be at the correct temperature, which is 1–5°C. The meat should also be at this temperature. If possible, do not handle the filling – use a piping bag or spoon.

Tying

Tying holds meat joints together before cooking, e.g. roast topside of beef, boned leg of lamb or stuffed pork loin. Tying the meat joint with butcher's string means it retains its shape during cooking, especially if the meat joint is stuffed. Untied, the stuffed joint would fall apart and the quality of the dish would be affected. Strands should be tied about a thumb's width apart. Tying a joint also provides you with a guide to portion sizes and portions will not fall apart. Do not tie the meat too tight. If you do, the juices from the meat will be forced out during cooking and leave the meat dry.

> ### Remember!
> Temperature is important when preparing meat or offal. The meat may contain harmful bacteria, which multiply rapidly at room temperature. Adding hot filling to a cool pork loin could lead to food poisoning.

How to tie a stuffed pork belly draft

① Pass butcher's string under the meat in the middle and tie a simple slip knot. The string should be quite loose. Cut the string.

② Tie a string at each end. These should be a little tighter.

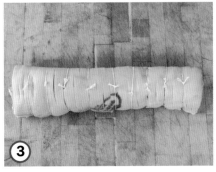

③ Fill in with more strings approximately a thumb's width apart. Keep the knots aligned as it is easier to remove the string afterwards.

Seasoning and marinating

Seasoning

Seasoning is the addition of ingredients such as salt, pepper and spices that help to bring out the flavour. Adjusting the quantities of seasoning will affect the flavour but you must be careful; too much of some seasonings, like salt, can make the dish or ingredients inedible.

Stewing

Stewing meat allows you to produce a good-flavoured dish from cheaper cuts of meat, e.g. mutton or beef shin. For more information see page 122.

Blanquette de veau

veal	700g
onions	2 medium
carrots	2 medium
lemon juice	a squeeze
bouquet garni	1
salt and pepper	to taste
butter or margarine	25g
plain flour	45ml
egg yolk	1
single cream	30–45ml
bacon rolls, cooked	4–6
chopped fresh parsley	to garnish
Cooking time	90 minutes
Serves	6

Method

1 Put the meat, onions, carrots, lemon juice, bouquet garni and seasoning into a large saucepan with enough water to cover. Cover and simmer for one hour or until the meat is tender.
2 Strain off the liquid, reserving 600ml. Keep the meat and vegetables warm.
3 Melt the butter. Mix in the flour.
4 Gradually add the liquid, ensuring the liquid is boiled after every addition. Cook until the sauce thickens.
5 Adjust seasoning, remove from heat and add egg yolks and cream.
6 Add the meat, vegetables and bacon rolls and reheat without boiling.
7 Serve garnished with parsley.

Frying

It is essential to control the temperature and regularly turn and check meat during frying. Pork must always be cooked right through. Red meat and offal can be cooked to the customer's requirements. For more information see pages 122–123.

Liver and onions

butter or margarine	25g
lamb's or calf's liver	450g
onions	450g
salt and pepper	to taste
mixed herbs (optional)	2.5ml
flour	for coating
Cooking time	5–10 minutes
Serves	4

Method

1. Melt the butter in a frying pan, add the onions and fry till brown. Add the herbs and seasoning. Cover and simmer for ten minutes.
2. Add the sliced liver to the onions and increase the heat slightly. Continue cooking for five to ten minutes.
3. Transfer to a warmed serving dish and serve.

Shallow-frying and stir-frying

Only good-quality meat should generally be fried.

To stir-fry meat, cut it into thin strips and place them into very hot oil in a wok. Cook the meat very quickly – normally for no longer than two to six minutes.

Find out!   **Worksheet 22**

List as many meat dishes as you can that require stir-frying, deep-fying or shallow-frying.

Remember!

Thicker pieces of meat will take longer to cook. For example, a sirloin steak will take longer than thin strips of pork for a stir-fry.

Remember!

Hot oil can inflict serious injury if you are not careful during cooking.

Video presentation

Watch the clip *Stir fry beef* to see this dish being made.

Grilling

Beefsteaks, lamb cutlets, pork chops, veal, liver and kidneys can all be grilled, but you must ensure that the cut of meat is appropriate. See the table on page 192.

The meat can be placed on a tray or directly onto a clean grill. The meat may even be on skewers, e.g. kebabs. The meat is usually brushed with butter or oil (olive) to baste the meat during grilling. Meat such as pork, which has been marinated, is suitable for grilling. The heat colours the meat and helps to develop flavour.

The cooking time will vary depending on the type and thickness of the meat and it must be cooked to at least 63°C at the centre. Cooked grilled meat or offal should be firm to touch and resistant to pressure. Beef and lamb are an exception to this rule, as they can be served pink. For more information see page 123.

Healthy eating

Grilling is a healthy way of cooking meat as some of the fat drips from it.

Barbecued pork spare ribs

vegetable oil	30ml
onions	2 medium
garlic clove	1
tomato purée	30ml
malt vinegar	60ml
dried thyme	1.25ml
chilli seasoning	1.25ml
honey	45ml
beef stock	150ml
pork spare ribs	1kg
Oven temperature	190°C
Cooking time	1¾ hours
Serves	4

Method

1. Heat the oil in a saucepan, add the onions and cook for five minutes until softened.
2. Add all the remaining ingredients, except the spare ribs, and simmer gently for ten minutes.
3. Place the spare ribs in a roasting tray in a single layer and brush with a little of the sauce.
4. Roast in the oven at 190°C for 30 minutes.
5. Pour off the excess fat and spoon the remaining sauce over the ribs.
6. Cook for a further 1¼ hours, basting occasionally.

Griddling

Some griddles have bars running across them. This enables the meat to be **charred** or **seared**, providing a distinctive flavour and colour. Too much oil on the griddle can lead to excessive smoke and can hamper the cooking process. For more information see page 124.

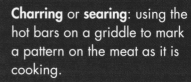

Definition

Charring or **searing**: using the hot bars on a griddle to mark a pattern on the meat as it is cooking.

Any type of meat or offal that can be grilled can also be griddled. The table below identifies what cuts from the meat types are suitable for grilling and griddling.

Meat or offal	Prime or tender cuts or joints
Beef	Rump, sirloin, fillet
Veal	Loin, best end
Lamb	Best end, saddle
Pork	Loin
Bacon	Gammon, loin
Offal	Liver, kidneys

Figure 7.19 Cuts of meat and offal suitable for grilling and griddling

Roasting

Roasting meat gives a joint a good natural flavour and colours it nicely through the cooking process which adds to the appearance of the final dish. Meat such as lamb or beef can be rare, well-done or medium. This refers to how much the meat is cooked. Pork must always be well cooked. Undercooked pork runs the risk of giving someone food poisoning.

Place meat for roasting in a sturdy tray with handles. Roasting is normally started at a temperature of 200–210°C. The heat is then turned down to 160–180°C once the meat has coloured. Oven cloths and personal protective equipment must be used. A probe should be used to check that the centre of the joint of meat has reached an acceptable temperature and is safe to eat. The temperature is usually 63°C.

A probe is not always available. If this is the case, the juice from the meat can be used to test its condition. If the juice is pink and the meat is pork then continue to cook. A well-done joint of meat cooked throughout will have juices that run clear. Touch is another test. A resistant surface indicates that the meat is cooked.

Let the meat relax for 30 minutes before carving to allow the meat to cool slightly and make it tenderer to eat. This is particularly important with red meat, e.g. lamb and beef.

The roasting times for the main types of meat are as follows:
- Beef: 20 minutes per 450g plus 20 minutes.
- Lamb: 15–20 minutes per 450g plus 20 minutes.
- Pork: 25 minutes per 450g plus 25 minutes.
- Veal: 20 minutes per 450g plus 20 minutes.

The table below lists the types of meat and cuts suitable for roasting.

Meat	Cut or joint
Beef	Rump, topside, sirloin, fillet, ribs
Veal	Cushion, best end
Lamb	Best end, leg, shoulder, chops, saddle
Pork	Loin, leg, ribs, belly, shoulder
Bacon	Gammon

Figure 7.20 Cuts of meat suitable for roasting

Classic roast beef

piece of beef (sirloin, rib, rump or topside)	2kg
beef dripping (optional)	50g
salt and pepper	to taste
mustard powder (optional)	5ml
horseradish sauce	
Oven temperature	200–210°C until meat has coloured, then 160–180°C
Cooking time	See guidelines above
Serves	8–10

Method

1. Weigh the meat and calculate the cooking times.
2. Place the meat in a shallow roasting tin, preferably on a grid with the thickest layer of fat uppermost.
3. Add beef dripping if the meat is lean, season with salt, pepper, and mustard if preferred.
4. Roast the joint at 180°C for the calculated time, basting occasionally.
5. Remove from the oven and allow to rest for 20 minutes before carving. Serve with horseradish sauce.

For more information see page 124.

Braising

The benefits of this cooking method are that the meat is very tender, flavours are able to merge and it allows cheaper, tougher cuts of meat to be used. The thickening agent for the liquid used when braising dishes is flour. A white or brown roux will be made and cooked into a sauce relevant to the dish. For more information see page 122.

Combination cooking

Lasagne is an example of a meat dish cooked using combination cooking. First the meat is sealed then it is stewed and finally it is finished by baking in the oven. For more information see page 125.

Combination ovens

A combination oven uses dry heat and an injection of steam to keep the food moist during cooking e.g. lamb chops can easily become dry if overcooked in an ordinary oven. In a combination oven, the steam coupled with the convection heat will help to keep the meat moist and good to eat. For more information see page 125.

Hot holding, finishing and serving

Once you have worked hard to prepare and cook a dish it is important to serve it with the correct garnish and at the right temperature.

Hot holding

Holding the meat at the right temperature is also about being compliant with the law. The Food Safety Act 1990 states that hot food must be served and held at a temperature of at least 63°C. This temperature makes sure that potentially harmful bacteria will not multiply and harm the consumer.

Food is usually held at the correct temperature by either storing in a hot cupboard or hotplate which is above 63°C. Be aware that you may only hot hold food for a maximum of 90 minutes. Keep checking the condition of the food whilst hot holding as it can tend to become dry if it is not monitored correctly.

Did you know?
The thickening agent for the liquid used when braising dishes is flour. A white or brown roux will be made and cooked into a sauce relevant to the dish.

Finishing

Finishing a meat or offal dish correctly is very important. You should always check a dish before it is served and ask yourself the following questions:

○ Is the meat or offal at the correct temperature for service?
○ Does the dish have the correct flavour?
○ Does it need more seasoning?
○ Do I have the correct **garnish** or accompaniment for the dish?
○ Do I have the right equipment to finish and serve the dish?

The following are all appropriate garnishes for meat dishes:
○ Other cooked ingredients such as Yorkshire pudding for roast beef.
○ Accompaniments and sauces appropriate to the dish, e.g. apple sauce for pork or mint sauce for lamb.

Definition

Garnish: adding the final touches required to enhance a dish.

Yorkshire pudding

plain flour	125g
salt	pinch
egg	1
milk	200ml
vegetable oil	30ml
Oven temperature	220°C
Cooking time	40–45 minutes
Serves	4–6

Method

1 Add the flour, salt and egg in a bowl and mix.
2 Add half the milk and beat until smooth.
3 Add the remaining milk and beat until smooth.
4 Put a small amount of oil in a small roasting tray and pre-heat it in the oven.
5 Pour the batter into the hot tray and cook until risen and golden brown.

Serving

The equipment required to finish and serve meat can include:

o serving platters (earthenware, plate or metal)

o serving utensils, e.g. spoons, tongs, slices or forks.

The surface of a dish should be clean and presentable and maintained in an appropriate condition during service so that it is appealing to customers.

The final dish needs to be appealing to you and your customer. This is an aspect of catering where your flair will play an important part in shaping your career.

Figure 7.20 Serving is as essential as the preparation and cooking in creating an appealing dish

Test yourself!

1 Where should a pork joint be stored and at what temperature?

2 What is offal? Name two different types.

3 What is the most preferred type of liver used in offal dishes?

4 Which meats are classed as high risk?

5 What are the quality points to check for when selecting a pork loin for roasting?

6 What is the minimum temperature for pork to be cooked to?

7 Why is it important to cook pork thoroughly?

8 What type of pig does bacon come from?

9 What are sweetbreads?

10 What are the accompaniments for roast beef, lamb and pork?

8 Poultry

This chapter covers the following NVQ units:
- Unit 2FP4 Prepare poultry for basic dishes
- Unit 2FC4 Cook and finish poultry for basic dishes

Working through this chapter could also provide evidence for the following Key Skills:
C1.1, C2.2, N1.1, N1.2, WO2.1, WO2.2, PS2.1, PS2.2, PS2.3

In this chapter you will learn how to:

Check poultry for type, quality and quantity	2FC4.1
Combine poultry with other ingredients	2FC4.1
Cook poultry and make sure it meets dish requirements, i.e. colour, flavour, consistency and quality	2FC4.1
Garnish and present the dish	2FC4.1
Make sure the dish is held and served at the correct temperature	2FC4.1
Safely store cooked poultry not for immediate use	2FC4.1

You will learn to prepare and cook basic poultry dishes, including:
- sauté chicken bonne femme
- poached breasts of chicken with mushroom sauce
- chicken in white wine sauce.

Types of poultry

What is poultry?

Poultry is the generic term used for domestic farmyard birds, e.g. chickens, ducks and turkeys. Geese and guinea fowl are also included in this group. Poultry is an increasingly popular source of protein, because it is versatile and adaptable in modern cooking.

Remember!

If you are unsure or have a problem with the poultry you are preparing or cooking then always seek advice from your supervisor, line manager or head chef.

Figure 8.1 Poultry includes many different species of bird (duck, turkey, chicken, guinea fowl, goose)

Chicken is the most popular type of poultry. It can be found in most domestic fridges as well in restaurants and industrial kitchens worldwide.

Did you know?

Corn-fed chickens are yellow. The cooked fat has a yellow tinge to it because of the food the bird is fed.

Quality points

The following quality points apply to all poultry:

○ There should be no bruises or cuts on the skin of the bird.
○ The skin should be dry and not slimy.
○ Good-quality poultry should be odourless or at least have a fresh smell to it.
○ The bird should be the right size for the dish you are to prepare. For example, a chicken for roasting should be about 1.3kg. Other birds, e.g. duck or turkey, can vary in weight but you should check the size against the requirements of the dish.
○ The **cavity** should not contain any excess blood or yellow fat, nor show any signs of damage to the inside of the carcass.

Definition

Cavity: the hollow space left inside the bird once all the innards have been removed.

Potential problems

Poultry is a high-risk food, as it can contain harmful bacteria, e.g. salmonella. Bacteria can multiply if poultry is not stored or cooked correctly and this could lead to food poisoning. It is important to follow these food safety guidelines strictly:

○ Poultry should be stored correctly at an appropriate temperature (1–5°C if fresh and -18–-25°C if frozen).
○ Always store raw meat on the bottom shelf of the refrigerator to stop the juices dripping onto the shelves below.
○ Thoroughly defrost frozen poultry before cooking. Otherwise the meat in the thickest parts may not be cooked through and the harmful bacteria could remain.
○ Always cook poultry to a temperature of above 63°C.
○ Check there is no sign of uncooked flesh before serving.

Chicken

Chickens are farmed or reared in three different ways:

1 **Free-range**: the birds are usually left to roam freely.
2 **Battery**: an intense method of farming where the birds are kept packed in pens with little if any freedom of movement.
3 **Organic**: birds are fed on natural and traditional foods. Information is always readily available regarding organic poultry from either the label or organisations relevant to the product.

There are many types of chicken for cooking; the most common are shown in the table below.

Did you know?
Chicken is high in protein and full of vitamins, especially vitamin B.

Healthy eating
The breast meat of chicken is low in fat and the leg meat has lower fat content than other more traditional red meats. The young age of the chicken (12 weeks) means that the meat is tender and very adaptable.

Type	Description	Average portion yield	Appearance
Poussin	4–6-week-old bird	1	
Double poussin	6-week-old bird	2	
Roasting chicken	12–14-week-old bird	4–8	
Boiling fowl	Older bird, over 14 weeks	6–8	
Large roasting chicken	Young fattened cockerel	8–12	

Figure 8.2 Types of chicken for cooking

a boiling fowl, b poussin, c roasting chicken, d capon

The bird you will most commonly prepare is the traditional roasting chicken, which may come pre-packed. It can range in size from 1.3kg to 3kg. The chicken will have already been plucked and cleaned of its innards. It will therefore be ready for dish preparation and cooking.

A chicken can be cooked:

○ whole
○ **jointed** from the carcass into two breasts and two legs (see page 204)
○ cut into eight pieces for sautéing (see page 205).

Checking quality of chicken

When selecting chicken for use in the kitchen, it is important to check for the following quality points:

○ It should be plump and of appropriate size (1.3kg–3kg).
○ There should not be any damage, breaks, blemishes or bruising.
○ It should be clean, with a fresh smell and it should not be slimy to the touch. An unpleasant odour indicates that the chicken may be unsuitable for use.
○ Make sure there is minimal fat and that the cavity does not contain a high proportion of yellow fat inside it, as this indicates poor quality or an old bird.

Using the wrong type of chicken will result in a poor quality dish and affect your kitchen's reputation. For example, you should not use a boiling fowl if you are supposed to be producing roast chicken.

Duck

It is believed that duck was first domesticated in China hundreds, maybe thousands, of years ago. Today many types of duck are reared for cooking. Some commonly used types of duck are:

○ Pekin or Long Island
○ Barbary or Muscovy
○ Aylesbury.

Barbary and Aylesbury are the most commonly used ducks in cooking. The Aylesbury duck has a higher fat content than the Barbary duck. Ducks are generally quite large birds. They should have long plump breasts and smaller legs in proportion to the breasts. The flesh is usually a deep red.

Healthy eating

A skinless chicken breast is an appropriate low-fat meat option as part of a healthy well-balanced diet. A chicken breast has only 120 calories per 100g.

Definition

Jointed: cuts of poultry removed from the carcass during preparation, e.g. legs and breasts.

Remember!

Chicken breasts can be expensive so there must not be too much wastage during preparation.

Figure 8.3 Duck breasts. Note the deep red flesh

Cutting poultry for sauté dishes

Sautéing is a relatively quick method of cooking and therefore the meat must be cut into small manageable pieces of approximately the same size. This preparation method is carried out on whole chickens.

How to cut a chicken into eight pieces for sauté

1

Make sure all the giblets have been removed. Clean the cavity – if necessary wash it out under cold running water and wipe it with a kitchen towel.

2

To remove the wishbone, pull the skin back around the neck area. Use an 8–10-inch chef's knife to rub the flesh on each side to expose the wishbone. You can see where the wishbone is joined to the shoulder blade.

3

Using the point of the knife cut through the bone on each side.

4

Run your finger along each side of the bone to the top. At the top there is an oval-shaped piece of bone attaching the wishbone to the breast. Pinch this and pull to remove the wishbone.

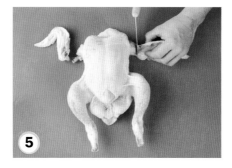

5

Cut above the wing joint. Scrape flesh back to expose a clean bone.

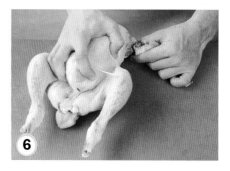

6

Snap off the wing at the joint. Repeat on the other side.

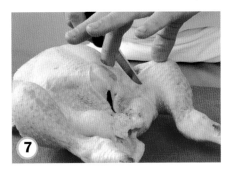

7 Pull out the leg and make a small cut through the skin to expose the flesh.

8 Push the thigh backwards to expose the bone. Hold the leg and pop the bone from the socket.

9 Work around the small piece of flesh on the back. This is the 'oyster'.

10 Remove the leg. Repeat to remove the second leg (2 pieces).

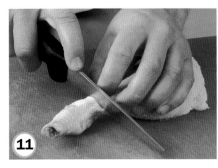

11 Cut the flesh at the bottom of the drumstick and scrape it back to the joint.

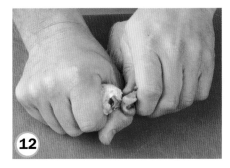

12 Snap the joint, leaving a small piece of clean bone exposed.

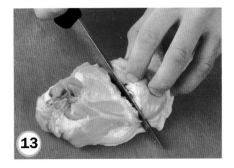

13 Smooth the skin. Put the meat skin side down. There should be a visible line of fat. Using this as your guide, cut through between the drumstick and thigh. Repeat on the other leg (4 pieces).

14 Remove the ball joint from each drumstick. Press down with the heel of the knife to cut off the bone. Repeat with the other leg.

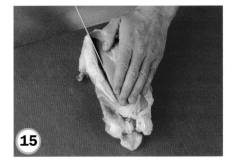

15 Have the cavity end towards you. Follow the feather lines along the breast, cutting through the shoulder.

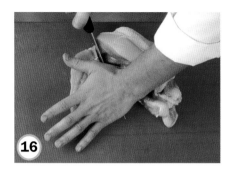

16 Put your hand over the front of the knife to steady it. Push the knife down to cut right through the bones. Remove the wing with part of the breast. Repeat on the other side (6 pieces).

17 Turn the chicken onto its side. Cut the remaining carcass from the breast.

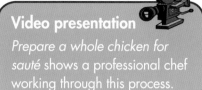

Video presentation

Prepare a whole chicken for sauté shows a professional chef working through this process.

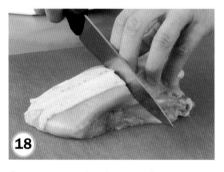

18 Cut across the breast bone. You will need to press on the heel of the knife to cut through the bone.

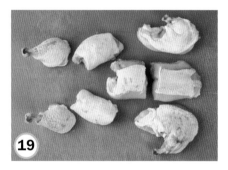

19 Reassemble the 8 portions on a tray, tidying the skin as you do this.

Stuffing or filling

Stuffing or filling poultry adds to the flavour, appearance and texture of the dish. Stuffing, e.g. sage and onion, is often put into the neck cavity. Legs can also be filled or stuffed. Before stuffing a cavity it is important to check it to ensure the quality of the bird. If necessary, wash and dry the inside of the cavity. The stuffing or filling should always be at the correct temperature, which is 1–5°C. If possible do not handle the filling; use a piping bag or spoon.

Remember!

Temperature is important when preparing poultry. The meat may contain harmful bacteria, which multiply rapidly at room temperature. Adding hot filling to a cool chicken cavity could lead to food poisoning. Always allow hot fillings or stuffing to cool below 8°C before adding them to the poultry.

How to stuff a turkey breast

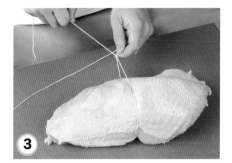

Remove the breast from the turkey. Cut into the fattest part of the breast along its length. This cut almost slices all the way through the breast, creating a pouch or envelope effect.

Put the cooled stuffing in this 'envelope' or 'pouch', using a spoon or your hands, as long as they are clean.

Tie the breast back to its original shape before cooking, using butcher's twine or another similar string. Do not use plastic-based string as this can melt and contaminate the meat.

How to stuff a leg

1 Remove the thighbone from the bird. This gives a natural cavity.
2 Put the stuffing in this cavity.
3 Sew, tie or wrap the leg in foil so that it keeps its shape during cooking.

Equipment and tools used to stuff a bird:

○ suitable knife
○ chopping board
○ piping bag to fill cavities in the meat
○ spoons to prevent unnecessary handling of stuffing
○ string to tie the bird or joint
○ gloves, which the food handler can use when stuffing poultry.

Seasoning and marinating

Seasoning

Seasoning is the addition of various ingredients, e.g. salt, pepper, and certain spices and herbs, to give a particular flavour to a dish or type of food. Adjusting the quantities of seasoning will affect the flavour, but you must be careful. Too much of some seasonings, e.g. salt, can make the dish or ingredients inedible.

A chicken or turkey for roasting is usually seasoned before cooking, during the preparation stage. If the poultry you are preparing is for a **wet method** of cookery, e.g. stewing or braising, the poultry should

Video presentation
Watch *How to stuff a chicken leg for ballotine* to see how its done.

Did you know?
The main seasoning in chicken chasseur is the herb tarragon.

Definition
Wet method: a dish which is cooked and served in a liquid.
Dry method: a dish which is cooked using a dry method of cookery (e.g. roasting, grilling).

be well-seasoned before cooking. The overall seasoning of the dish should be adjusted after cooking when all the flavours of the ingredients in the casserole have combined.

Marinating

Marinating is used to preserve or flavour foods. Marinating poultry is done by combining a cooked or uncooked liquid with the bird or joints in a dish. The liquid is called the marinade. It contains ingredients which will alter and enhance the flavour of the poultry. The poultry can be left in the marinade for between 30 minutes and 48 hours, depending on the dish. The poultry should be covered completely by the liquid.

Some marinades are cooked and then cooled before being combined with the meat. Most marinades, however, are cold and can be created very quickly using ingredients necessary to flavour the meat.

Some marinades are used after the meat has been removed from them to create a sauce to accompany the dish. Tandoori is a well-known chicken dish in which the sauce is created from the marinade.

As a chef you can experiment with creating your own marinades by combining flavours and adding those to different base ingredients, e.g. poultry.

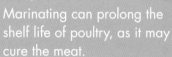

Did you know?

Marinating can prolong the shelf life of poultry, as it may cure the meat.

Basic marinade for chicken

chicken	1 portioned into 4 or 8
salt and pepper	to season
chopped shallots	2
thyme	1 sprig
bay leaf	1
chopped parsley	1 tablespoon
garlic clove, crushed	1 small
clove	1 small
black peppercorns	12
lemon juice	from 2 lemons
olive oil	375ml
Serves	4

Method

1 Season the chicken with salt and pepper.
2 Mix the other ingredients together in a bowl. Add the chicken and make sure it is covered in marinade.
3 Cover the dish and put it in a refrigerator for 2–12 hours.

Coating

Coating poultry can be as simple as covering it in seasoned flour during preparation. It can also refer to covering a piece of poultry in flour, egg and breadcrumbs to meet the requirements of a certain dish, e.g. Chicken Kiev.

Coating with seasoned flour

This is commonly done when preparing pieces of poultry for sauté. Dip each piece of poultry in a dish of seasoned flour and shake off the excess. The seasoned powder combines with the poultry to create a well-coloured and crisp texture when sealing the meat.

Coating with flour, egg and breadcrumbs

Coating poultry in flour, egg and breadcrumbs for Chicken Kiev allows the garlic butter to be held in the poultry leg or breast during cooking. A breadcrumb coating adds a different texture to the dish.

Always follow this process to make sure the poultry is evenly coated:

1. Take three bowls: one bowl of well-seasoned flour, one bowl of beaten egg and one bowl of fine breadcrumbs.
2. Coat the poultry with the flour and shake off any excess.
3. Place it in the beaten egg mix. Make sure the poultry is completely coated in egg mix. Shake off the excess.
4. Place it in the breadcrumb bowl. Make sure the meat is well coated.
5. Put the breadcrumbed poultry on a suitable tray until required for cooking.

Once the poultry has been coated it must not be left very long before cooking or the coating will become soggy. Do not stack portions of breadcrumbed products on top of each other or the quality of the coating and its appearance will be affected. Use greaseproof paper to layer many portions of coated poultry.

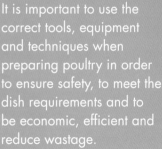

Remember!

It is important to use the correct tools, equipment and techniques when preparing poultry in order to ensure safety, to meet the dish requirements and to be economic, efficient and reduce wastage.

Find out!   Worksheet 23

List as many poultry dishes as you can that are coated in flour, egg and breadcrumbs.

Chicken Kiev

chicken breasts	2
butter	50g
lemon juice and zest	½ lemon
garlic clove	1
chopped parsley	20g
salt and pepper	to taste
flour	50g
white breadcrumbs	100g
eggs, beaten	2
watercress as garnish	
Cooking time	8–10 minutes
Serves	2

Method

1 Flatten the chicken breasts slightly.
2 Mix the butter, salt and pepper, lemon juice, crushed garlic and chopped parsley in a bowl.
3 Shape the butter mixture into fingers to fit inside the breasts.
4 Cut a pouch in each chicken breast big enough to put the butter in.
5 Put the butter into the chicken breasts and cover it with the surrounding flesh.
6 Coat each chicken breast in flour, egg and breadcrumbs. Make sure none of the chicken meat is left exposed. Refrigerate for one hour.
8 Deep-fry the chicken breasts for about six minutes until golden brown. Finish in a hot oven if required.
9 Serve with watercress.

Trussing

To **truss** a bird, use a trussing needle and butcher's string. A trussing needle is a long steel needle with a curved sharp end that is adapted for passing through poultry carcasses. Butcher's string is sturdy and will not alter when heat is applied. There are several ways to truss a bird and one method is shown below.

Definition

Trussing: a method of securing the bird in an appropriate shape during the cooking process.

How to truss a chicken

Use a string that is approximately four to five times the length of the bird.

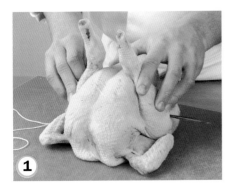

1 Insert the needle between the drumstick and the thigh on one side, through the cavity and out between the thigh and drumstick on the other side.

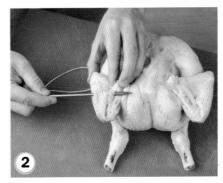

2 Turn the bird over and pass the needle between the two wing bones.

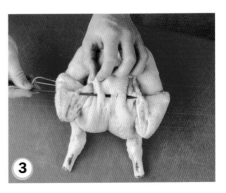

3 Sew down the neck flap.

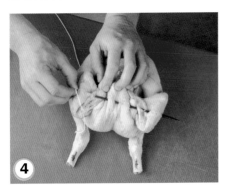

4 Come back through the opposite winglets.

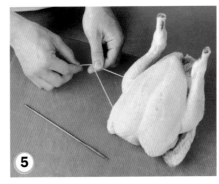

5 Tie securely producing a neat shape.

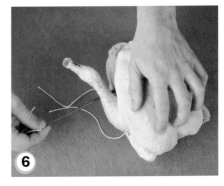

6 Insert the needle through the leg below the bone. Go through the cavity and exit through the other leg below the bone.

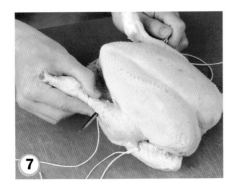

7 Go back through, just above the bone.

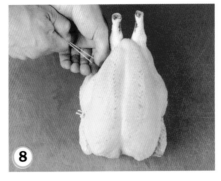

8 Pull the string tight to produce a nice neat shape and tie off.

9 A trussed bird.

Storing prepared poultry

Poultry can contain harmful bacteria, e.g. salmonella. This means it is necessary to store poultry correctly before, during and after preparation:

○ Ensure that raw poultry is stored at the bottom of a refrigerator. This will prevent any blood or liquid dripping onto other foods.
○ Clearly label poultry which has been prepared. The label should include the date so that it is possible to determine its shelf life.
○ Store prepared poultry at 1–5°C.
○ Do not stack prepared poultry on top of each other as it can affect the appearance and quality of the end product.

Cooking and finishing poultry dishes

Cooking methods

After poultry has been prepared correctly, it is important that the correct cooking method is used to ensure a quality dish. The cooking method adopted depends on the dish required. As the chef, you must make sure that you work in a safe manner and that the correct tools, techniques and methods are used.

It is useful to remember that a tough and fibrous bird is best cooked using wet methods of cookery, e.g. stewing, braising or boiling. For tender poultry, dry methods of cooking are appropriate, e.g. roasting, grilling, etc. Overcooking poultry makes it dry and unappealing to eat.

Steaming

For information on steaming, see page 120.

Poaching

White stock is usually used to poach poultry. See pages 121 and 261 for more information. To test whether the poultry is cooked, prick the meat gently. The juices should run clear or white.

Video presentation
Prepare a whole chicken for roasting takes you step-by-step through this procedure. You could also watch *Prepare a chicken for spatchcock*.

Chef's tip
Adding carrots and onions to the poaching liquor can give a delicate flavour to a poultry dish. Leeks and fennel are other good flavours for poultry.

Poached breasts of chicken with mushroom sauce

skinless chicken breasts	4
white stock	350ml
butter	25g
mushroom sauce	500ml
mushroom caps	8
salt and pepper	to taste
chopped parsley	to garnish
Cooking time	30 minutes
Serves	4

Method

1 Poach the chicken breasts in white stock for 20 minutes.
2 Slice the mushroom caps.
3 Shallow fry the mushroom caps in butter.
4 Heat the mushroom sauce.
5 Garnish the poached chicken breasts with the cooked mushroom caps, **napper** with the sauce and decorate by sprinkling the chopped parsley over it.

Definition

Napper: a French term meaning to coat or mask a tray of food.

Stewing

Stewing allows you to produce a good-flavoured dish from cheaper cuts of poultry, e.g. the legs or thighs. Vegetables and stock can be added and cooking slowly enables the flavours to infuse or merge.

Towards the end of the cooking time, you may need to thicken a stewed poultry dish. This can be done by **reducing** the liquid so it thickens itself or by using a roux or starch-based sauce method (see Chapter 11). For more information on stewing see page 122.

Definition

Reducing: to boil the liquid rapidly until it reduces in volume.

Coq au vin (chicken in red wine)

		For the garnish:	
chicken	1		
oil	50ml	button mushrooms	100g
bouquet garni	1	lardons of bacon	100g
red wine	100ml	button onions	100g
chicken stock	50ml		
meat glaze	12g		
butter	25g		
flour	25g		
heart-shaped croutons, fried	4		
chopped parsley	to garnish		
Oven temperature	140–160°C		
Cooking time	1–1½ hours		
Serves	4		

Method

1 Cut the chicken for sauté (see page 205).
2 Put the oil in a pan and heat it until there is a blue haze. Put the chicken in the pan.
3 Season chicken and **seal** and colour it quickly.
4 Remove the chicken and place it in a stewing vessel with the bouquet garni.
5 Sauté the onions, mushrooms and lardons in the same pan the chicken was coloured in.
6 Deglaze the pan with the wine and stock. Bring it to the boil.
7 Pour the liquid over the chicken and put a tightly fitting lid over the dish. Cook it in the oven until the chicken is tender.
8 Remove the chicken and garnish it with the mushrooms, lardons and onions.
9 Reduce the sauce by a third and add the meat glaze.
10 Put the butter and flour into a clean bowl. Combine the butter and flour into a paste (beurre manie).
11 Add small amounts of the paste to the liquid.
12 As the liquid boils whisk to obtain the required consistency: thick enough to coat the back of a spoon.
13 Adjust the seasoning.
14 Pour an appropriate amount of the sauce over the chicken and garnishes.
15 Serve with the fried croutons on top, sprinkled with chopped parsley.

Definition

Sealing: colouring meat in hot fat to prevent excessive juices leaking from the dish, e.g. the breadcrumbed breast of chicken for Chicken Kiev is sealed in hot fat to provide its colour and prevent the garlic butter from escaping during cooking.

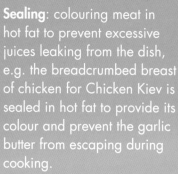

Definition

Deglaze: to add wine or stock to a pan used for frying in order to lift the remaining sediment to make a sauce or gravy.

Frying

Regular turning and checking of the poultry during frying is essential to ensure that the food is cooked right through. Remember that thicker pieces of meat will take longer to cook. For example, chicken drumsticks will require longer cooking than thin strips of breast.

Deep-frying

Pieces of poultry which are deep-fried must be closely monitored to make sure they are thoroughly cooked. Temperature probing or piercing the flesh at the thickest part to see if blood runs from the joint is a good indicator.

Shallow-frying, sautéing and stir-frying

Only good-quality poultry should be used for sauté as the pan is **deglazed** and a sauce is made from **residues**.

Definition

Deglaze: to add wine or stock to a pan used for frying in order to lift the remaining sediment to make a sauce or gravy.
Residue: the content left in the pan once the poultry has been cooked or sealed, including liquid and solid materials which all contain intense flavours which enhance a dish.

Sauté chicken bonne femme

chicken cut for sauté (see page 205)	1
lardons of bacon, blanched and sautéed	100g
white wine	100ml
demi-glace	400ml
button onions for garnish	100g
cocotte potatoes	100g
salt and pepper	to season
Cooking time	45 minutes
Serves	4

Definition

Bonne femme: dishes that are prepared in a simple rustic style and often served in the container they were cooked in.

Method

1 Sauté the chicken. Ensure that the poultry is cooked and coloured evenly. Keep an eye on the poultry as you do not want it to burn; regulate the heat if necessary. Fry off the lardons in the same pan, until they have a slight golden brown colour.
2 Deglaze the sauté pan with the wine.
3 Reduce the liquid by half.
4 Add the **demi-glace**, adjust the seasoning if required, add the garnishes (lardons, potatoes and onions), and serve.

Definition

Demi-glace: a sauce which is made up of equal quantities of brown stock and brown sauce (espagnole sauce), reduced by a third until the consistency coats the back of a spoon.

Trimming

Trimming fish means to remove the fins, gills, eyes, head and scales. Gills, eyes and fins are usually removed by cutting them out or off using kitchen scissors. Kitchen scissors are used as they are robust and sturdy.

Shellfish (e.g. mussels) have byssus threads (threadlike attachments) hanging from their shells. They use these to attach themselves to rocks or other static structures. Use a knife to pull away these strings, and wash the shellfish again.

Video presentation
Watch *Trim a whole salmon* for more information.

How to remove the scales from a fish

Here we use a medium-sized serrated knife which is suitable for the removal of scales from a large fish such as salmon. A filleting knife would be more suitable for a smaller fish, e.g. herring or trout. Fishmongers sometimes use a special type of wire brush.

Lay the fish on a blue chopping board. Cut off the fins using fish scissors.

Scrape the knife blade against the scales of the fish in the opposite direction to that in which they lie. Ensure you hold the fish firmly by the tail to prevent accidents. This scraping motion will lift the scales and any surplus slime from the fish's body. Wash the fillet.

Filleting

Filleting is a complex knife skill, which is an essential part of preparing fish. Filleting is the removal of the flesh from the bones and skin.

The equipment and tools used for filleting fish are:

o a blue chopping board, secured to a flat work surface
o suitable filleting knife with a sharp, flexible blade
o container for waste products
o tray for the fillets.

You may also need:

o tweezers to remove pin bones (small bones) left in the fillet
o kitchen scissors which can be used to trim away fins.

The process for filleting a flat fish is different from that of filleting a round one. Usually the preferred knife to use is a 7-inch blade which is flexible to aid the filleting process. If the flat fish is large (e.g. a turbot), a knife with a sturdy blade is needed for safety.

Figure 9.7 The tools required for filleting fish

How to fillet a flat fish

1 Lay the fish flat on the chopping board. Cut around the head with the point of the knife until you reach the lateral line.

2 Cut down the central lateral line until the knife reaches the rib bones. Then cut along the lateral line as far as the tail.

3 Bending the flexible blade, sweep the knife smoothly against the bones to remove the flesh. Cutting motions will leave flesh on the bone and affect the presentation of the fillet.

4 Cut the fillet away from the fins and place it on a tray. Turn the fish round and remove the other fillet in the same manner.

5 Trim up the fillet to remove the fins.

How to fillet a round fish

The fish must already be gutted and trimmed.

1 Lay the fish flat on the chopping board. Use a knife which has at least a 7-inch flexible blade and is sharp. Cut behind the fins and gills to give access to the backbone.

2 Cut along the backbone of the fish around the rib cage. Lift the fillet off the bones as you are cutting.

3 Continue to cut, lifting the fillet off the bones.

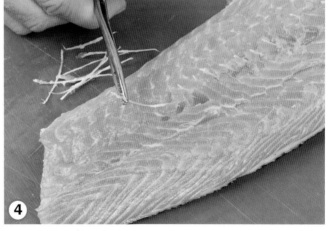

4 Place the fillet on the chopping board. Run your fingers along the flesh to locate any pin bones and remove them using tweezers.

Repeat the process on the other side of the fish.

Try this! Worksheet 28

Close your book and write down the five steps you should follow to fillet a flat fish.

Video presentation
Watch *Fillet a salmon* to see this in action.

Skinning

While skin is usually edible on fish, some dish requirements mean that it needs to be removed. This is quite difficult. When skinning, you must not damage the flesh of the fish, so specific knife techniques are needed.

Skinning usually occurs once the fillets of the fish have been removed. The exception is a whole flat fish. In this case the whole skin is removed by making an incision at the tail and then pulling the skin from the flesh to the head.

The equipment needed for skinning is:
○ a blue chopping board
○ a flexible filleting knife
○ salt or a clean cloth
○ a container for waste products
○ a tray to place the skinned fillets on.

Video presentation
Watch a skilled chef at work in *Skin a salmon fillet.*

How to skin a fillet

To provide grip when you grasp the tail end of the fillet either dip your fingers in some salt before you begin or use a cloth to hold the tail.

① Place the fillet on the chopping board. Cut into the end of the tail section until the knife is touching or lying on the skin at an angle of 45°.

② Take a firm hold of the tail skin and keep a firm grip on the knife. Use a sawing action, moving both the skin and knife at the same time. You will see the fillet come away from the skin and the angle of the knife will mean that no flesh will remain on the skin.

③ Trim any untidy pieces of fillet away to leave a neat, clean skinned fillet.

Fish stock or a court bouillon (see Chapter 11) is usually the appropriate liquor used to poach fish and this fish stock takes 30 minutes to prepare and cook.

When poaching fish or shellfish, bring the liquid to the boil and then simmer gently. The liquid may form part of a sauce to accompany the dish.

There are two types of poaching: deep poaching and shallow poaching.

Deep poaching is when a whole fish or cut is totally immersed in a special pan called a fish kettle (see Figure 9.9). The skin is left on to protect the flesh of the fish but it is removed later on. The liquid in which the fish or shellfish is poached is more acidic than when poaching in the conventional manner.

Shallow poaching is when the fish or cut is placed in a tray or pan. Liquid, either stock or milk, is added but does not cover the whole fish or cut. The liquid is brought to the boil the dish may be finished in the oven.

Before putting the dish in the oven, a cartouche (buttered piece of greaseproof paper) is placed over the fish to keep the steam in and to keep the fish moist during cooking.

Frying

Deep-frying

Fish or shellfish are usually coated in a batter (fish and chips) or breadcrumbs (scampi or goujons) before being deep-fried. These coatings provide a crisp texture to fish and shellfish and protect them from being damaged by the hot oil. Coatings include batters and breadcrumbs.

Batters consist of flour, eggs and baking powder or yeast mixed with water, milk or beer. The yeast or baking powder **aerates** the batter and makes it lighter.

Breadcrumbs – the fish is coated in flour and dipped in egg wash (beaten egg) before being passed through fresh breadcrumbs. The coating is sealed by the hot oil, keeping the fish or shellfish (scampi) moist. Breadcrumbs colour very quickly, so the temperature has to be checked carefully. Breadcrumbed fish can be deep-fried and then finished in the oven.

Video presentation

See how to poach salmon in court bouillion in *Poach a salmon fillet*.

Figure 9.8 A fish kettle is the perfect tool for deep poaching a whole fish

Chef's tip

Whole fish should be placed in cold court bouillon to cook. Fish cuts should be placed in hot court bouillon, as the heat seals the outer part of the cut, trapping the juices inside immediately.

Definition

Aerate: to introduce air into a mixture or liquid, making the texture lighter.

All fish can be deep-fried, as can many types of shellfish, e.g. cod, plaice, scampi (langoustines) and prawns (coated). Hot oil cooks the fish quickly. However, if the oil is too cool it will take longer to cook the fish and more fat will be absorbed. A thermostatically controlled deep fat fryer is required to deep-fry fish.

Deep-fried cod in batter

cod fillets	250g
seasoned flour	50g
vegetable/corn oil	to fill friture two-thirds
frying batter	75ml
salt and pepper	to taste
lemon wedges	2
parsley sprigs	
Cooking temperature	180°C
Serves	2

Method

1. Pass the fillets through the seasoned flour and shake off any excess.
2. Heat the oil.
3. Place the floured fillets in the frying batter. Allow a few seconds for any excess to run off and then place into hot oil.
4. Cook until golden brown in colour.
5. Drain off excess oil from the battered fillet, add salt and pepper to taste and serve with lemon wedges and a deep-fried parsley sprig.

Shallow-frying

Shallow-frying can make a fish or shellfish dish more appealing and also add colour to the product. Plaice coated in seasoned flour with the addition of a nut butter sauce (beurre noisette) is a traditional recipe for shallow-frying.

Fish and shellfish can be shallow-fried in pieces (medallions) as steaks, darnes, troncons, and even whole (trout). The length of cooking time will vary. A whole trout will take significantly longer to cook than monkfish medallions.

Some fish dishes require no coating on the fish. Shellfish such as prawns may be shallow-fried with just the addition of some chilli or garlic.

Video presentation

Watch *Deep fry goujons* to see a chef cook this dish and use a deep fat fryer safely.

Remember!

Safety when deep-frying is crucial as fat fires can cause major damage. Always have a fire blanket in the area in case of fire and never use a friture or industrial fat fryer if you have not been trained.

Chef's tip

When shallow-frying always lay the fillets in the pan presentation-side down first as the oil is cleaner and free of any impurities, apply colour, then turn over to avoid over-handling.

Fish such as sea bass should be placed skin-side down first and
cooked until crisp and golden.

To shallow-fry fish you will need:
○ a fish slice or palette knife and other utensils such as tongs to
  turn the fillets or shellfish
○ trays and wires to place the cooked fish or shellfish on.

Grilling

Overcooking fish or shellfish by grilling will make them dry. Your skill
and experience is required to identify when the fish is cooked. (Firm
flesh, correct core temperature, correct colour, crispy skin are all
signs.)

Cooking times will vary depending on the type and thickness of the
fish cut.

Grilled sea bass with capers

sea bass	4 fillets, each about 175g
salt and pepper	to taste
melted butter	25g
chopped parsley	15g
tiny capers	55g
shallot, finely chopped	1
garlic clove, sliced	1
grain mustard	2 teaspoons
lemon juice	¼ lemon
Cooking time	12–15 minutes
Serves	4

Method

1 Lightly oil a suitable tray for grilling.
2 Season the flesh side of the fish then lay the fillets skin-side
  up on the tray.
3 Brush the fish with melted butter.
4 Place the fish under a heated grill for about four minutes
  until just done (depending on the thickness of the fish flesh).
5 Place all the remaining ingredients into a pan and gently
  warm through.
6 Check the seasoning then pour the capers mixture over the
  cooked fillet and serve.

Most fish are suitable for grilling, as are crustaceans like prawns. Other shellfish like cockles, whelks and mussels are not usually grilled.

Some fish cuts that have been coated in breadcrumbs may also be grilled. Dip the fish in melted butter and breadcrumbs rather than flour, egg and breadcrumbs.

To grill whole fish and large fillets, score or make incisions on the skin side of the fish to enable the heat to penetrate the whole fish. Trout is a good example of a whole fish suitable for grilling.

Baking

Baking tends to dry out the fish, so various methods are used to keep the fish moist:

o Wrap the fish in foil.
o Place the fish or cut into a greaseproof bag (en papillote).
o Stuff the inside of the fish so moisture steams through the fish.
o Wrap pastry around the fish (en croute).
o Bake the fish in a sauce.
o Combine steam and dry heat in a combination oven.

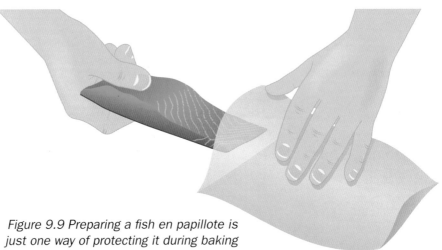

Figure 9.9 Preparing a fish en papillote is just one way of protecting it during baking

> **Remember!**
> When handling hot equipment:
> o wear protective clothing
> o have a dry oven cloth to hold hot equipment
> o have ready utensils such as tongs, palette knife or a slice to agitate and move the item.

> **Try this!**
> **As Asian foods are becoming more and more popular, try cooking fish with spices. Marinate some white cod fillets or other white fish with tandoori paste and natural yoghurt for 60 minutes and then bake in an oven. Served with rice and a salad it makes for a great alternative fish dish at a barbecue or a dinner.**

> **Remember!**
> Always use a dry cloth when handling trays from the oven to reduce the risk of burning yourself.

Serving

Fish and shellfish are high-risk foods. They must be cooked to a temperature of 63°C or above (except for oysters which are eaten raw).

Once cooked and held at service temperature of 63°C, fish will dry out quickly. Therefore it is important to cook and serve fish and shellfish as required or to order.

Garnishes for fish and shellfish are specific to the dish requirement. Garnishes are used to make the finished dish look more appealing. Accompaniments are other sauces or foods used to enhance the finished dish, or are simply good to eat with the cooked fish. Some traditional garnishes and accompaniments for fish and shellfish:

○ Tomato sauce (accompaniment)
○ Lemon slices or wedges (garnish)
○ Parsley chopped or deep-fried (garnish)
○ Tartare sauce (accompaniment)
○ Brown bread and butter (accompaniment)
○ Hollandaise sauce (accompaniment)
○ Beurre noisette (accompaniment).

Try this!   **Worksheet 29**

Using your book, the Internet and any other resources complete the crossword.

Test yourself!

1 Name three different types of shellfish.

2 What are the categories of fish?

3 What equipment is used to trim the fins of fish?

4 What equipment is required to fillet a round fish?

5 List three quality points to look out for when selecting fresh fish for preparation.

6 What equipment is used to poach a whole salmon?

7 What cooking methods are applicable to shellfish?

8 List some traditional accompaniments and garnishes for fish and shellfish.

9 What should you do if any problems occur while cooking fish or shellfish?

10 Game

This chapter covers the following NVQ units:

- Unit 2FP5 Prepare game for basic dishes
- Unit 2FC5 Cook and finish basic game dishes

Working through this chapter could also provide evidence for the following Key Skills:
C1.1, C2.2, N1.1, N1.2, WO2.1, WO2.2, PS2.1, PS2.2, PS2.3

In this chapter you will learn how to:

Check the game meets dish requirements	2FP5 and 2FC5
Combine game with other ingredients ready for cooking	2FP5 and 2FC5
Cook game	2FC5
Check flavour, colour and consistency and quantity of dishes	2FC5
Garnish and present the dish	2FC5
Make sure the dish is held at the correct temperature	2FC5
Store prepared game and cooked game not for immediate use	2FP5 and 2FC5

You will learn to cook basic game dishes, including:

- venison medallions with cherries
- rabbit fricassee.

Types of game

Game animals have been hunted to provide food for man as far back as history goes. Nowadays most of our meat comes from domesticated animals. Game animals are still hunted for sport, but usually only during the open hunting season (June–September for venison, August–December for grouse), although most game meats are now available all year round through specialist suppliers.

Problems can sometimes occur with freshness of game meat. If the carcass appears badly damaged it should be reported to your supervisor and replaced with a more suitable piece of meat.

Game is generally divided into two categories: furred and feathered.

Definition

Game: wild animals or birds which are hunted for food.

Furred game

Game animals with fur include:

Roebuck (small deer or fawn)

Wild boar

Rabbit

Hare

Healthy eating

Game meats are generally lower in calories and have less fat content than farmed meats (e.g. beef, lamb and pork). They are easily digested, as the meat fibres are short and fine. The meat is high in protein.

Figure 10.1 Game animals with fur

Venison

Meat from deer is called venison. There are four types of deer used for food in the UK – roe deer, fallow deer, red deer and sika deer.

Venison is one of the more common game meats. It is likely to come pre-prepared, jointed and packed. Specialist butchers may butcher cuts for you if requested.

Did you know?
The word 'venison' comes from the Latin term 'venationem' which means 'a hunt'.

Cuts and joints

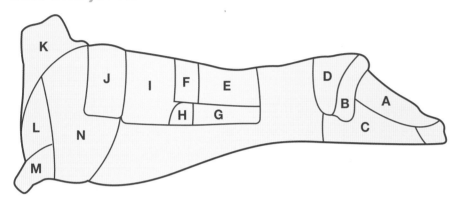

A Silverside		**H** Mignon	
B Rump		**I** Cutlets	
C Thick flank		**J** Chuck rib	
D Topside		**K** Neck	
E Loin		**L** Plate	
F Best end		**M** Shin	
G Fillet		**N** Shoulder	

Figure 10.2 The different cuts and joints you can get from deer

The table below identifies the cuts and joints from Figure 10.2 that you will use most often. It provides information on cooking methods (which are explained later).

Position	Cut	Gives	Cooking methods
A–D	Haunch	Joints (silverside, topside, thick flank, rump) Dice/mince Escalopes	Roasting, braising Stewing Frying, grilling
E, F	Saddle	Joint (best end of loin, loin) Chops Noisettes	Roasting Sautéing, grilling, braising Sautéing
E	Best end of loin (quarter)	Chops/cutlets	Frying, sautéing, braising
F, H	Fillet, mignon (from under the saddle)	Steaks/medallions	Sautéing, frying
M	Shin	Dice/mince	Stewing
K	Neck	Dice/mince Neck chops	Stewing Grilling, frying
N	Shoulder	Joints Dice/mince	Roasting Braising, stewing

Figure 10.3 Identifying and preparing the different cuts and joints of venison

How to portion a rabbit into 4 pieces

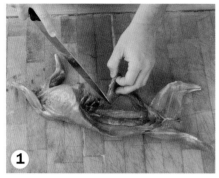

1

Using a chef's knife cut away the flap of flesh just below the rib cage.

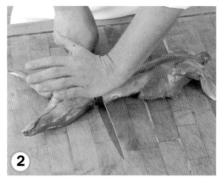

2

To remove the hind legs cut through the vertebrae just above where the hind legs join the backbone.

3

Cut through the rib cage and vertebrae just below the shoulder to remove the front legs.

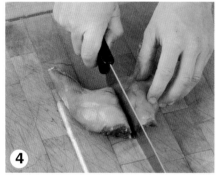

4

Position the knife between the hind legs.

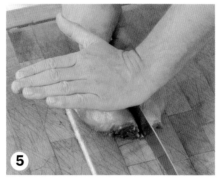

5

Split the backbone in two.

6

Position the knife between the front legs and split the neck and shoulders in two.

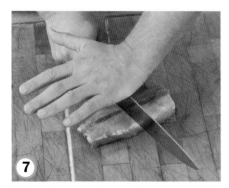

7

Take the saddle and reshape it by tucking the flaps underneath then cut it in half across the vertebrae.

8

The rabbit is now ready for the next process.

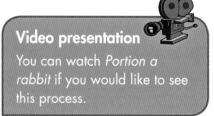

Video presentation

You can watch *Portion a rabbit* if you would like to see this process.

Feathered game

Game birds with feathers include:

Figure 10.11 Feathered game

Game birds

Game birds are very similar to domestic poultry. The styles of cooking are almost the same. The main difference is that the game bird can be hung, giving it a richer, stronger flavour.

Quality points for game birds

Consider the following points when checking the quality of game birds:
○ It should have a firm breast cage with a flexible breast bone.
○ There should be no tears in the skin.
○ The meat should have no patches of blue, which show bruising.

Some game birds are hunted for sport. This means some birds may have small holes in the skin. There may also be shot from the shotgun cartridge in the meat. This must be removed carefully before cooking. Use a small pair of tweezers or a small sharp pointed knife for this task.

Figure 10.12 You should always check for shot when preparing a game bird

248

Preparation

Hanging

Prior to plucking, the meat needs to hang to allow it to mature. Feathered game hang from their beaks or necks with feathers still on. Pheasant, grouse and quail should be hung for 3–4 days.

Plucking

All birds must be **plucked** in preparation for cooking. This can either be done by hand or by machine.

When plucking by hand, the bird is held tightly and the feathers are pulled away from the skin until none are left.

There are two machine methods: dry and wet.

The wet machine holds and dips the bird into hot water (50°C) for two to three minutes only. If you leave it any longer the skin begins to cook. The bird is then put onto the machine which has a series of rubber fingers on a barrel. The barrel spins and the fingers move over the bird to remove the feathers.

> **Definition**
> **Pluck**: to remove the feathers from a game bird, either by hand or by machine.

> **Did you know?**
> Pigeon can be cooked straight after skinning or plucking and cleaning. Hanging is not required.

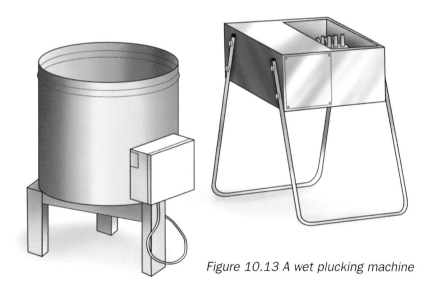

Figure 10.13 A wet plucking machine

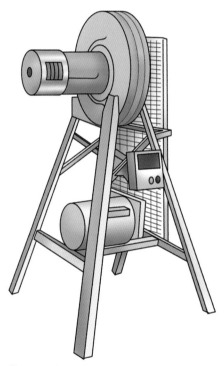

Figure 10.14 A dry plucking machine

The dry machine is made of a cylinder with a set of gripping blades that rotate at high speed. The bird's skin is held close to the spinning blades, which grip the feathers and pull them off into a bucket. This machine can pluck a pheasant in around 60 seconds and a large chicken in about 3 minutes.

Figure 10.15 A plucked partridge

Trussing

Most game birds can be bought whole, **dressed**, **trussed** and ready to use.

Smaller birds (e.g. quail or snipe) are served whole, one bird per portion. The cavities must be washed out before preparation.

A trussed game bird sits better on the roasting tray and is easier to baste and turn in the oven. You must remove the trussing twine before service.

Dressing

If you are dressing the birds yourself, you must ensure that the cavities have been cleaned thoroughly to remove any blood or tissue. All **innards** must be removed by hand carefully by placing your forefinger, index finger and thumb into the cavity and pulling out the innards.

You must clean the cavity under cold running water, until the water runs clear with no innards or blood deposits remaining. Do not use hot water!

The flavour can be improved by marinating the bird. This is often done before stewing or braising the meat. You can stuff the cavities and breasts with a variety of fillings and forcemeat stuffings.

Stuffed game bird breast is often sautéed and served over a bed of vegetables, usually two whole breasts to a portion as the breasts are small.

The methods of cutting, portioning and slicing game birds are the same as for farmed poultry (see Chapter 8).

> **Definition**
>
> **Dressed**: birds that have been cleaned, plucked and trussed.
> **Innards**: the internal organs of a bird.
> **Truss**: to thread one or two pieces of string or twine through the body of a game bird or poultry using a trussing needle, then tying them. This holds the legs and wings in place during cooking or following stuffing.

Figure 10.16 Grouse

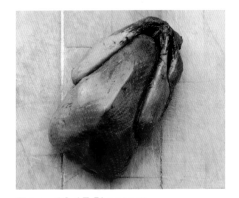

Figure 10.17 Pheasant

> **Video presentation**
>
> Watch the techniques used in *Prepare a whole chicken for roasting* and apply them to game birds.

11

Stocks, soups and sauces

This chapter covers the following NVQ units:

- Unit 2FPC1 Prepare, cook and finish basic hot sauces
- Unit 2FPC2 Prepare, cook and finish basic soups
- Unit 2FPC3 Make basic stock

Working through this chapter could also provide evidence for the following Key Skills:
C1.1, C2.2, N1.1, N1.2, WO2.1, WO2.2, PS2.1, PS2.2, PS2.3

In this chapter you will learn how to:

List different types of stock, soups and hot sauces	2NFPC3, 2NFPC2 and 2NFPC1
Identify the ingredients and quantities required in the preparation and cooking of different stocks, soups and hot sauces	2NFPC3, 2NFPC2 and 2NFPC1
List the tools and equipment required in the preparation, cooking, finishing and service of stocks, soups and hot sauces	2NFPC3, 2NFPC2 and 2NFPC1
Explain the methods of preparation and cooking of stocks, soups and hot sauces	2NFPC3, 2NFPC2 and 2NFPC1
List quality points to look for in the finished stocks, soups or sauces	2NFPC3, 2NFPC2 and 2NFPC1
Indicate the temperature for the cooking, holding, service and storage of stocks, soups and sauces	2NFPC3, 2NFPC2 and 2NFPC1

You will learn to cook basic stocks, soups and hot sauces, including:

- white beef stock
- white fish stock
- clear soup (consommé)
- purée of lentil soup
- cream of cauliflower soup
- béchamel sauce
- velouté sauce
- tomato sauce.

Basic stocks

A stock is a broth that is used as a braising liquid, a sauce base or as liquid for soup. A good stock should have a delicate flavour and a high proportion of natural gelatine. A gelatinous stock gives richness and body to a preparation without masking the flavours of the basic ingredients.

Stock is made by slowly simmering bones and/or vegetables with **aromatic** herbs in a juice, e.g. water or wine. During cooking the flavours of the meat, vegetables and herbs are released into the liquid. After cooking, the solid ingredients and any grease are removed and the liquid is strained until it is clear.

> **Definition**
> **Aromatic**: having a pleasant smell. Aromatic ingredients such as leaves, flowers, seeds, fruits, stems and roots are used essentially for their fragrance to enhance flavour of stocks.

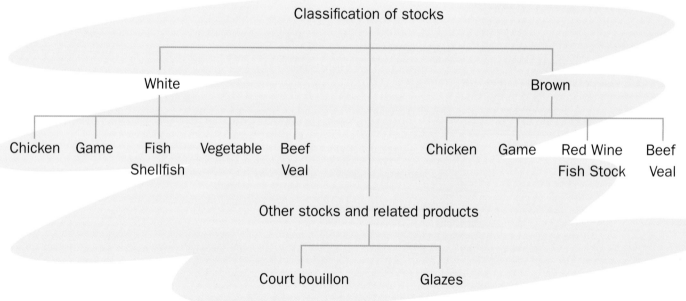

Figure 11.1 Classification of stocks

Types of stock

Stocks can be made from many different ingredients. The stocks covered in the NVQ Level 2 are: vegetable, chicken, fish, game and beef.

Stocks can be either white or brown. For a white stock, the ingredients are simply added to the stock pot. White stock is used as a liquid to make soups, white stews and **velouté** sauce for poached poultry and fish dishes. For a brown stock, any bones are roasted and the vegetables are sautéed before being added to the stock pot. Brown stock is used as a liquid in soups, brown sauces, brown stews and for braising large cuts of meat.

> **Definition**
> **Velouté**: a stock-based white sauce that is thickened with a white roux.

Vegetable stock or nage

This is a light neutral base, which can be used in many soups and sauces. It can be used with other stocks and is suitable for use in vegetarian cookery. For maximum flavour do not strain the vegetables out immediately after cooking, but allow them to steep in the stock for up to 24 hours. Vegetable stock is used as a liquid for soups, sauces and for all preparations in vegetable cooking such as braised rice.

Chicken stock

This is a very versatile stock. It should have a good amber colour, without being too strong in taste. If a stronger-tasting stock is required, boil the stock until the quantity of stock is reduced to half to produce double chicken stock. Use fresh carcasses and winglets and if possible add boiling fowl, which may be removed later. Some recipes may need a darker or brown chicken stock. To make this, roast chicken carcasses in a hot oven for 15–20 minutes until golden brown (remembering to turn them frequently) and drain off the fat before using. Sauté any vegetables used to a golden brown and drain this also before using.

Fish stock

The best bones to use for fish stock are turbot and sole. Other fish bones can be oily, strong and even taste of ammonia, although hake, haddock and cod can be used. Always remove the eyes and gills, as these can have an effect on the flavour and colour of your stock. Also remember to rinse the fish bones and trimmings under cold water to remove traces of blood. Fish stock is used in the preparation of soups, fish sauces, velouté or white wine sauce. Fish stock is also used for shallow poaching and braising fish.

Fish stock can also be prepared with red wine for poached fish dishes.

Veal stock

This forms the base of many sauces. It is possibly the king of stocks, offering excellent body, richness and colour with a subtle flavour. As the bones are large they should be chopped smaller to enable them to release their flavour. It is possible to produce a white or a brown stock from these bones, but careful roasting of the bones will give a stock greater colour and flavour.

Did you know?

The ideal temperature for the following is:

cooking of stock (except fish stock)	100°C
fish stock	98°C
holding of stock	75°C
storage of stock	4°C.

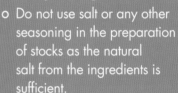

Healthy eating

o Do not use salt or any other seasoning in the preparation of stocks as the natural salt from the ingredients is sufficient.

o Make sure that all fat is removed from the meat and poultry bones before preparing stock.

o Always blanch the bones and refresh them in cold water to remove any excess fat (except fish bones).

Game stock

A rich brown game stock can be produced from any furred or feathered game. Chop the bones into smaller pieces so that they can release more of their flavour. Roast the bones in a hot oven or sauté them until golden brown. Sauté the vegetables and drain them before use. Game stock is used to produce sauces to accompany a game dish.

Beef stock

Beef stock can be produced in the same way as veal stock. Beef stock is not very versatile and is best suited for use in beef dishes.

Other stocks and related products

Court bouillon

This is a light aromatic stock of vegetables, herbs, spices and white wine vinegar. It is used for poaching fish, crabs and other shellfish. This stock can be used two or three times before being discarded. Like other stocks it may be cooled and frozen for use at a later date.

Glazes

A glaze ('glace' in French) is a concentrated stock which is made through a process of reduction. It is used to enrich the flavour of sauces and dishes such as Parisienne potatoes. Before the stock is reduced, it should be passed through a very fine sieve or better still a piece of wet muslin cloth. Care should be taken through the reduction period to remove any scum that rises to the surface. This will help the glaze achieve its characteristic shine. The consistency of the glaze should be just flowing when warm and solid when refrigerated.

Healthy eating

o Avoid rapid boiling of stocks as fats are emulsified and dissolved in the liquid making it milky and unhealthy.
o Avoid adding butter or oil while frying vegetables and bones for brown stocks. Always use the natural fat on the bones to give colour by roasting them in the oven.

Try this!   Worksheet 32

Close your book. List as many types of stock as you can remember.

Ingredients and equipment

White stock

White stock is a broth which has no colour. It has white meat bones and aromatic vegetables as a basis. The ingredients used are:

○ chicken, beef, veal or game
○ carrots, onions, leeks or celery
○ thyme, bay leaf or parsley stalks
○ liquid: water or white wine.

Remember!

If a small quantity of stock is required from a large pot in the refrigerator, never dip a utensil into it that is warmer than the stock itself.

Brown stock

This is a broth which has a light brown colour. The other term used to describe this stock is 'estouffade', which is a reduced brown stock. It has browned meat bones and sautéed aromatic vegetables as a basis. The ingredients used are:

○ chicken, beef, veal or game
○ carrots, onions, leeks, celery or garlic
○ thyme, bayleaf or parsley stalks
○ liquid: water.

Equipment

The equipment needed to make a stock:

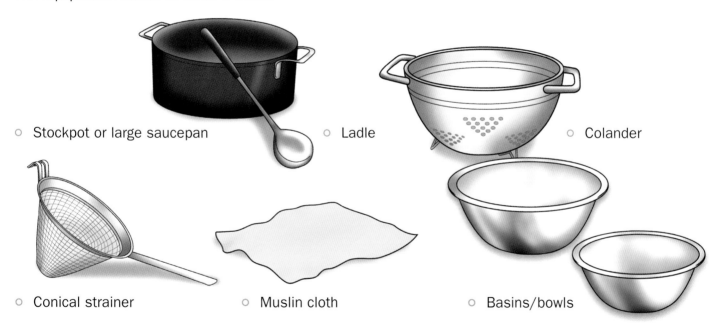

○ Stockpot or large saucepan   ○ Ladle   ○ Colander

○ Conical strainer   ○ Muslin cloth   ○ Basins/bowls

In addition, for a brown stock, a roasting tray or frying pan is needed.

Recipes for basic stocks

The minimum cooking times for different types of stock are:

- Vegetable stock – 30 minutes.
- Chicken stock – 2 hours.
- Fish stock – 20 minutes.
- Game stock – 2 hours.
- Beef stock – 4 hours.

Definition

Skim: to remove impurities from the surface of a simmering liquid with a ladle.

White beef stock

For the stock:		For the bouquet garni:	
beef shin bones	2kg	leeks	120g
water, cold	6 litres	celery	120g
carrots	240g	parsley stalk and root	30g
onions, stuck with two cloves	120g	bay leaf	1
		sprig of thyme	1
Cooking time	4 hours		
Makes	5 litres		

Method

1. Cut or break the bones into 10cm pieces. Remove any marrow.
2. Wash and place into stock pot and add 6 litres of cold water. Bring to the boil and **skim** off the scum.
3. Add 100ml of cold water and wipe the sides of the stock pot clean with a damp cloth.
4. Add the vegetables whole, and the bouquet garni.
5. Allow the stock to simmer gently for six hours, during which time the fat which rises to the surface must be constantly skimmed off. The vegetables should be removed from stock after three hours.
6. Pass the stock through a muslin.
7. Reboil and place aside to cool.

Points to consider when making white beef stock

All fat should be removed from the bones at the outset. The marrow should be put aside for use as a separate dish or as garnish. Stock should only simmer; if it is allowed to boil, it will become milky or cloudy.

Chef's tip

Six to eight hours is the maximum time required to extract the full flavour – if cooked too long the flavour will suffer. Bones from which the flavour has been extracted may be re-boiled for a further six hours to produce jelly.

The vegetables and bouquet garni should be easily accessible – tie bouquet garni to the handle of the pot with a long string and if there is a large quantity of stock, tie vegetables in a muslin or net. If allowed to remain in the pot too long the vegetables will begin to disintegrate and/or lose their colour into the liquid, causing the stock to discolour. Discard scum. Save the fat which can be later clarified and used as dripping, for braising.

Do not allow any fat to remain on the surface as this will stop the heat escaping and may cause the stock to 'turn', that is, become sour.

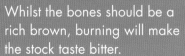

Chef's tip

Whilst the bones should be a rich brown, burning will make the stock taste bitter.

Brown beef stock

good meaty bones, beef or veal, and trimmings of meat	2kg
beef fat	60g
carrots, diced (mirepoix) and fried	240g
onions, diced (mirepoix) and fried	240g
bouquet garni	1
ham bone	240g
water	6 litres
Oven temperature	250°C
Cooking time	6–8 hours
Makes	5 litres

Method

1 Cut or break the bones into 10cm pieces and place in a roasting tray. Add the trimmings and fat.
2 Roast the bones and trimmings in a hot oven until a rich brown colour.
3 Remove bones from fat and place in a stockpot. Cover with 6 litres of water, bring to the boil and skim.
4 Add the fried carrot and onion, the bouquet garni and the ham bone.
5 Allow the stock to simmer for six hours, skimming from time to time to remove the fat.
6 Strain through a muslin, reboil and use as required.

Brown game stock

neck and breast of venison	2kg
trimmings of hare	1kg
old pheasant or partridge	1kg
carrots	180g
onions	180g
white beef stock or water	6 litres
dry white wine	0.5 litre
mushroom trimmings	120g
For the bouquet garni:	
leeks	120g
celery	120g
parsley stalk and root	30g
bay leaf	1
sprig of thyme	1
Oven temperature	250°C or 425°F
Cooking time	2–3 hours
Makes	5 litres

Method

1 Tie the meat and truss the game birds.
2 Make a **bed of roots** with the carrot and onion in the bottom of the roasting tray.
3 Place the meat and game on top of the vegetables in the roasting tray with a little **dégraisse** and brown quickly in the oven.
4 Transfer meat and game to a stockpot.
5 Pour off the fat from the roasting tray and deglaze the tray by pouring on the wine and a little stock and allowing it to simmer until all sediment has been dissolved.
6 Add the deglaze to the stockpot, together with the rest of the stock or water.
7 Bring to the boil, skim and add the remainder of the ingredients.
8 Simmer for three hours, skimming from time to time, strain, reboil and use as required.

Definitions

Dégraisse: the liquid fat which is removed from the surface of simmering stock using a ladle by the process of skimming.
Bed of root: chopped root vegetables which act as a base to put the bird on to prevent it sticking and burning on the tray.

Video presentation

Prepare a whole chicken for roasting will show you how to truss a bird.

Try this!

Worksheet 35

Close your book and list as many types of white and brown stock as you can.

5 Cook until all the ingredients are tender. Add tomato purée. Mix in well, remove the bouquet garni.

6 Add the cooked haricot beans; and the add tomates concassées. Reboil, taste for seasoning. Rectify the thickness. The consistency of this soup should be fairly thick.

7 Crush the skinned garlic with finely chopped pork fat, adding chopped parsley and fines herbes. Toss in little hot butter then added to the soup, mixing in well with a ladle.

9 Serve with toasted shredded bread or rolls, or toasted sliced flûte bread and grated parmesan cheese as an accompaniment.

Clear soup

Clear soup (*Consommé*)

minced shin of beef	1kg
egg white	1
mirepoix of onions	125g
mirepoix of carrots	125g
mirepoix of celery	125g
mirepoix of leeks	125g
cold, white beef stock	5 litres
bouquet garni	1
peppercorns	15–18
salt	to season
Cooking time	3 to 4 hours
Serves	6–8

Method

1 Soak the minced shin of beef in cold water for about 20–30 minutes, adding salt to withdraw blood. Add egg white and mix well.

2 Prepare the mirepoix of onions, carrots, celery and leeks. Add these vegetables to the beef and cover with good beef stock.

3 Add bouquet garni and peppercorns.

4 Bring it just to the boil slowly over a gentle heat, stirring occasionally.

5 Give a last stir and let the consommé simmer gently over a low heat. Cook it for approximately two hours without stirring.

6 Strain the consommé through a muslin cloth.

7 Use kitchen paper squares to remove all fat from the top.

8 Check the seasoning and colour, which should be a delicate amber.

9 Bring the consommé just to the boil again and serve in a warm soup tureen.

Chef's tip

Consommé can be prepared by using a variety of stocks such as chicken, game and veal. There are numerous classic garnishes which can be added to finish the soup.

Did you know?

Clear soup should never be boiled as this makes it cloudy. If it gets cloudy, the process of clarification must be repeated.

Healthy eating

Make sure clear soups are free from traces of fat.

Purée soup

Purée of lentil soup

lentils, red	250g
butter for vegetables	40g
pork or bacon rind	30–40g
onion, diced	30–40g
carrot, diced	30–40g
water	1.25 litres
bouquet garni	1
salt	to season
butter, clarified	40g
milk, boiling	150–200ml
bread for croûtons	100g
Cooking time	1 hour
Serves	6

Method

1 Wash the lentils well and soak for half an hour.
2 Lightly sauté the diced bacon or pork rind in 25g butter, using a thick-bottomed pan.
3 Add the diced carrot and onion, lightly colour.
4 Add the strained lentils and stir. Cook gently for 10–15 minutes.
5 Add water and bouquet garni. Cover with a lid, simmer until the lentils are tender and fully cooked, add salt in the last ten minutes.
6 Remove bouquet garni. Pass the soup through a sieve.
7 Reboil, pass through a fine chinois.
8 Reboil, taste for seasoning. Check the thickness, adding a little boiling milk if necessary. The consistency of the soup should be like thick double cream.
9 Add the clarified butter (15g) to complete the soup. Check the seasoning and add salt, if necessary.
10 Serve croûtons separately.

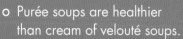

Healthy eating

o Purée soups are healthier than cream of velouté soups.
o Avoid the use of fresh cream, butter or cream and egg yolk liaison to finish the soups.
o Avoid over-seasoning the soups.
o Serve toasted croûtons instead of croûtons shallow-fried in butter.

Chef's tip

Omit the pork or bacon rind for a vegetarian option.

Cream soup

Cream of cauliflower soup

white of leek	500g
butter	300g
cauliflower, without leaves	2kg
water or cauliflower stock or white stock	2 litres
bouquet garni	1
béchamel, boiling	3 litres
cream, boiling	600ml
salt and pepper	to season
sprigs or leaves of chervil	
Cooking time	1 hour
Serves	6–8 portions

Method

1 Wash and shred the white of leek. Cook in half the butter without colouring.
2 Wash the cauliflower. Reserve 300g of cauliflower in small florets to be boiled and used for garnish.
3 Shred the bulk of cauliflower. Add to the leeks, mix well and season. Cover and continue to cook without colouring, until tender.
4 Add the liquid and the bouquet garni. Simmer for 15–20 minutes.
5 Remove the bouquet garni. Pass the soup through a sieve. Reboil and add boiling béchamel. Mix well, taste for seasoning. Pass through a fine chinois. Reboil then add the boiling cream and work in the rest of the butter.
6 Finally, add small cooked florets of cauliflower. The vegetable stock can be used to adjust the consistency of the soup. Taste again for seasoning. Cover and keep hot in a bain-marie.
7 Add the chervil on serving.

Chef's tip

Cooked leftover plain boiled cauliflower may be used for economy.
Blanched shredded onions can be used instead of leeks.

Cream of tomato soup

bacon trimmings	50g
onions, mirepoix	50g
carrots, mirepoix	50g
margarine	100g
flour	125g
tomato purée	220g
white stock	2 litres
bouquet garni	1
salt	to taste
pepper	to taste
double cream	100ml
For the gastric:	
vinegar	30ml
sugar	20g
Serves	10
Cooking time approx.	1 hour

Method

1 Cut bacon trimmings into 5mm dice.
2 Put margarine, bacon trimmings and mirepoix of onions and carrots in a pan. Sweat the meat and vegetables.
3 Add the flour. Make a blonde roux.
4 Remove the pan from the heat and add the tomato purée.
5 Place the pan back onto the heat and slowly add the hot stock.
6 Mix well in between each addition of stock to prevent the soup going lumpy.
7 When all the stock has been added and mixed in, add the bouquet garni. Season.
8 Bring to the boil and simmer for 1 hour.
9 Strain through a conical strainer.
10 Boil again and skim. Correct the consistency. Adjust the seasoning to taste.
11 For the gastric place the sugar and vinegar in a clean pan. Bring to the boil and reduce slightly. Add small amounts to the soup.
12 Add double cream just before service. Do not re-boil or the cream will curdle.
13 Serve with sippets.

Definition

Gastric: a reduction of vinegar and sugar which brings out the flavour of the tomatoes.
Sippets: 5mm cubes of bread, baked or fried to a golden brown colour.

Velouté soup

Velouté of asparagus

white of leek	500g
celery	50g
butter	100g
salt and pepper	to season
asparagus stock	2.5–3 litres
asparagus stalks (optional)	
bouquet garni	1
velouté chicken	3 litres
lemon juice and cayenne	to flavour
For liaison:	
yolks of eggs	4
cream	400ml
butter	100g
For garnish:	
green asparagus tips	250–300g
sprig of chervil	
Cooking time	1 hour
Serves	6–8 portions

Method

1 Wash and shred the leeks and celery; if they are old, blanch them. Cook slowly in 100g of butter, no colour, for 15–20 minutes. Season and stir occasionally.

2 Add asparagus stock and any available cooked asparagus stalks, both reserved from the cooking of same. Add bouquet garni and velouté. Simmer for 20–30 minutes covered.

3 Put the egg yolks, cream and butter in a china or plastic bowl. Prepare a liason.

4 Pass soup through a sieve, reboil. Taste for seasoning, then gradually pour onto prepared liaison. Mix thoroughly.

5 Reheat to thicken, without boiling. Add lemon juice and cayenne.

6 Pass through a fine chinois or tammy cloth with pressure, reserve in a soup bain-marie, covered; do not allow to boil.

7 Garnish with cooked green tips of asparagus, carefully mixed into the soup. Add sprigs of chervil at the moment of service.

Quality points to look for in finished soups

1 The colour and appearance is correct for the type of soup.
2 Correct consistency, in other words a proportionate amount of liquid added to the main ingredient.
3 Garnishes and accompaniments are consistent size and shape and are cooked correctly.
4 Well seasoned and appropriately finished.
5 Served at the correct temperature, hot or cold, depending on the type of soup.

Did you know?
The ideal temperature for the following is:
cooking of soup	100°C
holding of soup	75°C
service of soup	65°C
storage of soup	4°C.

Test yourself!

1 Name four different types of soup as they will appear on the menu.

2 Identify the main differences between the following:
  a Purée and cream soups
  b Broth and consommé
  c Velouté and cream soups.

3 Indicate the correct temperatures for the following:
  a Cooking of soup
  b Holding of soup
  c Service of soup
  d Storage of soup.

4 State four quality points to look for in the finished soup.

5 Suggest four ways of preparing, cooking and finishing basic soups to make them healthier.

6 Indicate the main difference between a garnish and an accompaniment. Give an example of each.

7 Indicate the finishing of the following soups:
  a Cream
  b Purée
  c Velouté.

8 Name four different thickening agents used in the preparation of basic soups.

Basic sauces

Types of sauces

Marinades were originally used to preserve and tenderise meat. Later they were also used to improve the flavour of dishes. Creative chefs transformed these marinades into sauces, to moisten a stew or accompany roast meats. Some sauces were originally devised to disguise the strong flavours of meat and game. Others, for example a creamy purée of beans or peas, helped to balance the saltiness of preserved meats.

The seventeenth-century in France was the 'golden age' of sauce creation. During that period famous chefs developed a small group of basic sauces, also known as 'mother sauces', from which hundreds of variations came. The original mother sauces were stock-based brown sauce, velouté, milk-based béchamel and hollandaise made from egg yolks. Another basic sauce was added a century later when tomatoes arrived from the New World. At first chefs believed that the scarlet flesh of the tomato was deadly poison. Soon they realised that the flesh can easily be broken down and made into a **piquant** purée sauce.

Did you know?
The word 'sauce' comes from the Latin 'salsus', meaning 'flavoured with salt'.

Definition
Piquant: a pleasant, sharp taste.

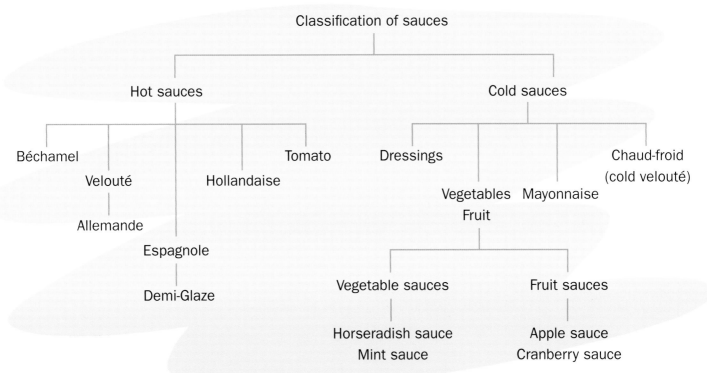

Figure 11.19 Classification of sauces

Thickening sauces
Thickening agents

Thickening agents used in the preparation of sauces include the following types:

1 **Roux**. This is an equal mixture of fat and flour, cooked slowly to break down the starch cells in the flour and allow thickening to take place. There are three types of roux:
   ○ white (used for e.g. Béchamel sauce).
   ○ blond (used for e.g. Velouté sauce).
   ○ brown (used for e.g. Espagnole sauce).
2 **Egg yolks**. These are used for hot and cold sauces, e.g. hollandaise sauce (hot), mayonnaise sauce (cold).
3 **Beurre manie**. This is a mixture of butter and flour kneaded together to form a paste. Small pieces of this mixture are dropped in boiling liquid and whisked together to form a sauce.
4 **Bread**, e.g. bread sauce.
5 **Vegetables and potatoes**.
6 **Fresh fruit**, e.g. apple sauce, cranberry sauce.
7 **Cornflour and fécule** (starch from potatoes). These are used to thicken roast gravy (jus-lié).
8 **Butter**. This is used in an emulsified form, e.g. butter sauce, white wine sauce for fish.
9 **Sugar**, e.g. caramel sauce.
10 **Various nuts**, including peanuts, cashew nuts, pistachio nuts, e.g. Satay sauce.

Vegetable-thickened sauces and coulis

Some sauces are produced without a thickening agent. Instead they are thickened by using the title ingredient which is puréed into the sauce, as in the case of vegetable-thickened sauces and coulis.

Type of sauce	Description
Carrot sauce	Carrots cooked in stock with thyme and garlic, sauternes and cream; liquidised and passed; finished with brunoise of blanched carrot.
Celery sauce	Celery cooked in bouillon, puréed in, mixed with cream sauce.

Tomato

Tomato sauce

diced bacon trimmings, blanched	80g
butter	125g
diced carrots for mirepoix	80g
diced onions for mirepoix	80g
plain flour	125g
tomato purée	300g
garlic, crushed cloves	2
white stock	3 litres
bouquet garni	1
salt	to season
pepper	to season
sugar	15g
Cooking time	2 hours
Makes	2 litres

Method

1. Place the butter and bacon into a thick-bottomed straight-sided pan. Allow to colour slightly.
2. Add the diced onion and carrot. Cook gently and lightly colour.
3. Add the flour and mix well.
4. Cook to a blond roux, then cool a little.
5. Add tomato purée and garlic.
6. Gradually add the boiling stock, mixing well.
7. Add the bouquet garni and salt.
8. When boiling remove the spoon, clean inside the saucepan with a palette knife.
9. Cover with a lid. Simmer for one hour.
10. Pass sauce through a sieve with pressure. Reboil, check the thickness and seasoning.
11. Add sugar to counteract the acidity of the tomato purée.
12. Pass the sauce through a fine chinois into a sauce bain-marie.
13. Butter the surface, cover with a lid, keep hot in the bain-marie.

Chef's tip

For large amounts this sauce can be cooked in a moderately hot oven.

Find out!   **Worksheet 34**

Find as many derivative sauces as you can for each of the following basic sauces: béchamel, velouté, espagnole, hollandaise and tomato.

Gravy

This is made from the meat juices after roasting, e.g. chicken, beef, lamb or pork. Gravy should not really be thickened. A good-quality gravy should be free from fat and have a strong meaty taste.

The flavour of gravy can be improved by the addition of alcohol such as white wine or red wine. It is normally served as an accompaniment with roast meat and poultry and the dish is described as 'au jus'.

Jus-lié

This is a rich, smooth and lightly thickened sauce made from meat juices. The thickening agent used in the preparation of Jus-lié is cornflour or arrowroot.

1 Mix the cornflour or arrowroot with a little cold water and then add slowly to the rich brown stock or reduced meat juices from the pot-roasting tray.
2 Bring to the boil and simmer for 20–25 minutes.
3 Strain through a conical strainer and use.

Temperatures for the cooking, holding and serving of sauces are:
○ Cooking of sauces   100°C
○ Holding of sauces   75°C
○ Service of sauces   65°C
○ Storage of sauces   4°C.

Finishing sauces

Methods of finishing sauces include:
○ Monter: this method involves finishing the sauce with a few pieces of butter at the last minute prior to serving, e.g. white wine sauce for fish dishes or Madeira sauce for tournedos.
○ Adding whipped double cream: this is folded into warm sauce as a glazing for a fish dish.
○ Adding fresh cream and egg yolk liaison: to finish sauces for dishes such as Chicken fricassee.
○ Adjusting consistency: e.g. adding potato flour diluted in cold water to meat juices from the roasting tray, e.g. Jus-lié.
○ Garnishing: e.g. adding short julienne of gherkins to Sauce charcutière.
○ Seasoning: e.g. adding mustard to Mustard sauce.

Definition

Jus: juice.

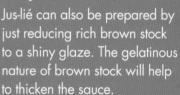

Did you know?

Jus-lié can also be prepared by just reducing rich brown stock to a shiny glaze. The gelatinous nature of brown stock will help to thicken the sauce.

Try this!   **Worksheet 35**
How many of the words can you find in the wordsearch?

○ It has been stored in a cool well-ventilated store free from damp.

○ It does not have any other physical contaminants, e.g. stones or anything that may have fallen into the storage container.

○ If it is still in the original packaging, that it is free from tears, rips or general damage.

Preparation methods

It is important to check the dish requirements before you begin preparing your dish. You should check what type of rice you need (long, short, round, brown) and the quantity you require, as this reduces unnecessary wastage.

Before cooking rice, wash it under cold running water to remove unwanted starch left over from milling and packaging. Also, as rice is tightly packed the grains rub against each other and leave a fine floury substance in the packet which needs to be removed. Washing the rice before cooking means it is less likely to stick.

It is important to weigh rice carefully to reduce wastage as rice gets larger and fluffs up as it cooks.

Cooking methods

Boiling

Boiling is the easiest and most usual way to cook rice. It is an ideal way to cook rice for serving with curries or meat dishes.

The rice (usually long grain) is plunged into boiling salted water for 15–20 minutes. When the rice is light and fluffy, but still with a little bite, it is cooked. Drain the rice in a colander and wash it off well to remove starch before service.

To safely store boiled rice for use in cold dishes, e.g. salads, drain the boiled rice under cold running water in a colander until cooled, allow to drain then put it in a covered container and refrigerate until required.

Steaming

Steamed rice is popular in Chinese-style cookery. It is simple and quick, and most types of rice can be steamed. Steamed rice is eaten plain or used as a garnish for meats and fish.

Did you know?
For a main dish the ideal portion of uncooked rice is 65g (2½ ounces) per person.

There are two ways to steam rice. The first way is to put washed rice over boiling water in a steamer; this takes 20–40 minutes.

The second, and more common, way is to combine boiling and steaming. Put the rice into a pan and cover it with 1½ times as much water. Cover with a tight-fitting lid, bring to the boil, then turn down the heat and cook until all the water has been absorbed by the rice or evaporated.

Stewing

Rice can be stewed in stock, water or milk. Set up as for boiling but keep the rice on the heat until most of the liquid has gone. It is important to keep stirring to prevent the rice sticking to the side or bottom of the pan.

Frying

Countries like China, Nepal and India use fried rice as part of many of their dishes. After you have boiled rice you can fry it, which is a good way to give the rice flavour. You can add other ingredients, e.g. vegetables or meat.

Find out! **Worksheet 36**

Visit the website for 'The Cook's Thesaurus' and go to the rice section. A link has been made available at www. heinemann.co.uk/ hotlinks. Just follow the links and enter the express code 9257P. Choose ten types of rice and find out:
o country of origin
o uses
o cooking method and time
o a recipe for each.

Fried rice

rice	5kg
oil	1 tsp
Cooking time	25 minutes
serves	40

Method

1 Boil and cool the rice.
2 Put the cooked rice in a deep frying pan with some oil or butter or margarine.
3 Heat it over a low heat and stir often to stop it sticking.

Egg fried rice

rice	5kg
eggs	25
Cooking time	25 minutes
Serves	40

Method

1 Boil and cool the rice.
2 Lightly scramble the eggs in a frying pan.
3 Add the cooked rice, season and mix with the egg.

Baking

This method is best suited to puddings. The best rice to use is round or short grain.

Milk is the most common liquid used with baked rice and forms the basis of rice pudding. Put the rice into the boiling liquid. Other ingredients may be added to help flavour the rice. Put this mixture into an oven and bake until the liquid has been soaked up by the rice.

Baked rice pudding

milk	500ml
round grain or pearl rice	160g
sugar	120g
nutmeg, grated	pinch
Oven temperature	190°C
Cooking time	30–35 minutes
Serves	4

Method

1 Put the milk into a medium-sized milk pan. Bring the milk to the boil and slowly add the rice. Remember to stir while you add the rice. Allow to boil for one minute.
2 Take off the boil. Slowly add the sugar and nutmeg.
3 Pour the mixture into an ovenproof baking dish, then put the dish into a medium/deep baking pan.
4 Pour boiling water into the baking pan so that it comes 1cm up the side of the baking dish, creating a bain-marie.
5 Cook in a preheated oven.
6 Remove the pudding from the oven, allow it to cool slightly.
7 Clean the outside of the dish and serve.

Braising

The common term for this method of preparing rice is pilaf or pilau. Long grain rice is the best type to use.

To prepare dishes such as pilaf, paella or risotto, sweat the rice in butter or oil to begin the cooking process. This coats the rice in fat. Add liquid, e.g. water or stock, and braise in an oven or over heat.

Pilaf or pilau of rice

onions, finely chopped	80g
butter	40g
white long grain rice, washed	260g
stock or water	750ml
Oven temperature	200°C
Cooking time	16–18 minutes
Serves	4

Method

1 Using a deep frying pan, sweat the onions in half the butter, being careful not to brown them.
2 Add the washed rice and stir until it becomes almost transparent.
3 Add the boiling stock or water and season.
4 Place a cartouche (buttered greaseproof paper) on to the liquid and rice, cover with a lid and put the pan into a preheated oven. Alternatively, transfer the rice and liquid to an ovenproof dish and proceed as before.
5 Remove the pan or ovenproof dish from the oven and allow the rice to stand for five minutes.
6 Stir in the remaining butter with a fork to separate the grains and transfer the rice to a serving dish.

Video presentation

If you would like to find out more about sweating food watch *Prepare fish stock (1) sweat.*

Did you know?

Au gras is cooked in the same way as pilaf rice but the rice is cooked with fat bouillon stock of chicken or beef.

In the table are examples of some popular pasta shapes:

Pasta shapes	Description of use
Rigatoni	Very good for heavier sauce dishes, e.g. bolognese or thick cheese sauce.
Cannelloni	Stuffed, covered with a sauce and baked.
Spaghetti	Good with almost any sauce, and can also be stir-fried after it has been boiled.
Linguine	A thin, long flat shape, good with sauce or in a salad.
Twists or rotini	The twist can hold meat, vegetables or cheese. This shape is ideal baked, as a pasta salad or stir-fried.
Farfalle	A 'butterfly' shape – ideal with a light sauce.
Vermicelli	Like thin spaghetti, this is ideal with light sauces.
Penne	This shape is a good choice to mix with a sauce, or use in a soup or salad.

Figure 12.7 Popular pasta shapes

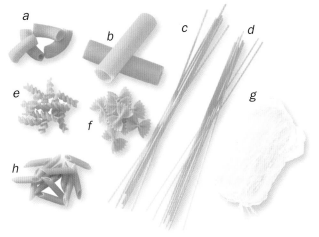

Figure 12.6 Pasta shapes: a rigatoni; b cannelloni; c spaghetti; d linguine; e twists; f farfalle; g vermicelli; h penne

Flat pasta

To make flat pasta, e.g. tagliatelle or lasagne, the dough is rolled very thin and then cut to a required shape: long strips, short strips or square sheets. The pasta dough can be passed through a machine which will flatten and cut it, or rolled out using a rolling pin and cut with a sharp 9-inch chef's knife.

Stuffed pasta

Stuffed pasta dishes are very popular as the pasta shapes are filled with meat, vegetables or cheese. This type of pasta makes an excellent meal on its own.

Stuffed pasta includes cannelloni, tortellini and ravioli, all of which can be served with a sauce and can be baked.

Cannelloni can be bought dried and filled with the stuffing of your choice. To make fresh cannelloni, follow the steps below.

1 Roll out some pasta dough to 10cm squares, 1.6mm thick.
2 Take a piping bag with a 12.5mm nozzle and pipe your filling in a line down the centre of the square.
3 Lightly egg wash one side of the square and roll it up like a sausage roll.
4 Put the cannelloni in a dish and cover it in a sauce ready for baking. Alternatively, you can cook flat sheets of cannelloni in boiling water for 15 minutes, drain them and serve with a separate sauce.

Figure 12.8 Rolled stuffed cannelloni ready for cooking

Quality points for dried pasta

The quality points for dried pasta are the same as those for rice. See page 304.

Cooking methods

To cook fresh pasta, plunge it into boiling salted water for 3–8 minutes depending on the variety. Filled pasta takes around two minutes longer to cook. Stir pasta regularly during cooking.

Cook dried pasta in the same way but for 8–15 minutes.

Certain varieties of pasta may be combined with other ingredients and baked, e.g. lasagne.

It is important to test pasta while cooking. To test whether pasta is cooked, remove a piece of pasta from the pan and taste it. It should be firm with no floury taste but still stiff enough to need chewing. This is called 'al dente'. It is easy to overcook pasta. When overcooked, pasta becomes stodgy, swells up, and then breaks apart.

Pasta can be cooked and cooled for use in salads or pre-cooked and used at a later date for stir-fries. Boil the pasta, strain it in a colander and refresh it under cold running water until cold. Store it covered in a refrigerator until it is needed.

Chef's tip
Dried pasta cooking times can vary. Always follow the instructions on the packet carefully.

Many pasta dishes are finished or accompanied by sauces, which can be light or heavy. These are some common sauces:

o **Carbonara**: a light binding sauce with a cream base, cooked bacon pieces or Parma ham. This sauce is traditionally seasoned with crushed black peppercorns. It has many varieties. Many chefs like to include mushrooms and onions to change the flavour of the sauce.

o **Napoletana** or **Neapolitan**: a tomato-based sauce, which is quite thick and often has other ingredients, e.g. ham, onions, mushroom, garlic, and herbs such as oregano or thyme. This sauce is often poured over the pasta allowing the customer to mix the sauce into the dish themselves.

o **Bolognese** or **Bolognaise**: traditionally this is a minced meat-based sauce; it contains a little tomato or tomato purée, onions, garlic and herbs, and is usually served with spaghetti.

o **Pesto**: a green sauce made with a mixture of olive oil, crushed pine nuts, basil and parmesan cheese. It can be served with pasta or Italian bread.

Try this!

Worksheet 37

Write out how to cook perfect pasta.

Spaghetti bolognaise

For the Bolognaise sauce:

onions, chopped	60g
olive oil	30ml
lean minced beef	280g
garlic clove, crushed	1
tomatoes, peeled and diced	220g
mixed herbs	pinch
beef jus	280ml
salt and pepper	to season
Cooking time	45 minutes

Method

1 Sweat the onions in the oil until tender. Do not colour them.
2 Add the garlic and the minced beef.
3 Cook until the beef separates into individual small pieces, then add the tomato and mixed herbs.
4 Add the beef jus and bring to the boil. Season and simmer for 30 minutes.

For the spaghetti:

spaghetti	600g
butter	60g
Bolognaise sauce (see above)	800g
salt and pepper	to season
Parmesan cheese, grated	60g
parsley	14g
Cooking time	15–18 minutes
Serves	5

Method

1 Boil the spaghetti in salted water for 10–15 minutes for dried pasta, 5 minutes for fresh pasta. When cooked, drain in a colander and lightly refresh under cold water.
2 Heat the butter in a shallow saucepan. Add the spaghetti, season well and stir until thoroughly reheated.
3 Place the spaghetti in a serving dish with the hot bolognaise sauce in the centre.
4 Sprinkle the spaghetti with Parmesan cheese, sprinkle the bolognaise sauce with chopped parsley. Serve.

Ravioli

pasta dough	250g
egg	1
filling of your choice (savoury mince, ricotta cheese, **duxelle**, shrimp and lemon, tofu)	100g
tomato sauce	200ml
Cheddar or Parmesan cheese, grated	30g
Cooking time	15–20 minutes
Serves	5

Method

1 Divide the dough into two equal pieces and roll out each piece to 1.5mm thick. Keep the pieces an even size.
2 Cover one piece in egg wash.
3 Put the filling into a piping bag.
4 Pipe portions of filling the size of a hazelnut 2.5cm apart onto the egg-washed piece of dough.
5 Cover with the second piece of dough and press down between each row of filling in both directions.
6 With the blunt end of a 2.5cm round cutter, press down around each portion of filling.
7 Cut the dough into equal-sized squares with the filling in the centre of each square.
8 Cook in boiling salted water for 10–15 minutes. Remove and drain in a colander.
9 Arrange the ravioli neatly in a baking dish and cover with the tomato sauce.
10 Sprinkle with cheese and lightly grill until the cheese melts.
11 Serve immediately.

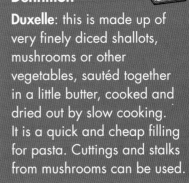

Definition

Duxelle: this is made up of very finely diced shallots, mushrooms or other vegetables, sautéd together in a little butter, cooked and dried out by slow cooking. It is a quick and cheap filling for pasta. Cuttings and stalks from mushrooms can be used.

Safe use and storage of pasta

The safe use and storage of pasta is the same as that of rice.
See page 296 for detailed information.

Pasta has a short shelf-life after cooking because of its high water
content. Use refrigerated pasta within two days. (Check information
on the label for the date.)

Test yourself!

1 List the three main ingredients used to make
pasta dough.

2 Give two cooking methods for pasta.

3 What happens to pasta when it is
overcooked?

4 How many days can you keep pasta in a
refrigerator?
   a One day
   b Two days
   c Three days
   d Four days.

5 What is Neapolitan sauce?

6 For how long should you cook fresh pasta?
   a 1–5 minutes
   b 2–8 minutes
   c 3–8 minutes
   d 5–10 minutes.

7 For how long should you cook dried pasta?
   a 5–10 minutes
   b 8–15 minutes
   c 10–15 minutes
   d 15–20 minutes.

8 Which of these pasta types can be stir-fried
after it has been boiled?
   a Penne
   b Farfalle
   c Linguine
   d Spaghetti.

9 Which of these pasta types has a 'butterfly'
shape?
   a Penne
   b Farfalle
   c Linguine
   d Spaghetti.

Grains

Grains are also known as cereals. They are grown in greater quantities worldwide than any other crop. They are cheap to produce.

Grains are the main source of carbohydrates for many developing countries but also contain some protein, fats and vitamins.

Types of grain

Barley

Barley is a cheap, very nutritious food. Barley is a good ingredient for soups and stews, where it is used to thicken the dish.

Two types of barley are available:
- **Pearl barley**: the most common form of barley. Pearl barley is stripped of a nutritious bran layer during processing, leaving just the 'pearl' inside. Even with this bran layer taken off, pearl barley is still a nutritious food.
- **Pot barley or whole grain barley**: processed exactly like pearl barley, but the bran layer is left on. This type of barley is the most nutritious.

Pearl and pot barley are very common in health food stores as they are normally sold in their natural form.

Figure 12.9 Processed pearl barley grains

Buckwheat

Buckwheat has a nutty, earthy flavour and gives dishes a rough texture. Buckwheat seeds are triangular after processing and are a light golden colour. It is commonly ground down into flour and used to make everything from pancakes and tortillas to bread and noodles. The seed when ground into flour is gritty and dark and makes an excellent healthy substitute to normal flours. Buckwheat is also popular in some countries, e.g. America and Scotland, as a breakfast cereal.

Corn or maize

This is the only grain that is normally eaten as a fresh vegetable. Corn is high in vitamin A, fibre and other nutrients. Corn is also known as maize in some countries.

Healthy eating
Buckwheat is high in fibre and protein but very low in fat.

Did you know?
Buckwheat is free from gluten, so it is perfect for people with a gluten allergy. For more information on gluten see page 321.

Corn bought fresh and raw in its husk (leafy outer covering) is called 'corn on the cob'. When buying corn on the cob fresh, break off one kernel (piece of corn) and bite it; the kernel should have a slightly sweet taste and be crisp. If the corn has no taste and is very dry, it is overripe.

Polenta

Polenta is made from ground corn called cornmeal. It looks like flour and can be rough or finely ground. It can be yellow or white. Polenta is very popular in Italy and is used in all sorts of recipes.

Polenta is most often served with simple meat dishes like pork chops, sausages or steaks. See page 313 for cooking instructions.

Figure 12.10 Polenta

Oats

Oats are highly nutritious. They contain protein, fat, iron, potassium, B vitamins and carbohydrates. They are high in fibre. Oats have a pleasant, nutty flavor and are fawn in colour.

Oats can be ground down into a meal and used to coat meat or fish. They can be rolled or crushed during processing and used to make breakfast cereals, e.g. porridge or muesli. They can also be used as an ingredient in biscuits or in crumble topping for pudding.

Figure 12.11 Rolled oats

Millet

Millet is very similar to wheat. It can be bought with its outer husk (hull) on or off. Millet seeds can be used to make flour, or used as part of breakfast cereals like muesli. The seeds are very tasty when toasted. Millet can be found in health food shops and is quite cheap.

Wheat

Wheat is used mainly in making flour; most flour available in the supermarkets is made from wheat. It can be used as grain in salads and also as an ingredient in pilaf dishes, muesli and cereal bars.

Wheat grain that has not been ground into flour has a nutty flavour. It is high in nutrients and gluten.

Healthy eating
Millet is very high in protein but is gluten-free.

Did you know?
Millet flour is very popular in India where it is used to make a flattened bread called bhakri.

Wheat is also processed into other ingredients like bulgar, semolina and couscous:

○ **Bulgar**: made from whole wheat that has been soaked and baked to speed up cooking time. It can be used as an ingredient in soup, bread and stuffing. It is a popular dish in the Middle East where it is used to make pilaf dishes. Bulgar comes whole, or cracked into fine, medium, or coarse grains. It is very high in nutrients and can be used as an alternative to couscous or rice.

○ **Semolina**: wheat that has been roughly ground or milled. It is often boiled and made into a pudding with sugar or another sweetener, e.g. jam. It can be flavoured with vanilla and eaten hot or cold.

○ **Couscous**: similar to semolina, but the wheat is ground a little finer. It is used as a side dish to meat or served under a stew or casserole. It is a very popular dish in Africa, Morocco and the Middle East where it is served with vegetables or as a separate side dish. To prepare couscous, soak it in cold water, then drain and wash it before steaming in a steamer or **couscousier**. Couscous can be served with meat or vegetable dishes.

Figure 12.12 Bulgar wheat

Quinoa

Quinoa is pronounced 'keen wah'. It is mostly used as an ingredient for breakfast cereals, but can also be cooked in the same way as rice. Quinoa contains more protein that any other grain. It is described as a perfect food because of the balance of nutrients.

Figure 12.13 A couscousier

Find out! **Worksheet 38**

Look at the list of grains: barley, buckwheat, corn/maize, polenta, oats, milet, bulgar, wheat, couscous, semolina, quinoa.
Can they be used for:
○ classic main course dishes
○ garnishes
○ desserts?

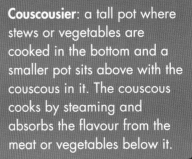

Definition

Couscousier: a tall pot where stews or vegetables are cooked in the bottom and a smaller pot sits above with the couscous in it. The couscous cooks by steaming and absorbs the flavour from the meat or vegetables below it.

Quality points for grains

The quality points for grains are the same as those for rice. See page 292 for more information. In addition, look for signs of pest infestation. Grains are a favourite food for vermin and other pests. Check the grains for signs of mould, especially if the grains is stored somewhere near moisture.

Problems

See page 292 for more information about what to do if you have problems with ingredients. Report any signs of pest infestation immediately.

Safe use and storage of grains

The safe use and storage of grains is the same as that of rice. See page 295 for more information. Grain dishes that are cooked and finished may be frozen for later use. Put them in a suitable dish and cover them. Label with the date of cooking and freezing, and place in a freezer. Thaw the dish properly before re-use.

Cooking methods

Boiling and simmering

Most grains can be boiled. Both types of barley take around one to two hours to cook, usually by boiling or simmering, although pot barley can take up to three hours to become soft.

Polenta is normally boiled and quick-cook polenta can take as little as five minutes. Traditional polenta can take as long as an hour to cook. Polenta may be served hot and creamy with a little butter added. Extra ingredients, e.g. cheese, can be added just before service.

Oats can be made into porridge, a hot breakfast cereal, if you boil them in milk or water.

Quinoa can be boiled, stewed or baked. It is an ideal replacement for rice and can be treated in much the same way. It takes about 15 minutes to cook.

Pilaf of pot barley

chicken or beef stock	440ml
pot barley (or pearl barley)	240g
spring onions, roughly chopped	3
celery stick, roughly chopped	1
mushrooms, sliced	220g
salt and pepper	to season
Cooking time	15 minutes
Serves	4

Method

1 Cook the barley in the simmering stock for approx. 45–50 minutes.
2 Drain the barley well and keep it warm. Keep around 100ml stock back.
3 Put the stock in a pan.
4 Add the spring onion and celery. Cook until the celery is soft.
5 Add the mushrooms. Cook until most of the liquid has gone.
6 Add the cooked barley. Mix gently.
7 Season with salt and pepper and serve.

This recipe can also be served cold as a salad.

Frying

Boiled polenta can be allowed to harden and then sliced and sautéed or fried before serving.

Grilling

Hardened polenta can also be sliced and grilled or fried before serving.

Baking

Millet croquettes

cooked millet	480g
celery, finely diced	120g
carrot, finely grated	60g
onion, finely diced	120g
chopped parsley	60g
dill	10g
oregano	5g
flour	120g
water	220ml
Makes	8–10 × 90g croquettes
Oven temperature	170°C
Cooking time	25 minutes

Chef's tip

This recipe can be used for vegans.

Method

1 Put the millet, celery, carrots, onion, parsley, dill and oregano into a bowl. Mix.
2 Add the flour. Gradually add the water and mix.
3 Form the mixture into even cigar-shapes, each 4cm long and approx. 90g.
4 Place on a lightly greased tray and bake.

Basic simple cornbread

cornmeal	240g
wheat flour	240g
baking powder	20g
corn oil	50ml
water	330ml
sugar	30g
salt	pinch
Serves	8
Oven temperature	170°C/350°F
Cooking time	20 minutes

Method

1 Put all the ingredients into a bowl and mix well.
2 Put in a greased casserole dish.
3 Bake in the oven.

Self-raising flour

Self-raising flour is a mixture of plain flour and baking powder in a ratio of 480g flour:10g baking powder. It does not produce a consistent product, as some recipes need more baking powder. Self-raising flour is best used within six to nine months.

Gluten-free flour

Some people are intolerant of gluten. They need a gluten-free diet. Gluten-free flour can be made from maize, rice, buckwheat, potato, tapioca or chickpeas.

Storage of flour

Flour is normally supplied in 16kg bags and should be transferred into mobile storage bins, with lids. Flour must be kept dry and cool. Always wash and dry the containers before storing new flour and never put new flour on top of old flour.

For more information on flour and bread, you can visit www.heinemann.co.uk/hotlinks and enter the express code 9257P.

Definition

Gluten: a protein found in flour which gives it its strength. The strength of the gluten is determined by the type of wheat and when and where it is grown.

Raising agents

Yeast

Yeast is a type of fungus and is a living micro-organism similar to a bacterium. Yeast is mainly used in breadmaking but may also be used in a variety of yeast batters, e.g. for fritters or blinis.

Like bacteria, yeast requires food, warmth, moisture and time in order to grow. Under the right conditions it produces carbon dioxide. This is what makes the dough rise.

Adding sugar to yeast will feed the yeast, but too much sugar will kill the yeast and prevent it producing carbon dioxide.

Adding tepid liquids like milk and water provides moisture and some warmth. A warm temperature during mixing and proving provides the warmth needed for yeast to generate carbon dioxide.

Salt improves the flavour and colour and stops the cooked products being sticky. Take care with the amount, as too much salt can kill yeast.

Warmth encourages the growth of carbon dioxide. Yeast starts to produce carbon dioxide at temperatures of 24–29°C. However, temperatures in excess of 49°C will kill yeast.

Yeast dough is usually left to prove in a warm, moist place, such as a prover. See page 336 for more information on provers.

Using cold ingredients to slow down the growth of carbon dioxide can be an advantage, as it can produce different textures for different dough products, e.g. enriched dough products like croissants and Danish pastries.

Fresh yeast is normally supplied in 1kg blocks. When open it should have a pleasant smell and the surface should have a grey plastic look. As yeast gets older the surface colour changes to brown and looks dry and cracked. Yeast in this condition should not be used. Yeast should be kept covered in cool, moist conditions, ideally in a fridge at a temperature of 4–5°C.

There are two types of dried yeast, commonly known as baker's yeast and dried active yeast. Baker's yeast has large particles of dried yeast and has to be reconstituted in liquid and then treated as fresh yeast.

Dried active yeast is powdered and can be added directly to the flour according to the manufacturer's instructions. Dried yeast is used in smaller amounts to fresh yeast. Check the manufacturer's instructions prior to use for the exact amount to use. Dried yeast also needs food, warmth, moisture and time.

> **Definition**
>
> **Prove**: to allow the yeast to develop carbon dioxide in the dough to make it rise before baking.
>
> **Prover**: a cabinet that creates heat and moisture, helping dough products to rise evenly and assists in preventing products from drying out and skinning.
>
> **Skinning**: when dough is left uncovered and the surface of the dough starts to dry out and oxidise.

Try this!   **Worksheet 40**

Write down seven points you need to remember about fresh yeast.

Baking powder

Baking power is a chemical raising agent that is made from one part bicarbonate of soda to two parts cream of tartar. When liquid is added, carbon dioxide is given off which makes products rise. Too much baking powder can have an adverse effect and cakes and sponges will collapse.

Bicarbonate of soda is an alkaline raising agent and needs acidic ingredients to work as a raising agent. Apart from bicarbonate of soda and egg white, all ingredients are acidic to various degrees, making bicarbonate of soda a good raising agent.

Cream of tartar is found in the juice of grapes, after they have been fermented in winemaking. It is classified as an acid and available in powder form. It cannot be used on its own as a raising agent.

Sugar

Sugar occurs naturally in all plants, in the fruit, the leaves and the stems. However, sugar for commercial use is obtained from two major sources, sugar cane and sugar beet. The sugar extracted from these sources is refined and cleaned to produce white sugar. It is then crystallised and sieved. The largest-holed sieve produces granulated sugar, the next size down produces caster sugar, and fine linen sieves are used to produce icing sugar. Loaf or cubed sugar is obtained by pressing the crystals together when slightly damp, drying them in blocks and then cutting them into squares. Sugar that has not been refined is coated in **molasses** and produces different types of brown sugar such as light brown sugar, soft brown and demerara sugar.

> **Definition**
> **Molasses**: a dark, thick brown liquid obtained from raw sugar during the refining process. It is used to make syrup, e.g. golden syrup and black treacle.

Sugar is used to add sweetness and texture to pastry products. Care needs to be taken to select the correct type of sugar for the dish you are making. Using the wrong type of sugar can affect the finished product. For more information you can visit www.heinemann.co.uk/hotlinks and enter the express code 9257P.

Granulated sugar is a white medium crystalline sugar that is best used in products that require the sugar to be dissolved prior to use, e.g. when making caramel. If granulated sugar is used in pastry products it will not dissolve during cooking and will leave tiny crystals on the surface of the finished item.

Caster sugar is a white fine crystalline sugar that is best used in cakes, pastry and meringues. This type of sugar dissolves during the cooking process and gives these products the sweetness and texture they require.

Icing sugar is a white powdered sugar that is mixed with an anti-caking ingredient. This type of sugar is best used for decoration and icing, but there are a few other occasions when this very fine product is required as granulated or caster sugar will not dissolve sufficiently, e.g. when making tuille biscuits.

Nibbed sugar is not widely available and is normally only used in specialist confectionery shops. Nibbed sugar is sometimes used as a topping, e.g. on bath buns and rock cakes.

Cubed sugar can either be white or brown, and is the purest form of sugar you can buy. White sugar cubes do not allow any impurities to penetrate them and this make them very suitable for boiled sugar work. Brown sugar cubes are generally used to sweeten coffee.

Dark soft brown sugar is a very dark sugar with an intense flavour, and soft in texture. It is used in sticky toffee pudding and various cakes and sponges. If it is not stored tightly wrapped up, it will go hard and lumpy.

Muscovado sugar is similar to dark soft brown sugar, but lighter in colour. If a recipe suggests using this type of sugar but it is not available, use dark soft brown sugar instead.

Light brown sugar is similar in texture to dark soft brown sugar, but much lighter in colour, and milder in flavour.

Demerara sugar is a light-brown coarse sugar used for caramelising crème brûlée or in coffee.

Golden syrup is made from molasses that has been clarified. You should weigh it into a greased bowl to make it easier to use.

Black treacle is a thick, sticky dark syrup made from unrefined molasses.

Preparation methods

Mixing the dough

First, carefully weigh and measure the ingredients and sift the flour. Next, prepare the yeast. There are two main ways that yeast is used to produce carbon dioxide in bread and bun products:

o sponging
o bulk fermentation time.

Sponging

Sponging is a method where the yeast is allowed to produce carbon dioxide before it is added to the bulk of the flour. Sponging is the fastest method for making bun and bread products and will result in a light and open dough texture.

Put the tepid liquid into a bowl. Dissolve the yeast and add the sugar. Add enough flour from the recipe to mix to a batter (the consistency of paint). This mixture is then allowed to ferment for 10–15 minutes before being added to the rest of the ingredients.

Bulk fermentation time

In this method, the yeast liquid is mixed with all of the flour at once.

Bulk fermentation time (BFT) describes the length of time that the dough proves from the end of the mixing time until the **scaling** time. It can take 1–18 hours, depending on the recipe and the dough temperature. The end product will have a tighter texture with an improved flavour.

Put the tepid liquid into a bowl. Dissolve the yeast and add the sugar. Mix. Add this mixture to all of the flour and mix to form a dough. Then allow to prove.

For both methods, the water used to mix the dough should be at body temperature (37°C). If the temperature is too high (above 49°C) it will kill the yeast.

The amount of liquid suggested in the recipes is only approximate. The actual amount of liquid needed will vary, depending on the quality of the flour. For example, the gluten content can result in more or less liquid being needed.

Remember!
All types of flour must be sifted. The ideal type of sieve is a drum sieve. Sieving ensures that flour lumps are broken up, leading to a better leavened product. It also identifies physical contamination.

Figure 14.2 A drum sieve

Definition
Scaling: cutting and weighing the dough into the required size, e.g. for bread rolls scale dough into 60g pieces.

Chef's tip
To test the temperature of the water, place a finger into the water. If the water feels warm or cold, the water is not at the correct temperature.

Kneading

Once all the ingredients have been combined, dough is **kneaded** by working it with the ball of the hand or by machine. This helps to develop the gluten in the dough. Strong gluten results in a better structure to hold the carbon dioxide produced by the yeast.

How to knead dough

① Use the heel of your hand to push the dough down and out.

② Lift the dough back with your fingertips.

Proving

Proving allows the gluten in the flour to relax after it has been stretched by the kneading process. Insufficient proving will make the dough difficult to shape and it will contract during rolling, leading to a close, heavy texture.

There are several stages when proving dough:

- **First prove**: after sponging, cover and prove in a warm place until the yeast mixture starts to bubble and looks like honeycomb.
- **Second prove**: after the kneading process, cover and prove the dough in a warm place until double in size.
- **Final prove**: after scaling and moulding but before baking, dough products are proved, usually in a prover, until they double in size.

Dough products can be proved without a **prover** by lightly sprinkling the surface of the dough products with water and covering them with oiled plastic and then placing them somewhere warm. A new plant spray bottle with a fine spray will help to give a light and even coating of water.

It is important to cover dough products when they are proving to prevent **skinning**.

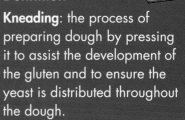

Definition
Kneading: the process of preparing dough by pressing it to assist the development of the gluten and to ensure the yeast is distributed throughout the dough.

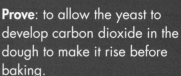

Definition
Prove: to allow the yeast to develop carbon dioxide in the dough to make it rise before baking.
Prover: a cabinet that creates heat and moisture, helping dough products to rise evenly, and assists in preventing products from drying out and skinning.
Skinning: when dough is left uncovered and the surface of the dough starts to dry out and oxidise. If this is then mixed into the dough it will leave dry pieces of dough in the finished product.

Remember!
Sponging method uses first prove, second prove and a final prove. BFT method uses second prove and final prove.

Definition
Oxidise: a chemical reaction when oxygen causes the surface of the dough to dry out.

Knocking back and scaling the dough

Knocking back means removing the air produced during proving. It is done by kneading the dough again. This ensures the yeast is working before shaping and provides an even texture during baking. Removing all the air also assists in shaping the dough after scaling. The dough is now ready to be scaled, or cut and weighed, into pieces of the required size.

Hand shaping

Shaping the dough is also known as 'moulding'. Hand shaping does take some practice but with time many different shapes can be achieved. The first two shapes to master are rounds and fingers.

How to shape rounds or balls

Mastering this shape will help you to make other shapes correctly.

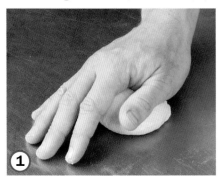

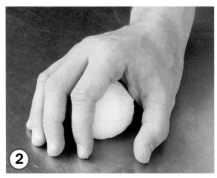

Take a scaled piece of dough and knead it briefly to remove any air. Then put the dough onto the work surface and cover it with the palm of your hand. Start to slowly rotate your hand while pressing down quite hard.

As the ball forms, slowly cup your hand until a nice smooth ball is achieved. The surface of the dough must be smooth with no cracks otherwise the roll will crack during proving and cooking.

Once the shape has been achieved, transfer the completed roll to a baking tray, lined with silicone paper, and repeat the process with the other pieces of dough. Allow them to prove until double their size. Unless you are using a steam prover, cover with oiled plastic to prevent skinning.

How to shape fingers

1 Shape as for rounds until the smooth ball has been achieved.
2 Roll the piece backwards and forwards until a finger shape has been made.
3 Transfer onto a baking tray and allow to prove.

Once the shaping of rounds and fingers has been mastered, there are many different shapes that can be achieved, including knots, double knots, three-strand plaits, five-strand plaits, twists, ropes, brioche shapes.

Cooking and finishing methods

Finishing methods applied before cooking

Before baking a product you may wish to apply a finish to the dough.

○ **Egg wash**: Use an egg wash to glaze dough products. Beat an egg well. Thin it down with a little milk or water if necessary. Brush onto the surface of products to give them a shine and a golden brown colour during baking. Dough products which can be egg-washed before baking include bread rolls, bread loaves, Bath buns. Dough products should be egg-washed before the final prove because they are fragile once proved and can collapse if touched.

○ **Toppings**: to give dough products an attractive finish, sprinkle them with different seeds, e.g. sesame, poppy, sunflower or pumpkin seeds, or oats.
For a more rustic look, dust bread dough products with flour.

○ **Cutting**: to achieve a different effect, make small cuts in the surface of the rolls or bread. Make the cuts before the final prove using a small sharp knife or a pair of scissors. Cutting the surface allows the cuts to expand prior to baking and gives the products an attractive finish.

Remember!
Do not allow the rolls to over-prove (no more than double their size) or they will collapse.

Figure 14.3 Bread rolls can be made in many attractive styles

Try this!
Cut an attractive pattern into bread roll dough using a pair of scissors or a small knife.

Chelsea buns

basic bun dough recipe	
butter, melted	to brush dough
dark soft brown sugar	30g
mixed spice	4g
sultanas	120g
currants	120g
mixed peel	30g
Oven temperature	200°C
Makes	10

Method

1. Follow the basic bun dough recipe.
2. Roll into a rectangle approximately 30cm × 20cm.
3. Brush with melted butter.
4. Sprinkle with the sugar.
5. Sprinkle with the mixed spice.
6. Sprinkle with sultanas, currants and mixed peel.
7. Roll up along the short end like a swiss roll. Brush with melted butter on the outside.
8. Cut into 10cm × 3cm pieces.
9. Turn the cut pieces so you can see the filling when put onto the table. Put into individual moulds which have been buttered and floured or a large cake ring, allowing space in between to prove.
10. Prove until doubled in size.
11. Bake until golden brown.
12. Allow to cool slightly before turning out the moulds onto a cooling rack.
13. While still warm glaze with bun wash.

Bun wash

caster sugar	100g
milk or water	100ml

Method

1. Put the ingredients in a pan and boil for about five minutes on a medium heat.
2. Glaze the warm buns with the hot bun wash.

Swiss buns

basic bun dough

Oven temperature	200°C
Makes	20

Method

1 Follow the recipe for the basic bun dough.
2 Scale the dough into 60g pieces and roll into finger shapes.
3 Place onto a greased baking tray.
4 Prove in a warm place until doubled in size.
5 Bake until golden brown.
6 Allow to cool slightly before placing onto a cooling rack.
7 When cooled, glaze with fondant icing or water icing.

Did you know?

Swiss buns can be filled with fresh whipped cream and/or fruit to make cream buns.

Video presentation

Follow these goodies being made step-by-step and learn more about fondant in *Make iced Swiss buns*.

Water icing

icing sugar	200g
water	30ml

Method

1 Sift the icing sugar into a bowl.
2 Add the water and beat using a wooden spoon.

Chef's tip

Add 20g cocoa powder to make chocolate icing.

Jam doughnuts

basic bun dough

caster sugar	to roll
red jam	

Method

1 Prepare the basic bun dough.
2 Scale 60g pieces and roll into round rolls.
3 Place on an oiled tray.
4 Prove in a warm place until doubled in size.
5 To deep-fry the doughnuts, heat the oil to 180°C.
6 Coat a wide spatula in the hot oil. Then place the oiled spatula under the doughnuts and carefully lift them into the oil.
7 Turn over with a spider. Remove with the spider when golden brown on both sides.
8 Place onto a cooling rack and allow excess oil to drip off.
9 Roll in sugar.
10 Pipe red jam into the centre once cooled down.

Chef's tip

As an alternative, you can glaze doughnuts with water icing or chocolate icing and fill them with whipped cream.

Steaming

Suet paste products are normally steamed. This is a long, slow method of cookery. It does not have any negative effects on the other ingredients, e.g. steak and kidney in a pie. The suet paste needs to be covered well to prevent water getting into the paste and making it soggy.

Modern steamers are self-contained and form part of a combination oven with a steam mode. Combination ovens can be adjusted to increase the amount of humidity inside the oven and this can provide an effective lift to the pastry, as the steam assists the layer to rise. Make sure the oven is switched to steam mode before placing the suet paste item to be cooked.

Use caution. Before opening the door to any steamer, make sure no one else is close to the oven door. Turn off the oven, slowly open the door and allow the steam to escape. Then open the door fully and place the item inside. Close the door and restart the cooking process.

> **Remember!**
> Opening the door of a steamer too quickly can cause very hot water to burst out and scald you or someone else.

Choux pastry

Choux paste

butter	65g
water	185ml
salt	5g
caster sugar	7g
eggs	3
strong flour, sifted	130g
Oven temperature	200°C
Cooking time	30–40 minutes, depending on product

Method

1 Dice the butter and place it into a saucepan with the water, salt and sugar.
2 Cook until the butter melts, then bring to the boil.
3 Crack the eggs into a bowl and whisk them.
4 As soon as the mixture boils add all the flour. Mix with a spatula until all the flour has been absorbed.

> **Chef's tip**
> Do not use a metal spoon in a metal saucepan as the spoon may scratch the saucepan and this will turn the paste grey.

5   Cook out the flour or the mixture will not absorb the correct amount of egg to make the final product rise sufficiently. To do this, cook until the mixture comes away from the sides of the saucepan. Then cook for a further minute.

6   Place the mixture (**panade**) into a clean bowl to cool. Do not start adding the egg while the mixture is hot, otherwise the egg will cook before the mixture goes into the oven.

7   When the panade has cooled, place it back into the saucepan and slowly add the egg. Beat well between each addition until the paste is smooth. The eggs give the finished cases the light and open texture.

8   Continue adding the egg until a dropping consistency has been achieved. Lift up the paste on the spatula and slowly count to seven. The mixture should drop off. Add more egg if required.

9   Shape the paste as required (see below).

10 Cooking times are shown below.

Products you can make with choux paste

Éclairs

These are 3cm- to 12cm-long pastries filled with cream and decorated with chocolate or fondant. Pipe the mixture onto lightly greased trays with a medium tube and savoy bag, about 7cm long. Keep the tube at 90° to the tray.

To make sure the éclair is completely round do not let the tube touch the tray or the top of the mixture coming out of the tube. To pipe the éclair straight, only move the tube as fast as the mixture is coming out of the bag. Apply consistent pressure.

Apply an egg wash to give an even colour during cooking. Cook for approximately 15 minutes.

Paris Brests

These are choux rings filled with hazelnut cream. The rings represent the car rally route between the cities of Paris and Brest. Pipe with a medium tube. Use the same piping technique as for éclairs. Cook for approximately 15–20 minutes.

Did you know?

The main raising agent in choux paste is water. The water in the pastry gets hot during baking and turns into steam which reacts with the flour and eggs causing the choux product to rise. Keep the oven door closed for at least 10–15 minutes, otherwise the steam will escape and will not be able to react with the eggs and flour. This will result in a flat end product.

Definition

Panade: a paste of flour, butter and a little liquid.

Figure 15.1 Eclairs

Figure 15.2 Paris Brests

Profiteroles

These are small cases filled with chantilly or pastry cream (crème pâtissière) and served with chocolate sauce. Pipe downwards onto lightly greased trays, to about the size of a ten pence piece. The tips will burn if they are allowed to remain proud; dampen a finger and press the mixture down to level it off. Cook for approximately 15–20 minutes.

Figure 15.3 Profiteroles

Choux pastry ring

Pipe in a large ring and decorate with flaked almonds. Bake for 20–30 minutes. Cut the ring in half. Fill with cream and dust with icing sugar.

Swans

1 Pipe a teardrop shape. This will form the body and the wings.
2 Pipe the neck with a small nozzle in the shape of a number 2.
3 Bake for approximately 15–20 minutes.
4 Cut the teardrop shape in half. Use one half for the body.
5 Cut the other half in half again lengthways for the wings. Dip the top in chocolate.
6 Fill the body with whipped cream and insert the wings into the cream.
7 Push the neck in between the wings to complete the swan.
8 You can decorate the body with fruit and dust with icing sugar.

Figure 15.4 Choux pastry ring

Choux paste fritters (*Beignets soufflés*)

These are small, walnut-sized pieces of choux paste, deep-fried in hot oil and served with apricot sauce.

1 Heat the oil to 190°C–200°C.
2 With two spoons, take uncooked choux paste about the size of a walnut and carefully drop into the hot oil.
3 Cook for approximately 10–15 minutes until brown.
4 Remove from the oil and drain well, sprinkle with caster sugar (it may be flavoured with cinnamon).
5 Serve fritters and apricot sauce separately.

Figure 15.5 Swans

How to check if choux pastry is cooked

1. Check the products are golden brown.
2. Open the oven door carefully and remove one piece from the tray, then close the door gently, leaving the rest in the oven.
3. Break open the product and touch the inside. It should feel slightly damp.
4. If it feels wet and sticky leave the products in the oven and check again in a few minutes.
5. Once cooked, cool on a cooling wire.

Storage of choux products

Filled choux cases must be stored in the fridge, unless they have been glazed with fondant icing; fondant icing will sweat in the fridge and fall off the case.

Unfilled cooked cases should be stored in airtight conditions to prevent them going soft and used within three days.

Puff pastry

This is one of the most complicated pastes used in patisserie. Few establishments make their own, because of the length of time needed to make it. Understanding how puff paste is made and works will help you when working with either commercial puff pastry or puff pastry made from scratch.

The proportion of fat to flour in puff pastry can be:
○ 1kg strong flour to 1kg of fat – full puff.
○ 1kg strong flour to 750g of fat – three-quarter puff.
○ 1kg strong flour to 500g of fat – half puff.

Between 80 and 90 per cent of the fat used in puff pastry is pastry margarine. Pastry margarine has a higher melting temperature than normal margarine. This creates steam during cooking, which gives the pastry its light crispy texture.

Puff pastry is made using a lamination method which gives the pastry its distinctive layered effect when cooked.

> **Chef's tip**
> If unfilled, cooked choux pastry cases go soft. Place them in an oven at 180°C (convection), 200°C or gas mark 6 (normal oven) for a few minutes to crisp up.

Methods of making puff paste

There are three different methods of making puff paste:

1. **French method**: a ball of paste rolled out to a shape similar to an opened-out envelope; the pastry margarine is placed into the centre. The folds are then used to seal in the margarine. Then the paste is pinned and folded.

2. **Scotch method**: this is a quick way to make puff pastry but its quality is not as good as the French or English methods. It can also be messy. All the fat is cut into small pieces and added to the flour. Then the liquid is added and mixed to form a dough, with the fat pieces whole. The paste is then pinned out and folded.

3. **English method**: three-quarters of a rectangle of paste is covered with pastry margarine and folded in thirds to seal in the margarine. The paste is then pinned and folded as described below. This is the most popular method.

Puff paste

lemon juice	5ml
salt	5g
cold water	315ml
strong flour	500g
margarine (block)	60g
pastry margarine	440g

Method

1. Add the lemon juice and salt to the ice cold water. Stir to dissolve the salt.
2. Sift the flour into a bowl.
3. Cut the block of margarine into smaller pieces and rub it into the flour.
4. Make a well in the flour. Add the acidulated water and mix to make a soft, pliable dough – similar to short paste.
5. Gently knead the dough to a smooth paste.
6. Cut a cross in the top of the dough and cover it with an upturned bowl.
7. Allow the paste to rest in the fridge for 30 minutes. This allows the gluten to relax.
8. Follow the instructions on the next page to fold in the paste.

Remember!

A high cooking temperature is needed to create steam to make the pastry rise as the layers of margarine melt during cooking.

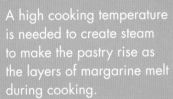

Video presentation

Did you know you can prepare puff paste by mixing it on the work surface rather than into a bowl? Watch *Prepare puff paste* to see how this is done. Then watch *Make puff paste (English method)*.

Did you know?

The lemon juice helps to strengthen the gluten.

How to fold puff pastry – English method

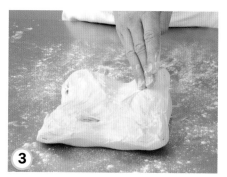

1 Take a clean plastic bag about the size of an A4 sheet and open it out. Put it on the work surface. Cover two-thirds of one half of the plastic in sliced pastry margarine.

2 Fold the other half of the plastic over the butter. Pin out to flatten the butter so that it fills the rest of the plastic and is of an even thickness. Put it to one side.

3 Lightly flour the work surface and place the prepared puff pastry dough onto it. Open out the corners of the cross in the top of the dough to make a square.

4 Pin out the dough into a rectangle a third longer and slightly wider that the pastry margarine.

5 Take the pinned out pastry margarine. Open up one side of the plastic. Put the margarine onto one end of the pastry and peel off the plastic. It should cover two-thirds of the pastry.

6 Fold the uncovered third of the pastry over to create 3 layers (2 pastry, 1 fat).

7 Use the pastry brush to remove any excess flour and fold over again creating 5 layers.

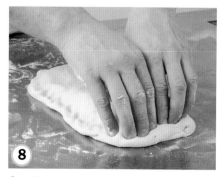

8 Seal the edges by pressing with your fingers.

9 Pin out the pastry again until it is just over 1cm thick.

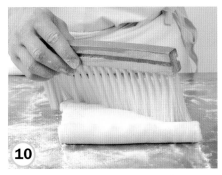

10 Fold one third down. Brush away any excess flour as you go.

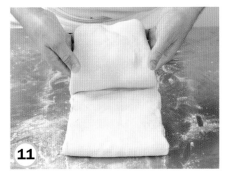

11 Fold the other third up and seal.

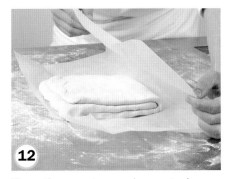

12 Turn the pastry and margarine envelope through 90° so the sealed edge is on the left. Wrap it in silicone paper and allow it to rest in the fridge for 20 minutes. This is one turn.

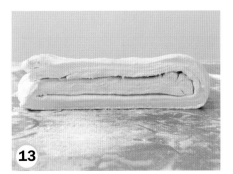

13 Repeat steps 9–12 until you have made 6 turns.

Cutting and cooking puff paste

When cutting puff paste use a guillotine method to prevent the layers of pastry causing distortion during cooking.

Do not twist pastry cutters when making vol-au-vents and bouches, as this will cause the pastry cases to rise unevenly.

Cooked puff pastry should be golden brown in colour, well but evenly risen, and have crisp texture. The bases should be cooked – turn them over and check.

Storage of puff paste

Uncooked puff paste should be covered in plastic to prevent skinning and stored in the fridge. All cooked puff pastry products not containing high-risk foods can be stored in airtight conditions to prevent them going soft. All products containing high-risk foods must be stored in the fridge.

Find out! **Worksheet 44**

What does salt and lemon juice do for puff pastry? Use the Internet to find five sweet and five savoury pastry recipes.

Convenience pastry

Any pastry that is available commercially, including pre-made pastry and pre-mixed pastry mixes, is called convenience pastry.

Puff pastry and filo pastry are the most commonly used commercial pre-made pastes. Puff pastry can be purchased either frozen, chilled or in a pre-mixed mix. Filo pastry is available chilled or frozen and is made up of very thin sheets of pastry, which are very crispy when cooked.

Filo pastry is made by rolling and pulling the dough until extremely thin sheets of the paste are produced. Filo is made in a similar way to strudel dough. It is often bought because the commercial product is of a high and consistent quality.

Because it is extremely thin, filo pastry needs to be kept moist or it dries and cannot be used. Melted butter is used to stick the sheets together and to keep the sheets moist until cooking. Any sheets not being used immediately should be covered with a damp cloth.

Dry pre-mixed mixes normally only require liquid. The method of production should be in accordance with the manufacturer's instructions. They should be stored in airtight conditions to prevent moisture and pest infestation.

Remember!
The manufacturer's storage instructions and 'use by' dates should be followed.

Test yourself!

1 When making short paste, what does the butter do to the flour?

2 Describe the creaming method for short paste.

3 When making short paste using creaming method 1, why should you not add all the egg in one go?

4 List five sweet and five savoury puff pastry products.

5 There are three ways to give pastry a lighter texture. What are they?

6 How is suet paste cooked normally?
   a Baked
   b Deep-fried
   c Steamed
   d Microwaved.

Rock cakes

Rock cakes are similar to scones but are more rustic.

Rock cakes

plain flour	500g
baking powder	30g
salt	3g
butter	125g
currants, washed and dried	60g
mixed peel, washed and dried	25g
caster sugar	60g
egg	1
milk	225ml
eggs for egg wash	2
granulated sugar	25g
Oven temperature	225°C
Baking time	15 minutes
Makes	16 cakes

Method

1 Sift the flour, salt and baking powder together.
2 Rub in the butter until a sandy texture is achieved.
3 Add the dried fruit and mix.
4 Make a well in the centre and add the sugar. Add the egg and milk and dissolve the sugar.
5 Draw in the flour and make a soft dough. Do not over-mix.
6 Break off evenly sized pieces and place onto a lightly greased tray. Do not make them too uniform.
7 Brush the rock cakes with egg wash and sprinkle them with granulated sugar.
8 Bake until golden brown. Once cooked remove from the oven and allow to cool slightly. Then transfer them to a cooling wire.

Raspberry buns are similar to rock cakes but are more formal.

Raspberry buns

plain flour	500g
baking powder	30g
salt	3g
butter	125g
caster sugar	125g
egg	1
milk	240ml
raspberry jam	100g
Oven temperature	220°C
Cooking time	15–20 minutes
Makes	16 buns

Method

1 Follow steps 1–5 for rock cakes.
2 Roll out the dough on a lightly floured surface and make it into a sausage shape.
3 Cut the dough into 16 pieces and shape each piece into a ball.
4 Dip the top of each ball into caster sugar and place them onto lightly greased baking trays.
5 Make an indentation on the top of each bun. Fill each indentation with raspberry jam.
6 Allow the items to rest for 15 minutes. Put them in the oven and bake to a golden brown colour.
7 Once cooked let the buns rest for a few minutes and then transfer them to a cooling wire.

Test yourself!

1 How many grams are there in one kilogram?

2 How many millilitres are there in one litre?

3 What protein is developed in flour during kneading?

4 What effect will it have in cakes?

5 Why is baking powder used?

17

Hot and cold desserts

This chapter covers the following NVQ unit:

o   Unit 2FPC14 Prepare and cook basic cold and hot desserts

Working through this chapter could also provide evidence for the following Key Skills:
C1.1, C2.2, N1.1, N1.2, WO2.1, WO2.2, PS2.1, PS2.2, PS2.3

In this chapter you will learn how to:

Check ingredients meet dish requirements and quality standards	2FPC14
Choose and use the correct techniques, tools and equipment	2FPC14
Prepare ingredients using the correct preparation methods	2FPC14
Cook ingredients using the correct cooking methods	2FPC14
Make sure the dessert has the correct colour, texture and finish	2FPC14
Finish the dessert to meet requirements	2FPC14
Make sure the dessert is at the correct temperature for holding and serving	2FPC14
Safely store any prepared desserts not for immediate use	2FPC14

You will learn to make basic cold and hot desserts, including:

o   ice cream
o   mousses
o   egg-based desserts
o   batter-based desserts
o   sponge-based desserts
o   fruit-based desserts.

Types of desserts

Desserts all have one thing in common – most people love them. The art of making desserts can be learnt by everyone, but some chefs have a particular passion for creating them.

Basic cold and hot and desserts include:

- **Ice creams**: made from milk, cream, sugar, eggs and flavouring, then churned in an ice-cream maker to achieve a smooth texture and consistency. Ice cream is available in many different flavours.
- **Mousses**: cold desserts such as chocolate or fruit mousse, generally light and airy in texture, often held together with a setting agent such as gelatine.
- **Egg-based desserts**: can be either served hot or cold. Cold desserts include crème brûlée, crème caramel and baked egg custard. Hot desserts include bread and butter pudding and cabinet pudding. Egg-based desserts also include meringues.
- **Batter-based desserts**: these are usually fried, e.g. pancakes and fritters.
- **Sponge-based desserts**: these include steamed sponges and bakewell tart.
- **Fruit-based desserts**: these include fruit flans, Eve's pudding, fruit crumble and summer puddings.

Ice cream

Ice cream is a very popular dessert, available in many different flavours. Ice cream is normally made using a sorbetière (ice-cream maker). It can be made using a normal household freezer, but the ice cream will not be such good quality.

A sorbetière slowly churns and freezes the ice-cream mixture. As the mixture freezes ice crystals are produced. These are kept small by the churning action. Small ice crystals mean high-quality ice cream with a smooth texture.

Freezing the ice-cream mixture in a normal freezer produces larger ice crystals so the texture is not so smooth.

Ice cream is generally made using high-risk products so it must be stored below –22°C. This temperature makes the ice cream hard to serve, so it is best to remove ice cream from the freezer and place

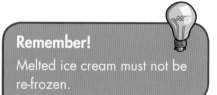

Remember!
Melted ice cream must not be re-frozen.

Hot meringue

1 part of egg white to 2 parts of caster sugar

Method

1 Put the sugar and egg white into a clean mixing bowl that will fit onto a machine. Combine using a hand whisk.
2 Put the bowl onto a bain-marie and whisk until the sugar has dissolved. To check this, remove the bowl from the heat and dip in a wooden spoon. Remove the wooden spoon and rub a finger over the spoon. If the mixture feels gritty return it to the heat and whisk until the sugar has dissolved.
3 Fit the bowl onto the machine, attach the whisk and whisk on the highest setting until the mixture is cold and in a stiff peak.
4 Use as required.

Video presentation

Watch *Finishing a flan* for an alternative method of making hot meringue. Try out both methods and see which you prefer.

Boiled meringue

granulated sugar	300g
water	90ml
cream of tartar	pinch
egg white	150g

Method

1 Put the sugar, water and cream of tartar in a clean saucepan. Combine with metal spoon.
2 Put the pan on a low heat. Wash the sides of the pan down with water and a clean brush (as for caramel for crème caramel).
3 Bring to the boil.
4 Boil the sugar mixture to 118°C. Test using a sugar thermometer. Do not stir the sugar, just let it boil.
5 In the meantime whisk the egg white to a stiff snow using a machine on the highest setting.
6 Once 118°C is reached remove from the heat and pour slowly into the whipped egg white while the machine is still running on full speed. Take care not to burn yourself.
7 Continue whipping until the mixture is cold and stiff peak.
8 Use as required.

Chef's tip

Meringues are normally one part egg white to two parts sugar. Weigh the egg whites and double the sugar to get the correct amount.

Granulated sugar is used in this type of meringue because it is a cleaner type of sugar with fewer impurities than caster sugar. In this method the sugar has to be boiled with the water and therefore the granulated sugar is more suitable.

Cream of tartar is found in the juice of grapes, after they have been fermented in winemaking. It is classified as an acid, available in the form of a powder and used in baking powder. It helps to stabilise meringue once it has been whisked.

Pavlova

Pavlova is a meringue dish that is soft and chewy inside with a crunchy outside. Cornflour and vinegar are added to the meringue.

Did you know?
Pavlova was named after Anna Pavlova, a Russian ballerina.

Pavlova

egg whites	100g
caster sugar	200g
vinegar	5ml
cornflour	5g
Serves	6–8

Method

1. Make meringue as previously described (cold meringue, steps 1–4).
2. Fold in the cornflour and vinegar.
3. Transfer onto silicone paper and bake at a temperature of 140°C for approximately two hours.
4. Cool and decorate with fruits and **Chantilly cream**.

Meringue shells, cases, nests and vacherins

These are all made with Swiss meringue and piped with star or plain piping tubes.

They can be dried on top of the oven overnight or dried in an oven on a low heat of about 90°C. This could take four to eight hours. Make sure that meringue products are not dried at too hot a temperature as they may discolour and lose their characteristic white colour.

Vacherins can either be large or individual round gateau-type meringues filled with fruit and cream and then decorated.

Definition
Chantilly cream: cream that has been sweetened, flavoured and lightly whipped (see Chapter 16 for recipe).

Batter-based desserts

Batter-based desserts can be as simple as a lemon pancake or a more classic dish like crêpes suzette. Batter can also be used as a light crispy coating used to protect fruit during cooking.

Pancakes

Pancakes should be cooked in **crêpe** pans, which are small flat pans which make tossing the pancakes easier. They can also be cooked in frying pans but tossing them is a little more difficult.

Definition

Crêpes: the French term for pancakes. Crêpes need to be as thin as possible.

Basic pancake batter

soft flour	240g
salt	a pinch
milk	565ml
eggs	2
melted butter	30g

Method

1. Sift the flour and salt together into a bowl.
2. Add the milk and eggs and whisk together until smooth.
3. Whisk in the melted butter.
4. Allow to rest for at least 60 minutes or the pancakes will be tough and rubbery. Whisk after resting.
5. Heat the crêpe pan, add a little vegetable oil (butter will burn and make the pancake taste burnt and bitter).
6. Coat the base of the pan with the hot oil and pour off any excess. (Too much oil will not only make the pancake greasy, it will also splash back and cause a serious burn.)
7. Fill a small ladle with pancake batter and pour the batter into the centre of the pan. Lift the pan and coat the base of the pan with the batter ensuring a thin even coat.
8. Put the pan back onto the heat, and cook the batter. When all the liquid has cooked, the pancake is ready to be turned over. Lift one edge of the pancake off the pan to check the colour; it should be a light golden brown.
9. To turn the pancake over, use a palette knife to run around the edge of the pancake to loosen it and make sure it has not stuck to the pan. Slide the palette knife under the pancake and turn it over to cook on the other side.
10. Once cooked turn onto an overturned plate if the pancake is to be served later, or onto a serving dish if being served straight away.

Figure 17.4 Crêpe pan

Ideas for service:

○ **Lemon pancakes**: prepare and cook pancakes as described, turn out onto a plate, sprinkle with caster sugar and fold into four. Serve with lemon quarters.

○ **Jam pancakes**: prepare and cook pancakes as described, turn out onto a plate and spread a spoon of red jam on each and roll up, sprinkle with caster sugar and serve.

○ **Apple pancakes**: apple pancakes are the same as jam pancakes, but with apple purée instead of jam. Refer to fruit-based desserts (page 413) for making apple purée.

American-style pancakes

American-style pancakes are made using a slightly thicker batter that has a raising agent added, normally baking powder. Due to their thickness the batter needs sweetening, unlike normal pancakes that have jam, lemon and sugar etc.

American-style pancakes

soft flour	135g
salt	3g
milk	140ml
egg	1 large
baking powder	10g
caster sugar	50g

Method

1 Follow steps 1–4 for basic pancake batter.
2 Add the baking powder just before cooking the pancakes, otherwise the effectiveness of the baking powder will be destroyed.
3 Cook the pancakes on a griddle. Pour the batter onto the hot surface about the size of a saucer. Cook and turn the pancakes.
4 Serve with maple syrup, fruit, ice cream, whipped cream or any sweet flavourings and accompaniments specified by the establishment.

Try this! **Worksheet 47**

Find out what faults there might be in pancake batters and the problems these can cause. Find out some possible recipes for yeast and pancake batters.

 Find out!

What else could be used to make the pancake lighter in texture?

Place all the fruit together and add sufficient stock syrup to cover the fruit. Just before service, peel and slice the bananas and add them. Gently stir to mix the fruit and syrup and serve.

The syrup could be a simple stock syrup or even an unsweetened fruit juice. Stock syrup is a mixture of sugar and water, dissolved and boiled together.

Stock syrup

sugar	720g
water	565ml

Method

1 Put the sugar and water into a saucepan.
2 Boil them and skim off any impurities.
3 Cool and use as required.

Stock syrup can also be flavoured with:

- cinnamon sticks
- lemons
- oranges
- coriander seeds.

Preparation of fruit

All fruit should be washed and dried before preparing or eating.

Apples need to be peeled, cored and quartered. Apples tend to turn brown very quickly once peeled. To prevent this, peeled apples should be kept in acidulated water. There are hundreds of varieties of apples, from the common Granny Smith to pink lady. Each apple has its own level of sweetness and crispness.

Bramley apples are normally used for cooking but eating apples can also be cooked. They require less cooking time and less sugar.

For Fruit salad the quarters should be sliced into small pieces.

Healthy eating
The vitamins and nutrients found in apples are just under the skin, so use a vegetable peeler to remove the peel. To increase roughage in people's diets leave the peel on.

Cooking apples should be peeled, cored, quartered and kept in **acidulated water** until ready for cooking. The time of year and the variety of apple used will determine whether the apple needs additional water and sugar added during cooking. As a rough guide only, 1kg of cooking apples needs 125g sugar. After cooking, taste the apples and add extra sugar if required, or if too sweet add some lemon juice.

> **Definition**
> **Acidulated water**: water with lemon juice added to it.

How to cook apples

1 Put sugar into a saucepan, add the drained apple slices and squeeze half a lemon over the top.

2 Put a tight-fitting lid on and place on the heat to cook. The steam created should provide enough liquid to cook the apples. Water can be added if necessary.

3 Test to see if the apple is cooked by tasting a small piece. If using the fruit in pieces it should be soft but still firm. For purée, cook slightly longer until there is no bite left.

4 Remove the fruit from the pan and allow to cool.

5 To purée the fruit, use a food processor. Purée can also be made using a potato masher, but it will not be so smooth.

Oranges should be peeled and segmented, but the most important part is to make sure there is no pith left on the segments.

How to peel an orange

1 To peel the orange, top and tail it first, so that you can see how thick the skin is.

2 Run a vegetable knife from the top of the fruit to the bottom, judging the correct thickness to remove all the pith and skin.

3 Once the first slice has been removed it will allow the next piece to be removed more easily, as you can then see how much skin to remove each time to remove all the pith and skin. Continue removing slices round the orange until all the skin and pith has been removed. Try to keep the round shape of the orange.

How to segment an orange

The orange is then ready to cut into segments which should be free from pith, pips or the membrane which divides up the inside of the orange. There are two different methods to achieve this:

Method 1

1

2

3

Place a container underneath the orange. Hold the peeled fruit in one hand and run a paring knife down towards the centre of the fruit just inside the segment membrane.

Once the centre is reached push the segment away from the centre.

The segment should come away from the membrane on the other side. Continue until all the segments have been removed. Squeeze the remaining pulp to remove any juice that remains.

Method 2 This is similar to method 1, but instead of pushing the segment away from the centre, cut the other side of the segment away from the membrane too. Method 2 is slightly easier but can cause more waste.

Bananas should not be prepared until required for service. Bananas turn brown very quickly and in fruit salad they will go black and spoil the presentation of the fruit. Bananas can be coated in lemon juice to slow down but not stop the browning process.

Peel the banana and cut slices about 3mm thick. If using bananas for fritters, cut them into three or four depending on the size of the fruit.

Grapes should be halved and the seed removed.

Kiwi fruit should be topped and tailed and peeled in the same way as oranges. Once peeled, slice and use as required.

Pears are either red or green and are also available in many varieties. Some are suitable for cooking. The normal method of cooking pears is poaching.

Pears can be peeled with a vegetable peeler and cored, then cut into quarters and then into smaller pieces to go into fruit salad.

Find out!   **Worksheet 49**

Find the names of four types of pears suitable for cooking and a suitable recipe for each.

To poach pears, do not core them until after poaching as this will help stop them falling apart. Pears can be poached in stock syrup, red wine or even sweet dessert wine. It depends on the dessert being produced, but the method of poaching is the same.

How to poach pears

1 Peel the pears and keep them covered in acidulated water.
2 Bring the poaching liquid to the boil and remove from the heat.
3 Put the pears into the liquid and cover with a cartouche.
4 Put back onto the heat and simmer gently for 10–25 minutes depending on the type of pear and the liquid being used.
5 The pears will change colour slightly to a translucent pale colour.

For more general information on fruits, visit www.heinemann.co.uk/hotlinks and enter the express code 9254P.

Fruit compote

Fruit compote is a mixture of stewed fruit which can be made with soft fruit, hard fruit and dried fruit.

Soft fruit should be chosen, washed and covered in hot stock syrup. Cool and serve as required.

Dried fruit should be washed and soaked overnight in cold water. Then sugar is added and the fruit is gently cooked in its juice. It is cooled and served as required.

Hard fruit should be washed, prepared, put in a shallow dish and covered in stock syrup. Put a cartouche on top and place in the oven to stew until the fruit is tender. Allow to cool in the syrup and serve as required.

Fruit compotes can be served at breakfast or with sweet sauces and ice cream. They can also be flavoured with alcohol. The fruit should retain its original colour, so the correct preparation method is important.

Fruit crumbles

Crumbles are a very popular but simple baked dessert. A crumble has fruit on the bottom and a topping of butter, flour and sugar.

Sometimes the fruit is cooked before the crumble topping is placed on top. This depends on the type of fruit used. For example, apples, rhubarb and gooseberries should be cooked, whereas raspberries, blackberries and peaches can be used raw.

Crumble

flour	450g
butter	200g
sugar	200g
fruit	1.5kg
Serves	8–10

Method

1 Rub all the ingredients together until you achieve a sandy texture.
2 Put approx 1.5kg of prepared fruit in an ovenproof dish.
3 Sprinkle the crumble mixture on top of the fruit. Do not press the topping mixture down as this compacts the topping and makes it soggy.
4 Bake in a moderate oven until the fruit is cooked and the crumble topping is golden brown.

Find out!   **Worksheet 50**

Find five ingredients that could be used to make the crumble topping healthier to eat.

Fruit flans

Apple meringue flan is a simple dessert, but care is still needed to produce it well. An apple meringue is a blind-baked sweet paste flan (see Chapter 15), three-quarters filled with apple purée and with meringue piped on top.

To finish the flan, sprinkle caster sugar on top and bake in a moderate oven until the top is golden brown and the apple is hot.

When piping the meringue, keep it even and level as any peaks will burn during cooking.

Lemon meringue flan is prepared exactly the same as apple meringue; just replace the apple with lemon filling. Lemon filling is available pre-made or in powdered form, or it can be made from fresh ingredients.

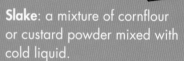

Video presentation

Watch *Finish a flan* to see this being produced. You may also find *Prepare sweet paste (rubbing in method)*; *Line a flan ring*; and *Bake blind* useful.

Lemon filling for lemon meringue flan

sugar	120g
water	150ml
lemon juice	60g
cornflour	25g
butter	30g
egg yolks	2

Method

1. Put the sugar and half the water into a pan over a low heat.
2. Dissolve the sugar. Add the lemon juice. Bring to the boil.
3. Dissolve the cornflour in the remaining water to make a **slake**. Add to the water and lemon juice and cook until the mixture thickens.
4. Add the melted butter.
5. Whisk in the egg yolks.
6. Remove from the heat. Pour into a cooked flan case and allow to cool.

Definition

Slake: a mixture of cornflour or custard powder mixed with cold liquid.

Apple flan is a blind-baked sweet paste flan, three-quarters filled with apple purée, topped off with sliced raw apple. Sprinkle with sugar and cook in a moderate oven until the apple slices are cooked and browned. Coat with apricot glaze.

Fruit flans are completed differently from apple flans. First the case is filled with pastry cream and then fruit is overlapped on top to completely cover the pastry cream. It is then coated in apricot glaze to protect the fruit from discoloration.

Pastry cream

milk	850ml
vanilla pod	1 (can be replaced with essence or extract)
egg yolks	8
sugar	240g
plain flour	120g

Method

1 Put the milk into a saucepan. Split the vanilla pod and put seeds into the milk, add the pod and infuse over a low heat.
2 Put the egg yolks and sugar into a bowl and whisk together until light.
3 Sift the flour and add to the egg mixture. Mix to a smooth paste.
4 Bring the milk to the boil and remove the pod.
5 Gradually add the milk to the sugar mix and stir well.
6 Put the mixture into a clean pan and bring it back to the boil, stirring continuously.
7 Pour into a clean bowl and cover with a cartouche to prevent skinning. Allow to cool.

These desserts are only a small sample of the vast selection available, but mastering them is the first step to understanding how to produce fantastic hot and cold desserts.

Figure 17.5 Dessert service

Test yourself!

1 What setting agent is used in mousse?

2 What is a sorbetière?

3 True or false? It is safe to re-freeze melted ice cream.

4 Why does milk boil over?

5 How would you prepare the following for a fruit salad:
 a bananas
 b kiwi
 c grapes
 d apples.

6 How can you reduce the risk of overheating the custard mix when making an egg custard-based dessert?

7 What ingredients do you need to make rhubarb crumble?

8 At what temperature should you store ice cream?

18

Prepare and present food for cold presentation

This chapter covers the following NVQ unit:

○ Unit 2FPC15 Prepare and present food for cold presentation

Working through this chapter could also provide evidence for the following Key Skills:
C1.1, C2.2, N1.1, N1.2, WO2.1, WO2.2, PS2.1, PS2.2, PS2.3

In this chapter you will learn how to:

Check food products and garnish dishes to make sure they meet requirements	2FPC15
Prepare ingredients and food products for cold presentation	2FPC15
Finish the cold products for presentation	2FPC15
Store food not for immediate consumption	2FPC15
Dispose of prepared food that is not used	2FPC15

Cold presentation of food

Cold presentation of food can be as simple as a display of bread for breakfast or as complicated as a plated starter for a banquet. Each is just as important. If food is presented well, it will attract people to eat it.

There is a fine line between making food look appetising and over-garnishing. Garnishing should be used to complement the dish and not to overwhelm it.

Pre-prepared food for cold presentation is generally high-risk food. It must be stored and held for service at the correct temperature otherwise the potential to cause food poisoning is huge.

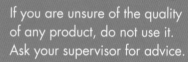

Remember!
If you are unsure of the quality of any product, do not use it. Ask your supervisor for advice.

If the establishment does not have a chilled service area, it is recommended that only products to be served immediately should be on display. Replace with new chilled food items as required.

This will help you to meet the current HACCP guidelines.

The storage temperature should be below 8°C, ideally 5°C. The food should be served at 5°C or below and food should not be on display for longer than four hours. Any high-risk product that has been kept on display for longer than four hours should be disposed of.

Bread products

See Chapter 14 for instructions on how to prepare and bake bread products. Bread displays should have a variety of bread shapes, toppings and types to appeal to the customer.

When displaying different types of bread for cold presentation in the service container, try and achieve different heights and ensure the bread products are the correct way up.

Bread loaves and French sticks can be sliced before being displayed in a service container. To make the slices look more appealing, slice them at a 45° angle using a serrated knife. Make sure the slices are kept even both for portion control and to ensure the most attractive presentation. A serrated knife will cut through the crust without damaging the bread and will help to produce an even slice.

Salads

Salads can be classified as simple or compound salads. Compound salads are any salad containing a mixture of ingredients bound together with a dressing or a sauce, e.g. a **vinaigrette** or **mayonnaise**.

Salads are only limited by your imagination and the ingredients available. They can be served as accompaniments to dishes, the main part of the dish, or as a selection of starters known as **hors d'oeuvres**.

Simple salads (one salad ingredient)

Cucumber salad

1 Check the quality points for cucumbers on page 140.
2 Wash the cucumber, then peel with a vegetable peeler.
3 Next top and tail the cucumber and slice it very thinly and evenly. Use a mandolin to slice it more quickly and easily.
4 Put the slices into a serving dish and decorate the top of the salad with slices of cucumber overlapping each other.
5 Wrap the bowl in cling film and store in the fridge until 15 minutes before service.
6 To serve, dress the salad with vinaigrette dressing and garnish with chopped parsley.

Tomato salad

1 Check the quality points for tomatoes on page 140.
2 Wash the tomatoes and remove the stem.
3 Blanch the tomatoes (see page 147).
4 Peel the skins off.
5 Put the tomato with the stem at 90° to the chopping board and slice thinly with a very sharp knife. Keep the slices in the order you cut them, to enable you to put them back into the tomato shape.
6 Transfer the tomato into a serving dish and fan out slightly but evenly.
7 Dress the sliced tomatoes with vinaigrette then place a fine line of finely chopped shallot onto each tomato. Complete with chopped parsley.

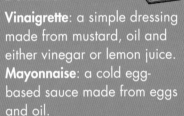

Definition

Vinaigrette: a simple dressing made from mustard, oil and either vinegar or lemon juice.
Mayonnaise: a cold egg-based sauce made from eggs and oil.
Hors d'oeuvre: a savoury appetiser that does not form part of the main meal. They can be served hot or cold.

Chef's tip

If you add the dressing too early the water to come out of the cucumber making it go soggy.

Remember!

A mandolin is a very sharp cutter. The blades can cause serious cuts so the guard must be used to prevent injury.

Capsicum (pepper) and onion salad

This can be made with any single colour capsicum or a mixture.

1 Remove the top of the capsicum and pull out the stalk. Remove the seeds and white pith from inside the capsicum.
2 Cut into quarters. Carefully split each piece into two giving eight pieces, then cut into julienne.
3 Finely shred some onion and mix with the julienne of pepper.
4 Dress with vinaigrette and transfer into a service dish. Sprinkle with chopped parsley.

Beetroot salad

This can be made with pre-cooked pickled beetroot, pre-cooked beetroot or fresh beetroot, which will need cooking.

1 Check the quality of the beetroot.
2 To cook fresh, raw beetroot, wash the beetroot well and put it into a pan of cold salted water. Bring to the boil and simmer until the beetroot is cooked. Test the same as for cooking potatoes.
3 Remove the beetroot from the water and allow it to cool slightly.
4 Peel the beetroot while it is still warm.
5 Slice the beetroot approximately 5mm thick, place into a serving dish and dress with vinaigrette. The beetroot will absorb the flavours from the vinaigrette while it is still warm.
6 Once cool, cover and place into the fridge.
7 To serve, place onion rings onto the top of the salad and garnish with chopped parsley.

Chef's tip

Keep the tops of the capsicums to make stir frys.

Couscous salad

Couscous is a cereal processed from semolina, rolled into small balls. Couscous does not need to be cooked; it does however need to be soaked. Couscous will absorb its own weight in liquid and the liquid can be used to help flavour it. See page 309 for more information on couscous.

Couscous salad

water or stock	300ml
garlic cloves	2
onion, finely diced	125g
couscous	250g
fresh coriander, chopped	a bunch
red capsicum, diced	60g
olive oil	15ml
salt and pepper	to season

Method

1. Put the stock or water into a saucepan and add the garlic cloves and finely diced onion.
2. Warm the stock until it just comes to the boil.
3. Put the couscous into a bowl and cover with the warmed stock/water. Cover and leave to absorb the liquid. (This should take about three minutes.)
4. Add chopped coriander, diced capsicum and olive oil and mix gently.
5. Season with salt and pepper to taste.
6. Allow flavours to infuse. Add more olive oil if required.

This salad can have other ingredients introduced to enhance and offer alternative flavours, e.g. dried fruits such as apricots.

Find out!   **Worksheet 51**

Find eight different salads from books, the Internet or your local restaurant. Record where the recipes are located and explain why you selected them.

Pre-prepared pies

Pies are a common commodity on buffets. They can vary from a chilled home-made chicken and ham pie or game pie to a simple bought pork pie.

These products are high-risk and must be stored in the fridge at a temperature below 8°C, ideally 5°C before service.

Pies are available in many different flavours and shapes; the garnish should complement the product inside. Your establishment will choose the most appropriate garnish, e.g. vegetables, fruit or herbs.

To serve, portion the pie according to the establishment's requirements. Place only sufficient portions on the service dish to meet the immediate service period.

Cooked red and white meat

Cooked meats can be sliced by hand or by machine.

When slicing meats, keep each slice in the order it is removed. This way the meat can be fanned and the shape of the meat will be uniform and will look more appetising on display.

Meat that is to be used for cold service is normally cooked the day before to allow it to cool and relax. This makes it easier to slice. Chicken, however, is normally cooked on the day, as this helps to retain moisture in the cooked bird.

Examples of meat that can be used for display:
○ **Gammon**: boil, cool, remove the fat, then glaze. The glaze is used to give flavour to the outside of the meat and to make it look more appetising. A popular glaze is brown sugar, honey, cloves and mustard. Gammon is normally served whole with the chef slicing the meat as required. To allow the customer to see the cooked meat, a slice is normally removed and placed onto the tray with the whole gammon. If the surface of the meat dries out, remove another slice and discard the dried piece. This ensures the best-looking meat is displayed to the customer.

Remember!
If slicing by machine you must be 18 or over and trained to use the equipment. Slicing machines are extremely dangerous.

- **Beef**: this is normally roasted, and can be served whole or pre-sliced.
- **Pork**: this is roasted and served whole or pre-sliced.
- **Chicken**: whole chickens can be roasted and served whole, ready to be carved, or pre-carved to speed up service. Breasts can be poached or even fried.
- **Turkey**: normally served whole and carved in front of the customer. Some establishments will only use the **crown** of the turkey, as most people prefer breast meat.

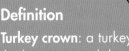

Definition

Turkey crown: a turkey with the legs removed, but leaving the breasts on the bone.

Pre-sliced meat can be displayed on trays. Keep the slices at an equal distance and allow enough space for the customer or serving staff to lift up the edge of one slice of meat for service.

The meat can be sparingly garnished with different things to complement the display. Some examples of garnishes:

- Parsley – chopped, picked.
- Tomatoes – rose, whole, wedges, slices, swans.
- Cucumber – slices, wedges, fans.
- Lettuce – leaves, chiffonade – very finely shredded.
- Fruit – carved, wedges, fans.

Each establishment will have its own preferred garnishes.

Figure 18.1 Cooked meats on display for a buffet

A selection of cold sauces can also be served as accompaniments. These are often bought ready-made. Some examples:

- Beef: horseradish sauce, English mustard.
- Pork: apple sauce.
- Chicken: satay, lemon, black bean, barbecue.
- Lamb: mint sauce, redcurrant jelly, cumberland sauce.
- Turkey: cranberry sauce.
- Duck: plum sauce, orange sauce.

Some of these sauces are the classic sauces normally served with hot cooked meat. However, with new tastes and modern trends the number of accompaniments is vast.

Fish

Fish can be smoked, poached or even fried before being served cold. Smoked trout and herrings are served with horseradish sauce and lemon wedges. Other cold fish can be served with dressings as determined by the establishment. They can be portions of fish or even whole fish, poached and decorated for display.

The skin can be removed to expose the flesh and make the fish look more attractive to the customer.

Examples of fish that can be served cold:

○ Salmon: poached whole, darnes, demi-darnes, smoked, normally sliced.
○ Trout: smoked or poached.
○ Tuna: seared.
○ Mackerel: smoked.

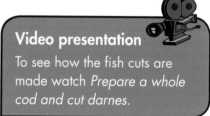

Video presentation
To see how the fish cuts are made watch *Prepare a whole cod and cut darnes.*

Find out!   **Worksheet 52**

Find three more sauces that can be served as an accompaniment to meat and fish.

Pre-prepared terrines

A terrine is made up of different textures of meat, fish or vegetables layered inside a mould, poached, chilled and turned out. During chilling it should set. It can then be sliced and served as a starter or as part of a cold buffet.

A terrine can be served with a sauce to enhance the dish or with salad items to enhance the presentation.

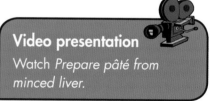

Video presentation
Watch *Prepare pâté from minced liver.*

Figure 18.2 A terrine for buffet service

The diagram below shows some sauces that can be made using mayonnaise.

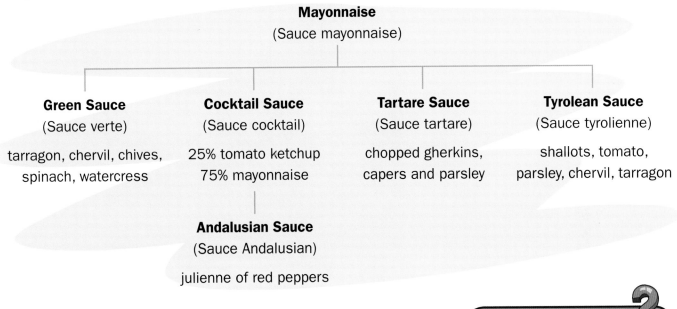

Mayonnaise
(Sauce mayonnaise)

Green Sauce
(Sauce verte)

tarragon, chervil, chives, spinach, watercress

Cocktail Sauce
(Sauce cocktail)

25% tomato ketchup
75% mayonnaise

Tartare Sauce
(Sauce tartare)

chopped gherkins, capers and parsley

Tyrolean Sauce
(Sauce tyrolienne)

shallots, tomato, parsley, chervil, tarragon

Andalusian Sauce
(Sauce Andalusian)

julienne of red peppers

Figure 18.4 Mayonnaise-based sauces

These sauces are basic and form a basis for learning about how different cold sauces can be produced.

Serve cold sauces separately – unless they are used to bind. Place the sauce close to the food item it is intended for.

Did you know?
Cocktail sauce is also called 'marie rose'.

Did you know?
If you add unwashed chopped parsley to a sauce the chlorophyll in the parsley will turn the sauce green.

Display and service

Display equipment

There is a vast amount of equipment that can be used to display cold food. This includes:

- slates
- mirrors
- tiles
- platters
- stainless steel trays
- crockery
- glass
- baskets
- chilled display cabinets.

Make sure they are clean before use.

Figure 18.5 Many different types of equipment can be used to display food

Service

When setting out a buffet for service, the following points need to be taken into consideration:

- **The type of service, waiting staff or self-service**: the type of service will affect portion control. If waiting staff are serving there is a greater level of control. If it is self-service, more food may be required as there is less control. To help with portion control when the food is being self-served, use serving spoons which are smaller than kitchen spoons and reduce the number of portions in the serving dish.
- **Number of covers**: the number of covers is very important to make sure there is sufficient food to feed all the guests. It can also determine the number of service points and how many of each item needs to be dressed ready for service.
- **Length of service**: the length of service can be important to determine how many service points and what type of service is required. For example, if 120 people are to be fed in an hour, how many service points will be needed to ensure all customers are fed?
- **Location**: the location of the buffet is important to ensure it is easy to replace any items that run out.

Find out! **Worksheet 53**

Choose four items that could be used to display cold food. Write about why you chose them and describe how they could be used.

- **Flow of customers**: it is important to ensure the customers can collect their plates and leave the service area in one direction. When placing food items in the direction of the customer, face the presentation side of the food item in the direction the customers are coming from.
- **Height**: when placing food items onto the service area, try to use different heights. This allows more food to be placed onto the service area and also provides a nicer-looking buffet.
- **Colour**: try not to mix too many of the same colours next to each other when placing items on the service area.
- **Texture**: try not to place the same food items next to each other. Look at the type of dressings and the type of food.
- **Type of buffet**: the type of buffet could include a hot section, uses chafing dishes to keep the food hot. You need to think about how dishes will impact on the service area and consider whether or not a separate area is needed.
- **Time of year**: the time of year will impact on the food choice customers make. In the summer more people are likely to go for the cold buffet, whereas in the winter more people are likely to choose the hot buffet.

Figure 18.6 An attractive buffet

Try this!   Worksheet 54

List five establishments where cold food is on display for consumption. Say why you chose the place and what you liked about the display.

Try this!   Worksheet 55

See how many of the salad-related words you can find in the wordsearch.

Test yourself!

1 What is the purpose of garnishing?

2 Name two simple salads and two combination salads.

3 What are the ingredients of a Waldorf Salad?

4 What ingredients make a popular glaze for gammon?

5 Pre-prepared pies are high-risk products. At what temperature should they be stored?

6 What is a terrine?

7 What is the difference between a pâté and a terrine?

8 Ideally, what should shellfish be served on?
   a Absorbent paper
   b Salad leaves
   c Lemon juice
   d Crushed ice.

9 Which of the following would you serve with beef?
   a Cranberry sauce
   b Apple sauce
   c English mustard
   d Mint sauce.

10 Which of the following would you serve with chicken?
   a Satay sauce
   b Cranberry sauce
   c Plum sauce
   d Redcurrant jelly.

11 Write down three sauces that can be made using mayonnaise.

12 Write down five pieces of equipment that can be used to display cold food.

13 There are ten points you must consider when setting out a buffet for service. Write down five of them and say why they are important.

Glossary

Acidulated water: water with lemon juice added to it.

Aerate: to introduce air into a mixture or liquid, making the texture lighter.

Alkaline: a chemical substance that is not acidic.

Appraisal: an assessment of performance providing feedback.

Aromatic: having a pleasant smell. Aromatic ingredients such as leaves, flowers, seeds, fruits, stems and roots are used for their fragrance to enhance flavour of stocks.

Bacterium: a single bacteria, which is a single-celled organism.

Bard: to place strips of fat onto or around a piece of meat while it cooks to slowly release juices over the meat. Mainly used for meat that has little fat.

Baste: to moisten with liquid, fat, gravy etc.

Baton: a cut of vegetable evenly sized 2.5cm long × 0.5cm × 0.5cm.

Bed of root: chopped root vegetables which act as a base to put a bird on to prevent it sticking to and burning on the tray.

Beurre manie: equal quantities of plain flour and butter mixed together to form a paste and added to a boiling liquid in small quantities as a thickening agent.

Bisque: a shellfish soup where the shellfish is puréed to add flavour.

Blend: to mix two or more ingredients together in the food processor or liquidiser.

Blind bake: to cook a flan case without the filling in it. The flan is lined with greaseproof paper (cartouche) and filled with baking beans. The beans help to keep the shape of the pastry during cooking.

Borsch: a traditional Russian soup made with beetroot.

Bran: the hard outer layer of a rice seed or grain.

Brioche: yeast dough that has been enriched with eggs and butter. It is similar to croissants.

Carcass: the dead body of an animal.

Cartouche: a round piece of greaseproof paper used to line or cover.

Castrated: testes removed before sexual maturity.

Caustic: a substance that will stick to a surface and burn chemically. It is used for heavy duty cleaning.

Cavity: the hollow space left inside a bird once all the innards have been removed.

Chantilly cream: cream that has been sweetened, flavoured and lightly whipped.

Char: to use the hot bars on a griddle to darken or pattern an item of food (e.g. meat, fish or vegetables) as it is cooking.

Clarify: to purify stocks, making the cloudy liquid clear using egg whites and albumen from the minced lean shin of beef.

Concassées: finely diced skinned tomato flesh (seeds and juice removed).

Condensation: a coating of tiny drops formed on the surface by steam or vapour.

Couscousier: a tall pot where stews or vegetables are cooked in the bottom and a smaller pot sits above with the couscous in it. The couscous cooks by steaming and absorbs the flavour from the meat or vegetables below it.

Crêpes: the French term for pancakes. Crêpes need to be as thin as possible.

Crimp: To give a decorative edge to pastry using forefinger and thumb or specialist tools.

Cross-contamination: the transfer of harmful bacteria from one food source to another by the food handler using the same equipment for different tasks, not cleaning their tools properly or not washing their hands before handling another food type.

Croûtes: sliced bread flutes toasted or evenly baked in the oven to a golden brown colour.

Croutons: 1cm cubes of white bread, shallow-fried to a golden brown colour in clarified butter.

Crustaceans: soft-bodied creatures with legs (and sometimes claws), whose exterior is a hard shell, e.g. crab.

Cull: to kill an animal.

Curdle: when food particles separate into curds or lumps.

Dariole mould: a small mould shaped like a flower pot.

Deglaze: to add wine or stock to a pan used for frying in order to lift the remaining sediment to make a sauce or gravy.

Degraisse: the liquid fat which is removed from the surface of simmering stock using a ladle by the process of skimming.

Demi-glaze: a sauce which is made up of equal quantities of brown stock and brown sauce (espagnole sauce), reduced by a third until the consistency coats the back of a spoon.

Dilute: to add extra liquid (usually water) to make the solution weaker.

Docker: a tool that has spikes that can be used to add decoration to products before cooking and to put holes into flan cases and puff pastry goods to prevent them rising during baking.

Document: make a detailed record of information.

Dormant: not active or growing.

Dough improver: adding ascorbic acid (vitamin C) assists the gluten development and can speed up the process of fermentation.

Dredge: to sprinkle or coat food with flour and sugar to enhance presentation.

Dressed: birds that have been cleaned, plucked and trussed.

Dry method: a dish which is cooked using a dry method of cookery e.g. roasting, grilling.

Duchesse potatoes: mashed potato piped onto trays and then grilled before service.

Due diligence: when every possible precaution has been taken by the business to avoid a food safety problem.

Duxelle: a ravioli filling made up of very finely diced shallots, mushrooms or other vegetables, sautéed together in a little butter, cooked and dried out using breadcrumbs. It is a quick and cheap filling. Cuttings and stalks from mushrooms can be used.

Escalopes: large slices of meat cut from the leg and flattened before cooking.

Excrement: solid waste matter passed out through the bowel.

Faeces: solid waste matter from the body.

Fines herbes: a mixture of aromatic herbs such as chervil, tarragon, chives and parsley.

Finger stall: a plastic tube that fits over a dressing (bandage or plaster) on an injured finger to protect it. It is secured by an elastic strap around the wrist.

Flambé: a French term used to describe cooking at the table in the restaurant and setting fire to the dish using alcohol to give a few seconds of flame.

Fricassee: a light, reduced meat stew bound with a liaison of cream and egg yolks.

Garnish: to add the final touches required to enhance a dish.

Germ: the heart of the rice seed or grain.

Gluten: a protein found in flour which gives it its strength. The strength of the gluten is determined by the type of wheat and when and where it is grown.

Hazard: something which could be dangerous.

Hors d'oeuvres: savoury appetizers that can be served hot or cold.

Hydrogenation: an industrial process in which oil is heated to a high temperature (260–270°C) to combine it with hydrogen. The liquid oil is converted to solid or semi-solid fat.

Immerse: to cover something completely in liquid.

Inedible: unable to be eaten.

Infuse: to soak something in liquid so that the liquid will take on its flavour.

Jointed: cuts of poultry removed from the carcass during preparation, e.g. legs and breasts.

Knead: to prepare dough by pressing it to assist the development of the gluten and to ensure the yeast is distributed throughout the dough.

Lamination: forming layers of fat in pastry to create texture and lift the pastry as it cooks.

Liaison: this is used to bind or thicken a sauce and is often based on egg yolks and cream.

Liquidise: to mix two or more ingredients together in the food processor or liquidiser.

Lost property: an item left behind by somebody else.

Mayonnaise: a cold egg-based sauce made from eggs and oil.

Micro-organism: a very small life form which cannot be seen without a microscope.

Molasses: a dark, thick brown liquid obtained from raw sugar during the refining process. It is used to make syrup, e.g. golden syrup and black treacle.

Molluscs: soft-bodied creatures contained in a hard shell.

Napper: a French term meaning to coat or mask a tray of food.

Organism: any living animal or plant.

Oxidize: a chemical reaction when oxygen causes the surface of the dough to dry out.

Panade: a paste of flour, butter and a little liquid.

Pass: to separate food from marinade, water or cooking liquor using a strainer, colander or sieve.

Pasteurisation: a method of heat-treating milk to a high temperature for a short period of time to kill any pathogenic bacteria. This makes it safe for humans to consume without spoiling its taste or appearance.

Pasteurised: has been heat treated.

Pathogen: an organism that causes diseases.

Paysanne: a small cut of vegetable in a variety of shapes such as triangles, squares, circles and oblongs.

Pectin: a natural setting agent found in fruit.

Plankton: a layer of tiny plants and animals living just below the surface of the sea.

Pluck: to remove the feathers from a game bird, either by hand or machine.

Portion: to cut meat or other food items into the correct size for it to be served. The correct size depends on the dish.

Prove: to allow the yeast to develop carbon dioxide in the dough to make it rise before baking.

Prover: a cabinet that creates heat and moisture, helping dough products to rise evenly and assists in preventing products from drying out and skinning.

Quark: a German cheese with the texture and flavour of soured cream.

Reduce: to boil a liquid rapidly until it reduces in volume.

Residue: the content left in the pan once the food, e.g. poultry, has been cooked or sealed, including liquid and solid materials which all contain intense flavours which enhance a dish.

Sauté: to cook meat, fish or vegetables in fat until brown using a sturdy frying pan.

Scale: to cut and weigh dough into the required size, e.g. for bread rolls scale dough into 60g pieces.

Sear: to use the hot bars on a griddle to darken or pattern an item of food (e.g. meat, fish or vegetables) as it is cooking.

Skim: to remove impurities from the surface of a simmering liquid with a ladle or similar equipment.

Skin: to remove the fur or skin from an animal in preparation for use in cooking.

Skinning: when dough is left uncovered and the surface of the dough starts to dry out and oxidise, it forms a skin. If this is then mixed into the dough it will leave dry pieces of dough in the finished product.

Slake: a mixture of cornflour or custard powder mixed with cold liquid.

Slaughter: to kill an animal for food.

Smoulder: to burn slowly with a small red glow and little smoke.

Spores: cells produced by bacteria and fungi.

Stiff peak: when the peaks of the whipped egg white stand up without falling to one side. The final test is to turn the bowl upside down to see if the white drops out.

Strain: to separate food from marinade, water or cooking liquor using a strainer, colander or sieve.

Swab: a sterile piece of cotton used to take a sample for analysis.

Toxin: a poison produced by bacteria.

Truss: a method of securing a bird in an appropriate shape during the cooking process. One or two pieces of string or twine are threaded through the body of a game bird or poultry using a trussing needle, then tied.

Tunnel boning: removing the bones without breaking the skin of a bird.

Turkey crown: a turkey with the legs removed but leaving the breasts on the bone.

Unpasteurised: has not been heat treated.

Vegan: a person who does not eat or use products that come from animals.

Velouté: a stock-based white sauce that is thickened with a white roux.

Vinaigrette: a simple dressing made from mustard, oil and either vinegar or lemon juice.

Wet method: a dish which is cooked and served in a liquid.

Wooden mushroom: a piece of equipment used to press the solid cooked food ingredients through a sieve to make a purée.

Zest: the outer coloured part of the peel of the lemon or other citrus fruit. It is often used as a flavouring.

Index

RADBROOK LRC